WOMEN'S CONTE

As increasing numbers of women return to work or education after starting or raising a family, it can no longer be assumed that education, employment and the family is a defining progression for women in the Western world.

Women's Contemporary Lives questions notions of success and equality as they are measured for women in and across the interconnected domains of work, education and family. Christina Hughes asks whether equal opportunity feminism is promising the impossible, and questions those who suggest that women's high achievement in education and the workplace means that there is no longer a need for feminism in social policy.

Exploring how age, class, race and sexuality have influenced and continue to influence women's expectations and assessments, *Women's contemporary Lives* points to a feminist agenda for social change based on a more inclusive and fluid interpretation of female subjectivity.

Dr Christine Hughes is a Senior Lecturer in the Department of Continuing Education, University of Warwick. She was previously co-editor of *Gender and Education* and currently serves on its editorial board. She is also assistant editor of *Gender, Work and Organisation*.

WOMEN'S CONTEMPORARY LIVES

Within and beyond the mirror

Christina Hughes

London and New York

First published 2002
by Routledge
11 New Fetter Lane, London EC4P 4EE

Simultaneously published in the USA and Canada
by Routledge
29 West 35th Street, New York, NY 10001

Routledge is an imprint of the Taylor & Francis Group

© 2002 Christina Hughes

Typeset in Baskerville by
Prepress Projects Ltd, Perth, Scotland
Printed and bound in Great Britain by
MPG Books Ltd, Bodmin, Cornwall

British Library Cataloguing in Publication Data
A catalogue record for this book is available
from the British Library

Library of Congress Cataloging in Publication Data
A catalog record has been requested

ISBN 0-415-23973-7 (hbk) 0-415-23974-5 (pbk)

CONTENTS

ACKNOWLEDGEMENTS

This book has been a long time in the writing, and it would never have been completed without the support and help from some dear colleagues and friends. In particular, I want to thank Lynn Clouder, Jane McKie, Jane Martin, Carrie Paechter and Arwen Raddon for taking the time in what I know are their very busy schedules to look through and comment so helpfully on earlier drafts. I also have to thank Loraine Blaxter not only for undertaking this same job, but also for being at the end of the telephone on those frequent occasions when I needed to sound out ideas. Indeed, I count myself fortunate to have had such a stimulating colleague and friend who took such an interest in the work I was undertaking. Finally, I have to thank my partner, Malcolm Tight, who walked the dog, made the dinner, read all my drafts, corrected my spelling, kept telling me I *was* going to finish and has been the rock at my side. What would I have done without you? Thank you all.

All errors, omissions, *mis*readings and so forth are, of course, my very own.

Christina Hughes
September 2001

INTRODUCTION
What's it about?

'What's it about?' my daughter asks as she enters the room half-way through a television programme. 'What's it about?' my colleagues enquire politely when they discover I am in the middle of writing this book. 'What's it about?' I say to a student who tells me she has decided on the topic for her dissertation.

'What's it about?' is not an invitation to supply a long and detailed exposition. My daughter does not want to know the aesthetics of the characterisation as they are played out through the twists and turns of the plot. My colleagues are not seeking a line-by-line, sentence-by-sentence or even chapter-by-chapter description. I do not want my student to tell me the life story of globalisation or empowerment or whatever is the topic of her dissertation. To do any of these things would be turgid in the extreme.

When we say 'What's it about?' we do not mean this literally in terms of 'What's it *all* about?' Rather the question is posed in a social context in which common phrases such as this carry particular sorts of meaning. When we ask 'What's it about?' we are seeking a brief, accessible summary. We want the reply to reveal the main story, the most salient points, an overview, a thumbnail sketch.

> A simple question, then, carries meaning beyond which a literal translation of the words would suggest. This meaning is context-specific. In this case, we are all in a hurry.

But, of course, we do not always get what we want or we expect. Instead, I reply to my daughter in terms of the relationship of the plot to wider social issues. I respond to my colleagues' kind enquiries by detailing how Chapter 6 is now part of Chapter 4, Chapter 3 has twelve key points and the conclusion draws on a breadth of scholarship that would fill twelve libraries. And my student begins by explaining the history of globalisation or empowerment or whatever and concludes by illustrating how her research will encompass several key theories in sociology, psychology and economics.

Thus, we cannot guarantee how each of us will take up these

meanings. In this way, meanings are not fixed. Sometimes we get the succinct summary. Sometimes we get the long version.

More problematically, we may decide to resist the expected response. When my colleagues ask me about my new book, I know that they are seeking a quick, brief reply. But, I think of myself as a scholar who has invested a good deal of myself in the project. Or, in the face of time-poor environments, I may have a commitment to creating developmental space for individuals. In either case I am impelled to go into great detail. It is cathartic for me. It is annoying for them.

How we respond to intended meanings is related to a sense of our identity and our political intentions. The long reply allows me to become, in those moments, the committed scholar. Or it allows me to redress the rush and hurry of academic life.

'What's it about?'

Origins and aims

The origins of this text lie in my research experiences as an academic and in an observation. My research has been focused in three areas: education, employment and family. This research has often been undertaken in separate phases, and in many ways this replicates ideas of these areas as distinct fields of scholarship. For example, there are innumerable texts that are concerned with women and education, women and employment or women and family. Nevertheless, demographic changes indicate how education, employment and family no longer constitute a simple linearity in women's lives. Increasing numbers of women form part of the paid labour force and combine family and employment. Women are also taking opportunities to return to education after the birth of their children.

There is no doubt that there is a range of excellent texts that offer analyses of the combination of two of these spheres. For example, there are texts that are concerned with the family–work nexus or the relations between education and employment. Similarly, there are also excellent texts that offer overviews of feminist research in a variety of key domains relevant to the analysis of women's contemporary lives (see, for example, Pascall, 1997; Pilcher, 1999). However, these texts do not offer the reader a synthesis of these domains in terms of a unifying framework that builds on feminist theory and debate. As a result, they maintain an academic separation of spheres that much feminist research has challenged and sought to overcome.

For those who are more interested in feminist theory there are, again, a number of excellent sources (see, for example, Tong, 1989; Clough, 1994; Evans, 1995; Brooks; 1997; Beasley, 1999; Freedman, 2001). In their primary focus on theory, these texts provide overviews of feminist positions and debates. Nonetheless, such texts do not relate these debates to more general feminist empirical research. In consequence, another form of separation is enacted. This is the separation of the more status-defined field of theorising from that of the less status-rich field of empiricism.

These observations of my own research experiences and the mirroring of these in terms of the development of academic publications led me to conceptualise this text in terms of the following two aims:

- to present an analysis of women's lives in contemporary Western societies that connects, rather than separates, the domains of education, employment and family;
- simultaneously to use this analysis to illuminate key feminist debates.

In this I believe that the text that I offer here is original. Nevertheless, a further problem remained. This relates to finding a framework that will not only hold theory and empirical research together within each chapter but also across the entire text. With some similarity to Skeggs (1997: 24) my search for a suitable framework has been lengthy and problematic as 'I moved through many theories'. My choice of the post-structural illustrates not only my growing understanding of how this offers a rich perspective of complex and contradictory phenomena but also how such approaches facilitate a 'feminist autocritique' (Stanley and Wise, 2000: 261) of the meta-narratives and universal truths of feminism.

Deconstructing the everyday

The meanings conveyed through simple phrases lie at the heart of this book. As the chapter contents indicate, these phrases are some of those commonly used to describe and generalise women's lives in contemporary Western societies. 'Women have made it', for example, conveys the idea of equality between women and men. Women are reaching the tops of career ladders and doing well in education. 'Best of both worlds' highlights the dilemmas involved in that equality when women still want to be mothers but also desire careers in paid employment. 'Women are caring' brings us to those ideas that women have innate nurturative qualities. 'Having it all' suggests that women can achieve all their dreams. 'Doing it all' implies that there are costs to that achievement.

In considering the meanings attached to particular phrases, I am making a distinction between two meanings of the term discourse. On the one hand, we can understand the term discourse as a string of, potentially innocent, words. On the other hand, as I shall illustrate here briefly using the phrase 'Women have made it', we can understand discourse to mean a way of being in the world which shapes who and what we are (see Gee, 1997, for a discussion of this kind of distinction).

'Making it' has a particular resonance in terms of goal achievement. I've 'made it', for example, because I now have the longed-for baby or because I have saved £1,000 or because I've run a marathon. Nevertheless, some meanings are more predominant than others. The main ways, I suggest, we understand women making it contemporarily are through their employment and educational successes. Women have made it because they are now reaching the tops of their professions. It is far more difficult to say that you have made it in twenty-first century Britain by staying within the confines of the family.

One way to analyse the meanings ascribed to discourses is to engage in a process of deconstruction. On a daily basis, most of our responses to discourses could be described as automatic. We do not spend great lengths of time thinking about how we will reply to questions or, indeed, how we will take part in everyday conversation more generally. Language has a taken-for-granted quality partly because we are so immersed in it. However, deconstruction encourages us to challenge the taken-for-granted.

Deconstructing discourses highlights the ways in which some meanings are dominant and some are subordinate. In the case of 'making it', given this speaks to employment and educational contexts, the economic is more dominant than the social. Deconstruction also facilitates a recognition of the political, social, economic and historic contexts from which discourses draw meaning. To say 'women have made it', for example, suggests something of its historical specificity in the later twentieth and early twenty-first centuries. Clearly, women have not made it in earlier times in terms of the current dominant meanings of this discourse. To preface 'making it' with the term 'women' also suggests something of the gendered nature of this achievement. It speaks to the realisation of some wider political goal. This is that of gender equality. To say 'women have made it', therefore, can also imply that there is no longer any need for feminism.

One of the purposes of deconstruction is to create a greater awareness of how discourses engage with us in terms of shaping who we are and what we might become. Discourses both authorise our experiences and deauthorise them. Here, we can see that the only women who are now defined as successful through the discourse 'making it' are those who are engaged in educational projects or employment spheres. Thus, I may be authorised to say I am successful if I have a well-paid job. As a mother without paid work, it is far more difficult to claim success as part of my identity.

How we might become successful is similarly defined for us. If I want to be a successful woman, for example, I need to work hard at my career. I must invest myself in this discourse, take it up fully as my own and create myself through it. To have success as part of my identity, then, I need to accept that the economic sphere is at least as important as the social. I need also to accept that to be successful requires adherence to a competitive and individualistic work ethic.

This brings me to a second purpose of a deconstructive project: to consider how we engage with discourses. What are our responses, for example, to the discourses of 'making it'? While, on the one hand. we may take up the dominant meanings fully, on the other we may seek to resist them. I may want to be a 'successful' woman through being a mother. In this, then, I may position myself within those discourses which state that motherhood is the epitome of womanhood or that selfless mothering is essential to children's well-being. These counter-discourses provide an alternative space within which we can place ourselves, though with more or less comfort.

I may not, of course, want to define myself as successful in any of these ways, and this brings me to a third purpose of a deconstructive project: by learning to read discourses and learning to recognise how they operate in a society we might seek not only to challenge them, but also to invent new discourses. For example, how might success be defined through discourses that do not separate the economic from the social? How might I 'make it' without subscribing to either a competitive work ethic or selfless motherhood?

The short, the everyday, phrases outlined above provide the framework to examine some of these issues. However, while I hope that this introduction indicates what I hope to achieve, it is similarly important to note what has not been attempted.

Themes and caveats

As a politics, feminism is concerned with notions of progression in women's lives. Are things getting better or worse or staying the same for example? To do this requires us to have some benchmarks for that progression. It requires us to marshal the empirical facts in order that some measures can be presented. 'Women have made it', for example, could be read as a statement of fact in just the same way as the dominant meaning of the discourses associated with 'making it' would have us believe.

What I present in this book are indeed some of the ways in which we might come to understand a little more of women's lives. Nevertheless, my central concern is not to prove whether or not women have made it, or whether women are caring or women are doing it all and so forth. My concern is to convey something of the actual and potential identificatory positions that each of the short phrases in the chapter titles represents and to link these to feminist theory and debate.

This is not to say that I do not seek to make clear the contingent nature of the knowledge that is presented in each chapter. In this, I hope to show that women generally have not made it; that there are dangers in assuming that all women are innately caring; that achieving a balance between family and employment has certain costs attached to it; and so forth.

In addition, it is important to say that the subject positions in the titles should not be taken to mean that women can take up only one of these positions, for example that a woman can be described either as a woman who has made it or as a woman who cares. The chapter titles do not, therefore, represent mutually exclusive positions. Indeed, they have been designed to reflect, support and contradict each other. In this way, we might understand women's lives in terms of the simultaneous nature of this circle:

Each chapter has been designed to take apart a little the discourses that each of the chapter titles represent. However, as I have already suggested, there is no one absolute way in which each of these phrases can be understood, and this is problematic in terms of maintaining accessibility and coherence in the text.

Moreover, the areas of feminist scholarship that I draw upon are those related to the spheres of education, employment and family. These areas are vast, and the relations between them are complex. Purvis and Hunt (1993: 475) use the term 'symptomatic studies' to refer to the selection process that they engaged in to illuminate the relationship between discourse and ideology. It is a term that is useful here because it denotes purposeful selection for heuristic purposes. This text could not aim to present a full literature review of research in the three fields identified. It could not aim to present a full account of the range of associated feminist theory. However, in presenting a variety of symptomatic studies the text does offer an introduction and an examination of feminist post-structural approaches in the three fields identified.

Chapter outlines

I have already indicated that what is offered here is based on a series of decisions that ultimately led to selecting what is and what is not included. Each of these decisions frames the knowledge produced in this text in terms of offering a particular perspective.

In Chapter 1, 'Gazing in the mirror', I elaborate on this further. I have used the metaphor of mirror to explore the main features of post-structuralist approaches in terms of the relations between discourse, subjectivity and power.

INTRODUCTION

The mirror is a classic metaphor in a range of texts. For example, in a discussion of premodern narratives and the mediaeval imagination, Kearney (1988: 124) notes how St Bonaventure, a celebrated philosopher of the Middle Ages, used the mirror to argue that 'human imagining is but a mirroring of the Divine act of creation ... The human creature is a simulacrum of the Divine Creator ... his [sic] highest vocation is to faithfully "mirror" the Supreme Artist of the universe.' Foucault (2000) explores the use of the mirror in Diego Velasquez's painting *Las Meninas* in terms of the relations between the visual and the verbal. Markson and Taylor (2000) draw on the mirror to explore gendered ageism in film.

More centrally for my purposes here, the metaphor of mirror has been central to post-Lacanian psychoanalytic understandings of the self. Specifically, I draw on feminist critiques to illustrate the problematics of humanist conceptions of the unified self. For example, these critiques ask us to consider who gazes back at us when we look into the mirror. They draw attention to the problematic notion of 'I' and they indicate how the images in the mirror are not to be taken as a simple reflection of reality. Feminist post-structural critiques also highlight issues of power by asking us to look into the shadows of the mirror and to notice how the judgements we make about the reflection presented there are influenced by those who haunt these shadows (Edholm, 1992).

In Chapter 2 I explore the discursive formations that contribute to ideas surrounding 'women have made it'. For those few women who have made it, this discourse is one of validation. For those women who are seeking to make it, it is aspirational and suggests potentiality. However, there are quite specific ways in which women can make it. These are in terms of a liberal feminist project in which the predominant concern has been to facilitate women's access to what traditionally have been men's spheres of employment and education. I begin, therefore, with a discussion of the discourses of liberal feminism to contextualise the discussion that follows. I illustrate how the discourses associated with 'women have made it' work in such a way that to take up an identificatory position in terms of making it in any other way is problematic. It places those women who do so in a counter-cultural position. In addition, I draw on research that explores a paradox in 'woman have made it' discourses in terms of women's continuing sense of inadequacy even though their lives bear testimony to success.

'Women have made it' is also an interesting discourse because it is used for backlash purposes. This backlash argues that, if women truly have 'made it', then there is no need for gender equity policies or feminist politics. Here, we can see the ways in which discourses do not stand alone. They reflect and work with the concerns of other discourses. For example, when 'Women have made it' is placed alongside discourses of masculinity in crisis we begin to get a rather different reading from the one suggested by the validatory and aspirational nature of liberal feminist politics.

INTRODUCTION

The framework of Chapter 3 relates to the dilemma many women face in terms of their employment options when they become mothers. In general, the feminist literature in this area relates these dilemmas to a tension between the needs of employers in capitalist economies and the needs of families. In managing these tensions women have little option but to strike a balance through part-time employment. Although I do not disagree with this analysis, my purpose in 'Best of both worlds' is to illustrate something of hegemonic discourses. I begin with a brief historical review of second-wave theorising on motherhood. A dominant perception of this era is of a feminism antithetical to motherhood. That this should be the dominant perception of this period suggests something of hegemonic discourses and the operations of power that demonised feminism in this way. Nevertheless, the effect has been that, when it comes to motherhood, feminism has since been on something of the defensive and has been determined to show its pro-natalist colours. As such, this review provides a useful case to illustrate the difficulties that women face in everyday life if they speak out against the sanctity of the mother–child bond.

The empirical research on women who seek to have the 'best of both worlds' indicates that they are 'living a contradiction' (Procter and Padfield, 1998). I also argue that they are also living an accommodation to liberalist and market discourses. I illustrate this through the changing nature of discourses that surround the 'good mother' and indicate how these have incorporated aspects of individualism. I argue that part-time employment is an attempt to resolve to two competing identificatory positions. These are the good mother and the independent woman of 'women have made it' discourses.

Chapter 4 takes us into an area fraught with difficulties for feminism. This is the place of caring as an aspect of women's subjectivity. The idea of the caring subject, for whom care is central to value and ethical systems and practices, is summarised in terms of the ethics of care debates. Ethics of care feminists argue for the concept of care as an alternative to the concept of rights that dominates in systems of ethical knowledge. They also argue for care as an alternative to the exploitative elements of market capitalism. In so doing, ethics of care feminists have taken up a counter-discursive position.

In exploring the discourses associated with 'women are caring' I consider the implications of counter-discourses or reverse discourses of this kind. I do this by exploring the convergence of the counter-discourses of care as a feminist politics with discourses in the field of management, which stress that to maintain competitiveness and productivity managers need the 'softer' skills associated with womanhood. In this respect, I demonstrate the dilemmas and dangers that are contingent within ethics of care debates. The connections of caring as a woman's domain reinforces essentialist views that can work to fix women into caring roles. In addition, its appropriation by managerialist discourses may herald opportunities for individual women, but it also means that, as women try to relinquish their primary responsibilities for domestic care, they take on the primary responsibilities for the care and nurturance of employment-based relations.

It was tempting, in Chapter 5, to leave the pages blank. After all, who does 'have it all'? Nevertheless, the discourses associated with 'having it all' are interesting in a number of ways. First, there is no definitive meaning to what the 'it' is in 'having it all'. In this way we can see how discourses work by retaining their ambiguity. Second, and because there is no one definitive meaning, this allows some space to make the 'it' your own. There is room for multiplicity and difference. Third, 'having it all' speaks to the promise of ultimate fulfilment. Such a promise is, of course, latent within feminist, and other, politics.

While post-modern theorising might deplore utopian visions, ideas of progression are implicit within emancipatory politics. However, given that feminists cannot (yet!) claim to have it all, I explore 'having it all' in terms of transition. In particular, I draw on two metaphors of the feminist subject: the exile (Benhabib, 1992) and the nomad (Braidotti, 1994). These metaphors have made important contributions to feminist debates that surround women in transition and the potential of the dis/locations that occur. Both the metaphors of 'exile' and 'nomad' as depicted by Benhabib and Braidotti emphasise issues of choice and agency in transitions. As discursive devices they are important in that they foreground the idea that women are not simply passive victims. For the development of her critical consciousness, the 'exile' chooses to take up a space 'beyond the walls'. For the purposes of constant renewal and to avoid assimilation, the 'nomad' chooses to keep moving.

I apply these metaphors to research into women 'returners'. Women who return to education can be seen as attempting to have a sequential form of 'having it all' as education and employment follow the raising of children. However, research in this area indicates how age, class and gender fix women in particular ways. Using the metaphors of exile and nomad I explore these aspects of fixity to illustrate something of the multiaxial nature of location with its cross-cutting points of identification and resistance. In so doing, my aim is to convey something of the difficulties of transition, the politics of locatedness and the 'fixity' and 'fixing' of aspects of difference.

The feminist literature is replete with examples of women 'doing it all'. It is the penalty for trying to 'have it all'. Mostly, this is understood in terms of unequal divisions of labour, with women, in addition to their roles in paid employment, retaining the major caring tasks associated with family life. In comparison with 'having it all', 'doing it all' foregrounds the structuring of inequality. Inequality is, of course, a dominant theme in feminist theory. I begin this chapter by focusing on the binary of sameness and difference that informs ideas of equality. I then take up the theme of 'doing it all' through feminist research that has focused on women's personal relationships in heterosexual and lesbian relationships. While research into heterosexual relationships indicates continuing inequalities, research into lesbian relationships suggests the potential for greater equality in household divisions of labour. Through a review of this research I show how each of the three concepts of equality, sameness and difference have a range of meanings and an associated range of practices. In particular, I indicate how notions of equality become transfigured into discourses of sameness, parity and fairness. These discourses inform the everyday of women's lives in their negotiation of household divisions of labour.

The final chapter brings together some of the many threads that have been left dangling in the text. The common, everyday phrases that I have selected are certainly discourses for contemporary womanhood. They offer identificatory subject positions for women, and in so doing shape choices and chances. In Chapter 7, 'Within and beyond the mirror', I consider more broadly the relations between each of these discourses. I also explore a variety of political responses within post-structuralism. In particular, I return to a key point from Chapter 2. This is that the meta-narrative within feminist politics is that of liberalism. This form of feminist politics has focused predominantly on legislative and juridical change. Consequently, it has taken legal and governmental institutions as the locus of power. Liberal feminist politics leave unchallenged the binaried nature of the discursive order, and they can also divert attention away from other sources of power that restrict and prohibit. Indeed, it could be said that liberal feminism 'promises the impossible' (Young, 1997: 5).

This is not to say that post-structuralism has not also been seen as intensely problematic for feminist politics. In its attention to deconstruction, post-structuralism has been accused of deconstructing woman out of existence. Nevertheless, I illustrate how post-structural theories of woman-as-a-subject-always-in-the-process-of-becoming offer the potential for optimism in terms of a feminist agenda for social change. Here, I demonstrate how a deconstructive project can promote the development of critical literacy, whereby women have the tools to facilitate social change. In fixing our gaze within the mirror, we might learn to look beyond it.

1

GAZING IN THE MIRROR

I have a fascination with mirrors. I search my eyes, trying to discover who I am. Who is this person looking back so intently at me? I am many things – some of them I know and recognize as I look back at myself, but others are strange to me.

(Jackson, 1998: 196)

Even when we as individuals reject the subject positions offered in dominant images, or see them as irrelevant, it is still difficult, in the absence of many powerfully visualized alternatives, to escape their influence and impact. The process of looking at our own reflections in the mirror is some indication of this; it is at some level uncomfortable. Gaining a sense of self-worth and autonomy against these dominant images and the values they represent can be difficult. So, the image in the mirror is shadowed by these other images – 'ideals' of Woman, of desirability – and by the gaze of others.

(Edholm, 1992: 156–7)

The *Daily Mirror*, a British tabloid newspaper, brings the world of news reporting for our gaze. Originally set up as a women's newspaper, one assumes its name was carefully chosen in order that women would identify with the newspaper as written *for* them. The *Daily Mirror's* title evokes many of the issues that have concerned feminist explorations of the self. The *Daily Mirror* re-presents a stereotype about women's natures. This suggests that it is mostly women who are concerned with their self-image. Drawing on such a stereotype is a familiar feature of media representations of womanhood. For example, Woodward (1997) illustrates how the mirror is used in women's magazines as a metaphor for constructing feminine identity. It is common to see photographs of women looking in the mirror while putting on their make-up or checking how they look in new clothes or jewels.

Through inviting the reader to gaze at its editorials and news stories, the *Daily Mirror* also suggests that its representations of reality are mirrors of the readers' own. No doubt the *Daily Mirror* also tells its readers that it reports the truth, though whose truths these are is what is really at issue. In this the pages of the *Daily Mirror* contain many cautionary tales that are designed to regulate behaviour. In myth and story the mirror has been similarly used. Through the mirror's associations with the perils of desire and self-love Narcissus warned us not to gaze at ourselves too much. Should we do so and

11

are not turned into a flower, then Alice provides a second lesson of the crazy mad world of Wonderland that exists when young women go beyond the surface of things and look too deeply.

Given that being overly concerned with one's look and madness are associated with womanhood it would be too easy to suggest that the mirror metaphor is solely representational of a negative view of womanhood or even fully equated with woman at all. Such a view would not convey the tentativeness and ambiguity of much discourse. Mirrors are the embodiment of pleasures both illicit and covert. Lovers place mirrors on their ceilings to enhance sexual pleasure, to catch a secret glimpse of themselves and their partner or to know themselves in unexpected ways. Police and social workers work behind one-way mirrors to observe suspects or family dynamics. There is also status in certain kinds of mirror. From the Hall of Mirrors (La Galerie des Glaces) at Versailles to the gilt mirror above the fireplace, mirrors can be as much a statement of who you believe you are as they are a design feature for creating an illusion of space. Of course, who you are or aspire to be is also reflected in the newspaper that you buy.

As a metaphor the mirror is useful because it brings together some important themes for feminist analyses. For example, the mirror both represents yet also calls into question the idea that there exists a core, independent, true self within each of us. As a representative of the self we cannot deny the person who stands before the mirror. However, through the idea of reflection, our attention is drawn to exploring the idea of the self, or selves, as constituted through an other or others. To be 'I' requires 'you' (Belsey, 1997). In feminism, this other has broadly been taken to be men. Thus, by looking in the straight mirror of masculinity (Irigary, 1985) is the woman I see his reflection? Does my womanhood imitate, pass for, copy, mimic or mirror man-made images? Is it that, as a woman, I can only truly be known through the curved mirror of the speculum that allows access to that which is neither visible nor given voice to in man-made cultures? Or, are masculinist representations so hegemonic that, as Edholm (1992) indicates, even when I try to create myself anew my selfhood is shadowed by phallocentric images of the ideal woman?

The mirror's association with gazing at ourselves or being gazed at by others also highlights our status as subjects and objects. As subjects we have agency to act in ways that we think appropriate. We are not so totally colonised by the other that we turn out as 'Stepford Wives', those identical models unable to resist. If this were the case then the panoptic gaze of masculinity that the mirror represents would be so totalising that we could never be other than othered. Yet the gaze of the other does work to regulate and discipline us. Being watched or being looked at changes the way we behave. This may be for just a moment. When the looker stops looking we revert to what we were doing before. Or it may be permanently. There is no need to watch us. We have internalised the other's gaze to such an extent that it has become part of our own self-regulation. We take our everyday feelings, thoughts and behaviour as if they were of our own making.

Paradoxically, the mirror represents both the self and its opposite. However, unless we move beyond the simple reversals and binaries that mirror-image implies, the mirror as a suitable metaphor lets us down. A mirror-image is an identical image but with the structure reversed. Woman–man is often viewed as a mirror-image. Woman is warm and soft. Man is cool and hard. Nevertheless, the mirror can too easily deny the diversity that exists within each sex and within us. When we look in the mirror the person we see before us is not just a gendered body but one who is marked by a range of social divisions. We need to be mindful, as fairground mirrors exemplify, that different mirrors reflect us in different ways.

The mirror-image can also deny that others are also objects and not simply always subjects. Men also look at themselves in the mirror. As objects men are shaped and regulated by the gaze of other men and women. It is often too easy to fall into the trap of thinking that man is always a subject able to operate with free will to the cost of womanhood. The operations of power are not quite so straightforward.

My purpose in this chapter is to offer an introduction to the post-structural thinking that has provided the theoretical framework of this text and through which these issues of subjectivity and power are explored. The interrelational nature of discourse, power and subjectivity has made it difficult to create neat and distinct separate subsections. Nevertheless, although there is overlap, I have endeavoured to ensure something of a distinct focus in the organisation of the text. Indeed, I hope that any repetition will only facilitate understanding of what can be a highly abstract discussion.

This chapter begins, in 'Why post-structuralism?', with a brief overview of the reasons why post-structuralism has been seen to offer radical potential for feminism. In 'Language and the instability of meanings' I indicate how post-structuralism views language as hierarchically arranged, relational yet not fixed in the transference of meaning. There are three purposes of the section 'Discourses and the hollows of meaning'. One is to introduce the concept of discourse. Another is to highlight the importance of the 'not-said' that is significant to feminist post-structuralist approaches. The third purpose is to illustrate the connections between discourse and subjectivity. In 'Discourses, power and Foucault' I set out the main elements of Foucauldian conceptualisations of power. I also illustrate the implications of these for understandings the working of discourse. Finally, in 'Mirrors of subjectivity' I discuss two ways in which mirror metaphors have been used to convey the psychoanalytic processes associated with the construction of subjectivity.

Why post-structuralism?

Butler and Scott (1992) caution that post-structuralism is not a position such as socialist feminism, radical feminism or liberal feminism commonly found within feminist theorising. One cannot say, for example, 'I am a post-structuralist' as one does say 'I am a feminist'. One might say instead 'I do post-structuralism'. Thus, post-structuralism is 'a critical interrogation of the exclusionary operations by which 'positions' are established' (Butler and Scott, 1992: xiv). As such, and of course marked by variety, post-structuralism can be viewed as a methodology that is used to examine, for example, how commonly accepted 'facts' about women's lives come to be established and maintained.

There are two aspects of post-structuralism that I seek to draw attention to here. First, post-structuralist analyses seek to explore the relations between discourse, subjectivities and power. In so doing, post-structuralism views the subject as one of process rather than fixity. Because of the centrality of language that is accorded within post-structuralism to the creation of the subject, post-structuralism also views the subject as a site of contradiction rather than unity. Second, post-structuralism is predominantly a *both/and* rather than an *either/or* approach to understanding social relations. For example, predominant within social analysis questions are posed in terms of whether a phenomenon is *either* agency *or* structure or whether it is *either* oppression *or* empowerment. Post-structuralist analyses focus on the ways in which social phenomena exhibit evidence of *both* agency *and* structure or *both* oppression *and* empowerment. In this way, post-structuralism seeks to go beyond the binaried thinking that has marked much social analysis.

The view of the subject, as a process, as contradictory, as in flux, is one that has offered an answer to some of the problems that have beset feminism. In particular, it provides an alternative explanation to notions of resistance and contradiction which have proved to be so problematic for the sex role theories that formed much second-wave thinking (Francis, 1998).

Sex role theory has been important in feminism because it recognises the social, as opposed to the biological, production of gendered beings. Sex role socialisation, for example, indicates the ways in which girls and boys are treated differently from the moment of their birth. The operation of a 'hidden curriculum' in schools also highlights differential treatment, with boys, for example, receiving more attention than girls. What remains unexplained, however, is how things change if such roles are so fixed and why some girls and some boys refuse to take up or resist taking up their gendered identities in the ways prescribed.

Through the relations of discourse, subjectivity and power, post-structuralism facilitates a recognition of how power is exercised within groups as well as between them and how, for example, women exercise power over other women. In addition, because it calls into question the concept of a fixed identity, it also provides the potential to overcome some of the essentialism inherent in much womanist discourse. Moreover, its focus on *process* gives rise to the potential for creating new gender discourses and, by implication, new subjectivities.

The following sections are intended to explore these issues further.

Language and the instability of meanings

The meanings attached to words have long been a feminist concern. Spender's (1980) research, for example, highlighted the maleness of the English language, with its dominance of the generic 'he/man'. Irigaray (1993), similarly, has made this point in relation to French, and other languages, in which nouns are ascribed as either feminine or masculine. As they and others have pointed out, language, and its patterning through narrative structures and characterisation, is not a neutral arbiter of the social world. The generic 'male' in language denies the existence of much of women's lives by rendering this invisible. The use of gender-specific nouns also signifies the hierarchical order of that which is valued or prized and that which is not.

These features of language have been applied in feminist writings to the meanings associated with both family and work. For example, the term 'family' is overwhelmingly associated with a heterosexual married couple living with their own children. For some feminists, therefore, the term household is a more accurate description of the variety of living arrangements that exist and can work to subvert the dominance of 'family' in everyday discourse. Others, of course, disagree and consider it important to retain the term 'family'. This is because the term 'household' has been used to downplay the significance of the gendered and hierarchical relationships implicit in widely held notions of 'family' (see, for example, Delphy and Leonard, 1992). In this way, 'household' presents as rather apolitical. Similarly, feminists have highlighted how the term 'work' is commonly equated with paid labour. This denies the work that women do in the home. For this reason, qualifying phrases are used, such as 'paid' and 'unpaid' work or 'paid' and 'unpaid' employment.

Language is of political importance for feminism as it highlights both material and subjective aspects of women's lives. Indeed, it is logical to extrapolate from the foregoing that in denying and denigrating women language is denying and denigrating women's senses of self, their everyday practices and their ways of being in the world. There is a danger in this nonetheless. To do so would suggest that all women are so denigrated and all women experience a sense of invisibility and low self-esteem. How then do we recognise the contradictory ways in which language works when at a general level we can also recognise its hierarchical ordering? It is here that we need to consider theories about the primacy of language from which post-structuralism draws.

Post-structuralism places considerable emphasis on the role of language in shaping both how we know and who we might become. In this, post-structuralism emphasises that 'language is first born' (Hartmann, 1981). Nevertheless, in contrast to structuralism, which considers language as having a fixed structure, post-structuralism destabilises this view. Thus, post-structuralism tends to 'stress the shifting, fragmented complexity of meaning (and relatedly of power), rather than a notion of its centralised order' (Beasley, 1999: 91).

This focus on the lack of fixed and universal meanings in language comes particularly from the work of Derrida. As Smith (1998) notes, Derrida drew on the work of Heidegger, who indicated that the concept of Being had undergone so many changes that it could not be used to convey any universal meaning. Yet, with no other suitable word available, it was necessary to continue to use it. Thus, Heidegger identified the ambiguous status of meaning by placing the word under erasure: ~~Being.~~

From a Derridean perspective language is organised in terms of hierarchical binaries. The most classic example of this is that of the binary male–female. It is this relational nature of meaning that is seen to give rise to its instability. Here we need to extend the idea of instability of meaning in language by considering how this arises. We have noted that language is organised in terms of hierarchical binaries. This is important not only to signify what might be dominant and what might be less so, but also because it draws attention to how meanings are derived. To be a woman, for example, requires there to be a man. Without this relation the terms alone would have no reference point from which to derive their meaning. Nonetheless, it is the relation between these binaries that gives rise to the instability of meaning production and reproduction. In particular 'the first term in a binary opposition can never be completely stable or secure, since it is dependent on that which is excluded' (Finlayson, 1999: 64). As understandings of female change, so do those of male.

Nevertheless, while meanings cannot be fixed, we live our lives as though they are. How can this be? The appearance of fixity is maintained through 'the suppression of its opposite' (Finlayson, 1999: 63). As I have indicated, what it means to be masculine relies on what it means to be feminine. However, in everyday discourse this relationship is hidden from view. We are not conscious, for example, that every time we use the word woman we are using the reference point of man to derive our meanings. As Davies (1997a: 9) notes 'This construction operates in a variety of intersecting ways, most of which are neither conscious nor intended. They are more like an effect of what we might call "speaking-as-usual" ...'

It is, of course, 'speaking-as-usual' that has been an important site of feminist critique. In seeking to explore the relations of domination that are underpinning our 'speaking-as-usual', feminist post-structuralism turns to understanding the silences and 'hollows' of discourse.

Discourses and the hollows of meaning

... all manifest discourse is secretly based on an 'already-said'; and that this 'already-said' is not merely a phrase that has already been spoken, or a text that has already been written, but a 'never-said', an incorporeal discourse, a voice as silent as a breath, a writing that is merely the hollow of its own mark.

(Foucault, 1972: 25)

The lack of universality of meaning that is a mark of language can be seen when we look at the term discourse. Indeed, Bacchi (2000: 55) remarks that 'there is no single or correct definition of discourse; we define it to suit our purposes, though this usually happens without conscious intent'. Thus, we find that the term discourse has been used in a number of ways in academic research and writing. It may, for example, refer to the analysis of spoken dialogue or written text or both. It may focus on the patterning of speech or be concerned with the effects of that speech on the receiver. It may be concerned with a very short sequence of speech or with the structuring of narrative and characterisation. It may have as its concern the relationship between reader and text. Or it may refer to non-verbal signs. Or it may have nothing to do with language but with wider forms of representation such as film, art or the body.

In addition, the term discourse is used in a variety of disciplinary contexts – sociology, psychology, linguistics, literature, history, law, anthropology, to name a few. And, within and across these, the term will be employed in a range of paradigmatic, theoretical, political and conceptual frames. Wodak (1997), for example, indicates the range of ways in which feminists in the field of socio-linguistics apply the concept of discourse in their work. This may be through conversation analysis or analysis of the written text. Feminist linguists may be concerned with analysing sexism in language or, more recently, the relation of language and subjectivity. They may emphasise dominance or difference positions.

In her analysis of policy-as-discourse positions, Bacchi (2000) notes that the most common purpose of such research is to challenge relations of domination. Similarly, it is this political potential of discourse that has drawn it to the attention of feminist scholars. As Foucault (1972: 25) makes clear, 'The manifest discourse, therefore, is really no more than the repressive presence of what it does not say; and this "not-said" is a hollow that undermines from within all that is said'. What is 'not-said' and, in consequence, that which threatens to undermine dominant discourses is a key site of attention for feminism. Thus, what we might say is general to conceptualisations of discourse within post-structuralism is that when the term is used it usually indicates a broadening from a narrow focus on language as a string of words (Gee, 1997) to 'the way language systematically organizes concepts, knowledge and experience and to the way in which it excludes alternative forms of organisation' (Finlayson, 1999: 62).

Gee (1996: 132 passim) draws a distinction between discourse as a focus on the speech and Discourse as a focus on what lies in the hollow of the 'not-said' by using the capital 'D' for the latter. He indicates that there are several important points that can be made about Discourses:

- Discourses involve a set of values and viewpoints about the relationships between people and the distribution of social goods, at the very least about who is an insider and who isn't, often who is 'normal' and who isn't.
- Discourses are resistant to internal criticism and self-scrutiny, as uttering viewpoints that seriously undermine them defines one as being outside them. The Discourse itself defines what counts as acceptable criticism.
- Discourse-defined positions from which to speak and behave are not, however, just defined internally to a Discourse, but also as standpoints taken up by the Discourse in its relation to other, ultimately opposing, Discourses. The Discourse we identify with being a feminist is radically changed if all male Discourses disappear.
- Any Discourse concerns itself with certain objects and puts forward certain concepts, viewpoints and values at the expense of others. In doing so it will *marginalize* viewpoints and values central to other Discourses. In fact, a Discourse can call for one to accept values in conflict with other Discourses of which one is also a member.
- [Dominant] Discourses are intimately related to the distribution of social power and hierarchical structure in society. Control over certain Discourses can lead to the acquisition of social goods (money, power, status) in a society. These Discourses empower those [dominant] groups which have the least conflicts with their other Discourses when they use them.

Use of the term 'discourse' signifies reference to something that is more than language. Discourse foregrounds a focus on the systematisation *and* instability of meanings. Importantly, it also draws attention to the practices and subject positions that arise from our relationships with and to language. As Henwood (1998: 39) notes:

> The common point being made ... is that discourses are not merely people's assumptions, ideas and definitions expressed through language but also the practices, formations and subject positions which follow from these.

This is how post-structuralism seeks to understand how the idea of a unified fixed self is so pervasive. Post-structuralism represents a critique of the notion of the fixed self of humanism. Post-structuralism suggests that the self is positioned by and, importantly, positions itself within the socially and culturally constructed patterns of language that we label discourse. Thus, 'practices create subjectivities so that no real human subject exists prior to the social practices within which she is subjected' (Walkerdine, 1989: 206).

A predominant discourse in Western societies is that of the autonomous, unified subject. Such a discourse is represented in the term 'I' that is invoked whenever we refer to our*selves*. It is indeed difficult to get rid of the idea of a solid person or a true self that the mirror appears to reflect back to us. It is also difficult to rid ourselves of the either/or positions of exterior and interior that these uses of the mirror as a metaphor give rise to. From a post-structural viewpoint, this sense of solidity is itself an effect of subjectivity. In this sense it is a 'fiction'. It is one that is sustained through the very language we have available to us. Within post-structuralist analyses, the 'I' is thus a discursive creation that arises through the subject being taken up by, and taking up, such a dominant discourse. In consequence, it is very difficult to overcome the idea that there exists within each of us a true authentic self, because each time we speak 'I' we are reproducing the fiction that 'I' exists.

Nonetheless, and although it has all the appearance of fixity, post-structuralism argues that the 'I' is not fixed but is one of process. This returns us to the discussion above in terms of the instability and variety of meanings in language. As I shall elaborate further below, there are clearly many discourses within language. Some are dominant, some are marginal, some are 'fleshing' (Haw, 1998) and some are counter or reverse. Discourses also come together and combine through discursive formations that are always changing and are internally very diverse (Epstein and Johnson, 1998). This means that, just as there are contradictory discourses, the subject is not one of unity but of contradiction. And, as there are multiple discourses, so too we take up multiple subjectivities. Indeed, Gee (1996: 132) notes that 'the individual is the meeting point of many, sometimes conflicting, socially and historically defined Discourses'. As discourses shift and alter so do subjectivities. Belsey (1997: 661) puts it thus:

> The subject is thus the site of contradiction, and is consequently perpetually in the process of construction, thrown into crisis by alterations in language and in the social formation, capable of change.

The idea of the subject-as-process is central to the political potential of feminist post-structuralism as 'the fact that the subject is a *process* lies the possibility of transformation' (Belsey, 1997: 661, emphasis in text; see also Munro, 1998). While the point of a post-structuralist political project is not to set up a new binary of humanist subject and anti-humanist subject, such a project is concerned to 'show how the humanist self is so convincingly achieved' (Davies, 1997a: 272). Thus, post-structuralism illustrates how language prevents us from conceptualising the subject as only ever in process. As Davies (1997b: 275) indicates, language traps us back into a pre-existing choosing subject:

... in attempting to reconceptualise the subject as process, we are limited by the images and metaphors we can find to create the new idea. Pronoun grammar is a good example of this. We cannot yet see how to do without it. We see the power of gendered pronouns, for example, to reconstitute the male/female binary in the very language we use in our attempts to move beyond gender ... the text/discourse relentlessly writes us as existing, even when our intention is to enable the reader to disattend the active subject/writer and to attend to the constitutive force of discourse.

Yet language does not operate on the subject simply as a force outside ourselves in a deterministic way. While we cannot get outside language, we are not trapped by it either. Thus, in addition to a lack of universality in the meanings of language there is also a lack of fixity in the transference of meaning. For example, I cannot assume that my intended meanings in writing this text will be those that are taken up by readers. Readers bring their own knowledges, experiences, values and meanings to the text. This means that, as author, I cannot guarantee the authority of my words. As Smith (1998: 260) notes:

> Post-structuralist discourse analysis undermines the idea that language is a transmission device for carrying the intention of the author, with the reader trusting an authoritative voice. If the author is no longer the authoritative voice of truth and authenticity, readers can be seen as participating in the production of meaning by constructing their own stories.

We are each involved in both the production and reproduction of meanings ascribed through language. We can see this when we consider the concept of desire. Desire is the term used for those processes associated with investments in particular identity positions. Those positions we take up and identify with are those which constitute our identities (Woodward, 1997). Thus, in identifying as a woman we may be identifying with discourses that suggest that womanhood is (any, and all of) nurturative or vulnerable or sexual or oppressed or strong, and so forth. Of course, we can, and do, resist particular subject positions. For everyone who identifies as feminist, for example, there are many more that do not!

Laws and Davies (2000: 206) note how the dual nature of simultaneously being subjected to forces external to us and at the same time becoming an agentic subject is difficult to grasp. They comment:

> The dual nature of subjectification is hard to grasp: one is simultaneously subjected and at the same time can become an agentic, speaking subject. The speaking/writing subject can go

beyond the intentions of powerful others and beyond the meanings of the discourses through which they are subjected while necessarily and at the same time being dependent on their successful subjection for becoming someone who can speak/write meaningfully and convincingly beyond the terms of their subjection. To grasp this requires a capacity to think outside our more practiced, linear patterns of thought.

Nevertheless, this is a significant aspect of post-structuralist approaches. A post-structuralist conception of identity formation stresses the contradictory and precarious processes through which we come into being because of the ways in which discourses operate. In these ways, post-structuralism takes up a view of power and resistance that draws from the work of Foucault.

Discourses, power and Foucault

There are four elements of Foucault's conceptualisation of power which are important to understanding the attention given to the significance of discourses and the ways in which they operate within post-structuralist writings. These four elements are: power can be understood in terms of a matrix or capillary; where there is power we will find resistance; the operations of power, through disciplinary practices, regimes or techniques, give rise to self-surveillance or self-discipline; and, finally, power is productive rather than repressive.

Foucault's analysis highlights the multiaxial locations of power:

> Power is everywhere; not because it embraces everything, but because it comes from everywhere. And 'power,' insofar as it is permanent, repetitious, inert, and self-reproducing, is simply the over-all effect that emerges from all these mobilities, the concatenation that rests on each of them and seeks in turn to arrest their movement. One needs to be nominalistic, no doubt: power is not an institution, and not a structure; neither is it a certain strength we are endowed with; it is the name that one attributes to a complex strategical situation in a particular society.
>
> (Foucault, 1978: 93)

Rather than turning our attention to government or economy or patriarchy, the statement that power is everywhere means that we need to look at the social relations that occur everyday between people. It is here, according to Foucault's conceptualisation, that we will know power more adequately. In moving from the macro to the micro, Foucault challenges several ideas. First he challenges the idea that power is exercised only by those who have 'more' power in a society, for example men as opposed to women, White people as opposed to Black, bosses rather than workers, adults rather than children. Second, he challenges the idea that power is exercised in one only direction, i.e. from the top down. Rather, power is also exercised from below. Third, he indicates that power is not located in one source but is embedded in networks of relations, the total effect of which may, indeed, be that certain forms of power are self-reproducing.

In addition, Foucault argues that power and resistance coexist:

> Where there is power, there is resistance, and yet, or rather consequently, this resistance is never in a position of exteriority in relation to power. Should it be said that one is always 'inside' power, there is no 'escaping' it, there is no absolute outside where it is concerned, because one is subject to the law in any case? Or that, history being the ruse of reason, power is the ruse of history, always emerging the winner? This would be to misunderstand the strictly relational character of power relationships. Their existence depends on a multiplicity of points of resistance: these play the role of adversary, target, support, or handle in power relations. These points of resistance are present everywhere in the power network.
>
> (Foucault, 1978: 95)

This means that, rather than one single resisting force, we should understand resistance, like power, in terms of its multiplicity and, again like power, embedded in the everyday of social relations. Whereas revolutions, for example, are possible through the strategic codification of these many points of resistance, resistance takes many forms:

> spontaneous, savage, solitary, concerted, rampant, or violent; still others that are quick to compromise, interested, or sacrificial ...
>
> (Foucault, 1978: 96)

For Foucault, power also acts through forms of self-discipline. It is internalised. This means that although, of course, coercive forms of power can be visibly exerted, for example smacking a child, in the everyday there is no need. This is most usefully illustrated through Foucault's attention to the panopticon. The panopticon was designed as the perfect prison. Through a central tower, it offered the prison authorities the possibility of continual surveillance, and hence discipline, of prisoners. Moreover, the panoptic gaze is not relevant solely to understanding disciplinary aspects of power in the context of prisoners. It is also relevant to understanding the operations of power in a whole range of disciplinary institutions, be they schools, families or employing organisations.

The gaze (*le regard*) is one example of the ways in which technologies of surveillance operate at a micro level. We need think only of the existence of cameras in shopping centres or on motorways to see the relevance of this. Through being watched, monitored, evaluated, one is controlled. Moreover, it is the knowledge that you *might* be watched that gives rise to its self-disciplining effect. The speed cameras may or may not have film in them. You slow down nevertheless. In these ways power is exercised independently of the person who exercises it. Yet power is also visible but unverifiable:

> Visible: the inmate will constantly have before his eyes the tall outline of the central tower from which he is spied upon. Unverifiable: the inmate must never know whether he is being looked at at any one moment; but he must be sure that he may always be so. ... The Panopticon is a machine for dissociating the see/being seen dyad: in the peripheric ring, one is totally seen, without ever seeing; in the central tower, one sees everything without ever being seen.
>
> (Foucault, 1977: 201–2)

The notion that power is productive offers an alternative understanding of the operations of power to that traditionally used in feminist analyses. Feminism has, more commonly, understood power in terms of repression and illegitimacy. The weight of these analyses has focused on how women are oppressed through the operations of patriarchal power. This power has in some way been seized from women, rendering them powerless. Paechter (2000: 27) draws our attention to a neglected but important aspect of power when she comments that 'Power is not simply repressive, but is bound up with our desire, the desire to know and to understand ... we cannot conceive of power as simply a great negative, only to be resisted, but must also see it as empancipatory, as producing pleasure and a sense of mastery, which, even if based on an illusion, allows us a glimpse of freedom'.

In defining power as productive, Foucault was emphasising the fact that power 'is producing knowledge rather than repression' (Ramazanoglu, 1993: 21). Again, the Panopticon indicates how the operations of power give rise to new forms of knowledge, which in turn gives rise to new targets for the operation of that power:

> ... the Panopticon was also a laboratory; it could be used as a machine to carry out experiments, to alter behaviour, to train or correct individuals. To experiment with medicines and monitor their effects. To try out different punishments on prisoners, according to their crimes and character, and to seek the most effective ones. ... The Panopticon may even provide an apparatus for supervising its own mechanisms. In this central tower, the director may spy on all the employees that he has under his orders: nurses, doctors, foremen, teachers, warders; he will be able to judge them continuously, alter their behaviour, impose upon them the methods he thinks best, and

it will even be possible to observe the director himself. An inspector arriving unexpectedly at the centre of the Panopticon will be able to judge at a glance, without anything being concealed from him, how the entire establishment is functioning. ... The Panopticon functions as a kind of laboratory of power. Thanks to its mechanisms of observation, it gains in efficiency and in the ability to penetrate into men's behaviour; knowledge follows the advances of power, discovering new objects of knowledge over all the surfaces on which power is exercised.

(Foucault, 1977: 203–4)

The panoptic gaze gave rise to two kinds of visibility: synoptic and individualising (Fraser, 1989). The synoptic gaze allowed whole populations to be observed. And within whole populations individuals came increasingly to be objects worthy of study. The growth of the case history is one example given by Foucault of the ways in which individuals, inspected, supervised and observed, became the objects of new forms of enquiry – through, say, medicine, social work and education. This, in turn, has given rise to new knowledges and new sciences. Sociology, psychology and psychoanalysis would be classic examples.

Finally, let us consider the relations between power and discourse that are central to understanding a post-structuralist conception. Foucault points out that there is an implication that, lying behind the masquerade of ideology, there are pre-existing, objective truths waiting to be found. The phrase 'the ideology of motherhood', for example, suggests that once we have unpicked this ideology we will find a 'true' motherhood. Foucault bracketed off questions of validity and truth. He left them to one side as it were. This is because, from a Foucauldian perspective, knowledge:

... is always bound up with historically specific regimes of power and, therefore, every society produces its own truths which have a normalizing and regulatory function. ... Rather, it is the task of the genealogist to discover how these discourses of truth operate in relation to the dominant power structures of a given society.

(McNay, 1992: 25)

In place of ideology Foucault used the terms 'discourse' or 'discursive formation'. This was because it was in discourse that we can see the ways in which power and knowledge are joined. As the following indicates, the relation between power and knowledge means that discourses cannot be viewed as stable or uniform. Discourses should be perceived as multiple. Because of their multiplicity they can be drawn on in terms of a variety of strategies. Discourses give voice and they silence. Discourses can give rise to differential effects dependent upon who is the speaker and the position of the speaker.

Discourses do not always work in the ways expected but can have contradictory effects. They cannot therefore be seen to be mere instruments of power. Discourses produce power but also hold within them the possibilities of undermining power. Discourses are:

> ... discontinuous segments whose tactical function is neither uniform nor stable. To be more precise, we must not imagine a world of discourse divided between accepted discourse and excluded discourse, or between the dominant discourse and the dominated one; but as a multiplicity of discursive elements that can come into play in various strategies. It is this distribution that we must reconstruct, with the things said and those concealed, the enunciations required and those forbidden, that it comprises; with the variants and different effects – according to who is speaking, his [sic] position of power, the institutional context in which he [sic] happens to be situated – that it implies; and with the shifts and reutilizations of identical formulas for contrary objectives that it also includes. Discourses are not once and for all subservient to power or raised up against it, any more than silences are. We must make allowance for the complex and unstable process whereby discourse can be both an instrument and an effect of power, but also a hindrance, a stumbling-block, a point of resistance and a starting point for an opposing strategy. Discourse transmits and produces power; it reinforces it but also undermines and exposes it, renders it fragile and makes it possible to thwart it.
>
> (Foucault, 1978: 100–1)

In addition, discourses are not understood as static or unchanging. Changing discourses of women's role as mothers and paid workers have given rise to discourses of the 'new woman', who is able to combine her responsibilities for care with employment (Woodward, 1997). Given that caring is integral to the 'new woman', this discourse involves a rearticulated version of older discourses of the caring mother. Moreover, it indicates the relation of discourses to changing economic and social conditions as the discourse of the 'new woman' arose at a time of women's increasing participation in paid labour. Nor are discourses predictable in their effects and the ways in which they are understood. To maintain their hegemonic effect they may incorporate elements of disruptive discourses. Blackmore (1999), for example, notes how new management theories that emphasise a 'softer' approach to managing organisations have incorporated emancipatory feminist leadership discourses.

These issues of power, language and hierarchy are resonant in the use of mirror metaphors in psychoanalytic understandings of the subject. It is to these that we now turn.

Mirrors of subjectivity

The mirror metaphor has been classically used in psychoanalysis to explain the processes of acquiring a sense of identity. Lacan, for example, used the metaphor of mirror to describe the stages of identity formation. Irigaray has used the metaphor of speculum to refute the phallocentricism of Lacan's straight mirror of masculinity.

Lacan's straight mirror of the father

> ... several functions are served by the mirror ... First, it provides a point outside the self through which the self is recognised. Second, it provides the infant with his or her first experience of corporeal unity, although an illusory one. Third, the infant is introduced to an order of imaginary relations. There is a split between a glimpse of perfect unity and the infant's actual state of fragility. Though based on an ideal, the mirror episode gives the child an imaginary experience of what it must be like to be whole. It is in the mirror phase that the child begins to acquire language. And it is through the entry into language that the child is constituted as a subject.
>
> (Sarup, 1996: 36)

Grosz (1990: 31) notes that Lacan's account is 'widely recognised as the basis of his questioning and subversion of dominant, i.e. humanist, social sciences and of the reign of the Cartesian cogito'. Wright (2000: 55) comments that Lacan 'has launched a powerful critique of stable identity without getting rid of it altogether'. Lacan argued that the unified subject that has been so powerfully articulated through the work of Freud was a fantasy. Rather the self is split. This splitting occurs because the self is constituted through others. The differentiation of the child from others relies on points of reflection. What we see in the mirror is an illusion. Just as we might say 'How do I look in the mirror?' or 'What does this mirror make me look like?' the self is a reflected image. It relies on others to constitute itself. Not only do I require 'you' to be 'me', I' can only exist through 'you' (Belsey, 1997).

According to Lacan, the child constructs a self in terms of a reflection in the eyes of others or in a reflection in an actual mirror. This sense of self, however, does not happen suddenly 'But at the same time, the baby is fascinated by human faces and figures and he makes an initial identification with these whole and unified figures as later he is to gain his own unified image in the mirror' (Mitchell, 1974: 386). Nevertheless, although the subject is a series of reflections of others it still desires to be unified. As Mitchell (1974: 386, emphasis in text) comments:

> The baby is helpless ... but the image he is given of himself, through others and then in the mirror, is not helpless – on the contrary it is

whole and coordinated. The mirror-image must be more perfect than itself – the itself that is not yet constituted – as Narcissus discovered to his cost.

Battersby (1998: 87) notes that for Lacan 'To see oneself as a unitary subject involves a form of visual repression. What is blanked out is everything that would disturb the illusion of the "I" as controlling and autonomous'. Nonetheless, the desire for unity leads to powerful identifications with particular subject positions and with significant others outside ourselves. It occurs at those moments that you say, as Belsey puts it, 'I'm just like that'. By being 'you', of course, I cannot be 'me'.

These processes of identity formation occur at the point of entry into the language. Language does not simply signify identity. Language constitutes it:

> In order to speak the child is compelled to differentiate; to speak of itself it has to distinguish 'I' from 'you.' In order to formulate its needs the child learns to identify with the first person singular pronoun ... it is language which provides the possibility of subjectivity because it is language which enables the speaker to posit himself or herself as 'I', as the subject of a sentence. It is in language that people constitute themselves as subjects. Consciousness of self is possible only through contrast, differentiation: 'I' cannot be conceived without the conception 'non-I', 'you,' and dialogue, the fundamental condition of language, implies a reversible polarity between 'I' and 'you'.
>
> (Belsey, 1997: 659)

Lacan argued that women always enter the social world in a negative way. This is because the phallus, as *the* privileged signifier, occupies '*the* central discursive position, [that] forever constitutes women in terms of what they lack (the phallus), and men in terms of the threat of lack (fear of castration)' (Woodward, 1997: 201, emphasis in text). As Battersby (1998: 87) notes:

> ... for Lacan, there is no speaking or viewing position which is that of woman. Indeed, in so far as women speak or gaze ... they are positioned as masculinized. 'Woman' and the 'female' do not exist, except in so far as they act as the necessary limit to the oedipalized self. Women can speak; but they cannot speak (consciously) from the position of woman. This is because self-identity is first prefigured in relation to a 'cut' from the Other; that which eventually gets characterized as not-self, but which is only thrust into Otherness as the infant experiences non-completion or lack in the absence of the mother. Thus, the eyes of the mother serve as a kind of mirror against which identity is constructed and boundaries determined. What is

prefigured in that mirror is established more firmly later as the child is inducted into language.

Walkerdine (1989: 276) comments that 'Lacan argued that "woman" exists only as a symptom of male fantasy. What he meant was that the fantasies created under patriarchy (or the Law of the Father or Symbolic Order, as he calls it) create as their object not women as they really are but fantasies of what men both desire and fear in the Other'. Women, then, 'become the Other, that is, what men are not' (Weedon, 1999: 104). 'For Lacan there is no other of the Other' (Battersby, 1998: 98). It was this issue that Irigaray challenged through the metaphor of the speculum.

The curved mirror of the speculum

> But which 'subject' up till now has investigated the fact that a concave mirror concentrates the light and, specifically, that this is not wholly irrelevant to woman's sexuality?
>
> (Irigaray, 1985: 144)

Woman as Other of Lacanian psychoanalytic discourse is, for Irigaray, 'the image that he wishes to reflect himself against' (Whitford, 1991: 28). She is the image that constitutes him as whole and maybe as 'perfect'. Grosz (1990: 173, emphasis in text) similarly comments that Irigaray 'attempts to traverse the Lacanian mirror of male self-representation which confirms woman in the position of *man's* specular double or alter-ego. His is a mirror, she implies, that can only reflect the masculine subject for whom it functions as a form of self-externalization.'

For Irigaray, such an image reflects the need of patriarchy to 'contain' woman. It was in rebuking the phallocentrism of Lacan's analysis that Irigaray used the metaphor of the speculum. Lacan's analysis views women in terms of what they lack, as a 'hole', rather than in terms of what they have. The emphasis in Lacan on what can be seen, i.e. the phallus, was countered by Irigaray's use of the speculum, the curved mirror that enables internal inspection of the body. As a metaphor the speculum demonstrates that what *is* is not always on view. What woman is or could be cannot simply be known through a dominant phallocentric view represented by a looking-glass mirror. The speculum allows access to those sites that are hidden from (male) view and that are beyond the phallus.

Battersby (1996: 262) notes how 'Speculum as a whole reverses the direction of gaze, using woman's body as the apparatus through which to regard the philosophers' accounts of being'. For example, Irigaray opposes the Lacanian image of woman as 'hole' with the symbolic image of '*contiguity*, of the two lips touching' (Whitford, 1991: 28) This image is designed to show

how a woman's desire does not need to be seen through male representations but can be seen for itself. In addition, Irigaray draws on ideas of fluidity to oppose notions of woman as a 'container'. Thus:

> The/a woman never closes up into a volume. The dominant representation of the maternal figure as volume may lead us to forget that woman's ability to enclose is enhanced by her fluidity, and vice-versa. Only when coopted by phallic values does the womb preclude the separation of the lips.
>
> (Irigaray, 1985: 239).

Weed (1994: 81) notes that 'Irigaray's texts permit multiple and ... often contradictory readings'. Thus, the image of fluidity can imply an essentialism associated with Nature or it can imply a symbolic counterpoint to notions of fixity. Yet readings of essentialism belie an interpretation of Irigaray as deconstructing 'the explanatory power of psychoanalysis in relation to the construction and reproduction of patriarchal forms of subjectivity. Moreover, not only does it analyse the human subject, it is also able to make explicit the "stakes" involved in *all* phallocentric knowledges' (Grosz, 1990: 169, emphasis in text). For example, as many commentators have noted, Irigaray never mentions Lacan's name in the *Speculum of the Other Woman*. Grosz (1990: 169) argues that this is a strategic move and 'a mimesis of Lacan's and Freud's relegation of the question of femininity to a side issue in the exploration of the Oedipus complex and the name-of-the father. She attempts to undo psychoanalytic phallocentrism by insinuating the question of sexual specificity into its most central assumptions and propositions.' Certainly 'In exposing this appropriation of woman (especially of woman as mother) as a mirror of masculine resemblance, Irigaray's concern is to free woman from her one-dimensional, reflexive position within phallocentric culture' (Berry, 1994: 230).

In that, therefore, there is no doubt that Irigaray keeps us focused on the political as a project within feminist post-structuralism. To this end it is worth noting, as a postscript to this section, that on publication of *Speculum* Irigaray was dismissed from the Vincennes Department of Psychoanalysis of the University of Paris, where she had been a close associate of Lacan.

Summary

This chapter has been designed to set out the main tenets of feminist approaches to post-structuralism. Central to post-structuralism are the relations between discourse, power and subjectivity. Post-structuralism interrogates the idea that gender identities are fixed and unified and posits in its place the idea of the subject-as-process. As a politics, feminism post-structuralism also seeks to interrogate the taken-for-granted 'facts' and practices that constitute gender, and other, relations. As Weedon (1987: 12) notes, it seeks to 'understand why women tolerate social relations which subordinate their interests to those of men and the mechanisms whereby women and men adopt particular discursive positions as representative of their interests'. Throughout this chapter I have endeavoured to keep a focus on the political. The implications of post-structuralism for feminist politics is a topic I explore more fully in the final chapter.

2

WOMEN HAVE MADE IT

Opportunities are available to women that would have been unimaginable twenty years ago. All professions are open to women. Legislation has been passed to prevent the more blatant attempts at discrimination. And many women have made it to the top.

(Coward, 1993: 3)

In short, with some exceptions, education is a success story for women in the 1990s.

(Walby, 1997: 43)

Discourses that attest to the fact that 'women have made it' are prevalent in contemporary Western societies. These discourses cite evidence of widening opportunities, choices and potential in women's lives. They point out that more women are in paid employment; more women are achieving ever higher educational qualifications; more women are choosing to delay having children or are choosing not to have them at all; and there are increasing numbers of women in managerial and professional positions. At the level of political representation, in 2000 there were more women representatives in the British parliament than ever before.

These discourses are supported through a plethora of writings on issues related to women and gender, giving a new sense of consciousness to women who have 'never been near a women's liberation meeting' (Coote and Campbell, 1987: 253). Bulbeck (1997) also comments that the lack of consciousness about the low numbers of women taking their place in the public spheres of life has not only been reversed, but would now be unthinkable. In a 'new millennium' celebration of female success the first issue of the *Independent on Sunday* for 2000 (2 January 2000: 3) devoted a whole section to 'Women on Top'. This contained photographs of 100 successful women that were reproduced 'to give a sense of the multiplicity of ways – unthinkable a century ago – in which modern women can reach the heights of power, wealth and influence.'

Similarly, in a trade magazine aimed at business professionals, R. Johnson (2000) reviewed the evidence of futurologists who claim that women are likely to overtake and eventually replace men as leaders at the top of organisations.

These discourses are also supported through legislative change. Over a decade ago the achievements of feminism were listed as including the legislation relating to abortion, the Equal Pay and Sex Discrimination Acts, greater representation of women in political parties and equal opportunities policies in small and large organisations alike (Phillips, 1987; Eisenstein, 1991). There is, indeed, much to suggest an optimistic future for some of feminism's goals. Or is there?

Given this weight of evidence, discourses that women have made it appear to be self-evidently true. However, in an article accompanying the *Independent on Sunday* photographs, D. Orr (2000) was cautious to remind readers not to believe that too much had changed. The arenas in which most of the women who were featured found their success – the arts, media, fashion and retailing – were available to women 100 years ago. These are traditional sources of paid labour for women. And so, Orr notes, 'There were Judi Denches back then, and Joan Collinses and Kathy Burkes' (p. 6). Moreover, Orr continues, while there may be more women in employment, little has been achieved in terms of the provision of childcare facilities or to shift the balance of responsibilities for domestic work between women and men. Similarly, R. Johnson (2000) questions how the future can be female when the 'glass ceiling' remains so firmly intact.

Wilson (1999: 529) goes so far as to say that the idea that we are now living in a gender-equal society 'is a convenient assumption men and women wish to believe'. She suggests that the alternative view that, despite all these changes, gender inequality is persistent and unending is too unpleasant to behold because such a view contradicts Enlightenment ideas that the steady progress of history is leading to a better world. Yet a belief in the Enlightenment is not the only way in which we are encouraged to believe that women have made it. 'Women have made it' discourses comprise four highly persuasive elements that in themselves reflect dominant ideas in society. When they are put together they operate in such mutually sustaining ways that they are difficult to resist.

The first of these elements is a definition of equality that views women and men as the same. In the discourses of feminism's third wave, this position is occupied by 'sexy ... power feminists [who] have won the battle of the sexes by embracing strategies their foremothers refused' (Drake, 1997: 107). Moreover, some perceive that they have done so without even breaking a nail (ibid)! The more erudite would much more strongly identify this position with liberal feminism. Based on a form of competitive individualism, it is hardly surprising that this has never been the most politically correct of feminist positions. It has, however, been the most populist. Indeed, Beasley (1999: 51) points out that liberal feminism is both the most widely known form of feminism and also commonly 'seen as synonymous with feminism *per se*'.

Eisenstein (1984) illustrates that the roots of feminism lie in liberalist thought. In so doing, this form of feminism has taken up the discourses of liberalism and shaped them to make it its own. For example, liberalism and feminism share 'some conception of individuals as free and equal beings, emancipated from the ascribed, hierarchical bonds of traditional society' (Pateman, 1987: 103). Given that liberalism 'is the most successful ideology in practice' (Browning, 2000: 161), it is no wonder that liberal feminism has become the most dominant discourse found within feminism. It accords with many pre-existing 'truths' about the world in terms of particular conceptions of equality, fairness, liberty and choice. Thus, achieving greater access to employment opportunities not only demonstrates women's right to leave the kitchen sink but also offers a sense of freedom of choice and autonomy.

The second persuasive element of 'women have made it' discourses is that they speak to mainstream ideas of what it is to be successful in Western societies. Success is defined through the ability of individuals to navigate the social system in an upwardly mobile way. This is achieved through education and paid employment, the two main institutional arenas where, though importantly not unambiguously, competitive individualism is celebrated. Through the connections between definitions of success and the arenas of education and employment, 'women have made it' discourses draw in several other discursive strands. For example, they contain meritocratic assumptions that education and employment should operate in symbiosis. Thus, gaining more, and higher, qualifications enables women to compete more ably for well-paid jobs. They draw on the split between public and private life, which in themselves reflect the values of the masculine and feminine. It is, for example, appropriate to be ambitious in educational and employment terms. The family, on the other hand, is a place for nurturance and care. And, 'women have made it' discourses presage a feminist future. Gaining access to higher levels of organizational decision making produces images of power sharing across the sexes and the potential for more women-friendly ways of organising.

Linked to these aspects of success, the third element that persuades us to believe that women have made it is the notion of woman as a universalist category. 'Women have made it' discourses attempt to speak for all women. In asking us to celebrate 100 named women as a collective of success, the *Independent on Sunday* photographs invite all other women to identify with them. In doing so, they present a view of desirable womanhood that links this desire with the kind of success that is achieved through fame, wealth and institutional power. This unity of womanhood masks any claims for difference. Instead of asking which women *can* make it in terms of their class, 'race', (dis)ability and sexuality, we are drawn into a cosy view of the sharedness of women's experiences. This sharedness, moreover, relates to assumptions that all women desire to be like this. In other words, 'women have made it' discourses assume that they are speaking for all our desires.

The legitimacy of statistics provides the fourth element of persuasion. Statistical evidence is presented with all the hallmarks of classical scientific enquiry, which is itself a dominant way of knowing. Statistics appear hard, rigorous and objective. In so doing, they suggest that there is an external reality that can be measured. They provide a view of the social world as composed of measurable packages. School league tables, for example, delineate the worth of a school through a series of performance measures. They mark out good schools from bad ones. As an aspect of science, statistics draw on Enlightenment discourses to illustrate the degree of change. Thus, measuring the changing positions of women and men is part of a continuing evaluation of the progress of a more gender-equitable society.

Nevertheless, in presenting particular views of reality in this way, statistics are themselves discourses that shape responses to this reality. Parents choose 'good' schools rather than bad ones. Government ministers argue that 'failing' schools should be closed or they need to learn from the successful ones now designated as 'beacons'. As women, the statistics provide a measure of our own positions as 'successful' or 'non-successful' people. For feminism, the question that is asked is 'If women really are making it, have we reached a post-feminist age where the "battle of the sexes" can cease?'

These elements, drawn on singly or multiply, form particular discursive formations. These are combinations of discourses 'with different histories, but combined in particular relations of force, in process in the same place and time ... always being produced, always changing and internally very diverse' (Epstein and Johnson, 1998: 16). This is true not only of 'women have made it' discourses, and indeed the other discourses discussed in this text, but it is also true of the elements that constitute them. For example, it would be a mistake to assume that liberal feminism is a single discourse or that some of the assumptions of liberal feminism are not common to other feminist politics. Nor should it be assumed that there is consensus about where the borders and boundaries of different feminist positions lie.

Although the final section of this chapter does refer to studies that have been concerned with confirming, or challenging, the fact that women have made it, this is not my overall aim here. In accord with Walkerdine (1994: 59) I argue that 'we have to move away from a simple empiricism to a position in which we understand fact, fiction and fantasy as interrelated'. We should not, for example, take 'women have made it' discourses as simple facts to be proven or otherwise. Rather, we should be concerned with how such discourses work on our desires and aspirations and how they present certain 'truths' about who we are and the world we live in. For this reason, my aim is to deconstruct 'women have made it' discourses by asking 'How is this truth constituted, how is it possible, and what effects does it have?' (Walkerdine, 1994: 59).

As Wilson (1999) has indicated, ideas that women have made it are rather seductive. This chapter begins, in the section 'Women can make it: liberal feminism's promise', by indicating how 'women have made it' discourses draw on a conception of equality that is part of wider political discourses associated with individual rights, choices and opportunities. This view of equality is such that the goal of feminism is to become equal to men through the exercise of the same rights, choices and opportunities. I offer a post-structuralist critique of this position by paying attention to the concept of the unitary subject at the heart of liberal feminist discourses and through the notions of power that such discourses draw on.

In the next section, 'Successful women: a contradiction in terms?'. I turn to a paradox in 'woman have made it discourses' as I explore research that explores women's continuing sense of inadequacy even though their lives bear testimony to success. Here, I draw on research that explores how the values of success in 'women have made it' discourses shape subject positions 'in the way of men'. I illustrate how a series of contradictions, which are polarised around views of femininity and masculinity, create dissonance. The internalisation of this dissonance is reinforced through everyday acts that teach women their inferiority.

Finally, in 'Women are doing too well' I explore the operations of hegemonic masculinity through the work of feminists who have responded to these discourses. My purpose here is to illustrate that, although it remains important for feminists to continue to assert the 'facts' of women's continuing inequality, this is an insufficient political tactic for those feminists who seek to create new discourses and potentially new ways of being.

Women can make it: liberal feminism's promises

> ... there is the gender script of professional success, the gender-neutral 'I', built upon the notion that 'my success is due to hard work and merit and sheer professionalism alone'. This is the ultimate expression of the freely operating individual, who makes choices, and who, through her capacities as a person, not a woman, 'makes it'.
>
> (Blackmore, 1999: 83)

When we hear that women represent over 50% of students in higher education at first-degree level (Higher Education Statistics Agency, 1996) or that the numbers of women achieving professional qualifications have risen substantially, we are listening to 'women have made it' discourses. Similarly, when our attention is directed to the fact that more women are finding themselves in positions of authority in organisations, as leaders and managers, and that young women are delaying child bearing in order to forge a career, we see a 'women have made it' view of the world. In each case, we are learning that women are achieving equality with men in the worlds of education and employment.

Equality is a tremendously pernicious word. It has all the appearance of ready accessibility and legitimacy. Equality is not, of course, a concept that is the sole preserve of liberal feminism. As a way of becoming, or as a political goal, one will find feminists (and of course non-feminists) of all persuasions pursuing equality's promise. Drawing on the tenets of positivism, 'equality' presents itself as such a safe word. It appears comparative. I am as equal as you are. It appears measurable. You are richer than I am. Equality also has heart. It is just. Having better health care than me is unfair. In these ways, equality is certainly not as slippery as, say, conceptualisations of difference. Difference raises much more difficult questions. Are you different from me because I am Black and you are White? Does it make a difference that I am gay and you are straight? What are the differences between two White women?

It would be a mistake to believe that equality is a reliable and certain concept. Or that there is only one way in which it can be defined. Nevertheless, 'women have made it' discourses certainly present equality in these ways. They do so in terms of the extent to which women and men are essentially the same and therefore should have equal opportunities. This view of equality accords with a liberal feminist perspective.

Such a perspective argues that all human beings have the same potential. Women can run boardrooms, nations and galaxies as well as (actually better than) men. The feminist task is to find ways to achieve these equal potentials. In undertaking this task, liberal feminists have used the social facts of gender inequality to put forward a case that this inequality is an injustice. This case is based on the rights arguments of liberalist thought more generally. Liberalism argues that it is a basic human right for all individuals to participate fully in the organisation of society. As fellow human beings, women should have the same natural rights that men have traditionally enjoyed. Women have a right to equal civil liberties; they have a right to economic independence; they have a right to the same positions and employment spheres as men; they have a right to the same levels of education and training; and so forth.

In addition, liberal feminism argues that women are individuals with rights to freedom of choice (Eistenstein, 1993). In this regard, some liberal feminists would fully subscribe to liberalist arguments that the individual should be free of unwarranted restriction and restraint through, for example, government interference. However, it is freedom from the 'bonds of custom or prejudice' (Beasley, 1999: 52) that is most commonly invoked. Women should be able to choose to be mathematicians, engineers or scientists should they wish. These should not be the traditional preserves of men. They should be able to choose both paid employment and motherhood. Women should not be confined to the house simply by virtue of prejudicial assumptions related to their physiology.

One major area where these liberal feminist arguments have been forwarded is in respect of the low numbers of women in science and engineering. For example, in making the case for girls taking up science subjects, Kelly (1987: 7–8) powerfully illustrates the liberalist connection between choice of educational subject, liberty and life chances:

If children's choices are limited by what they themselves consider to be suitable for girls or boys, or what their teachers, parents, peers or employers consider to be suitable, then they are not able to develop their potential to the full. Stereotyping reduces liberty. Both the individuals concerned and the society as a whole lose from the restriction of talent ... there are additional reasons why girls' under-involvement in science is of particular concern. These have to do with power and influence in society. Science qualifications help individuals to get jobs – often well-paid secure jobs – in a way that other subjects do not ... There may be jobs for temps in London offices, but their earnings will never match those of car mechanics throughout the country; we may need more social workers, but the papers are full of vacancies for computer programmers.

In order to secure these rights to equality of opportunity, liberalism has also been strongly associated with changes in the legislature. Thus, rights are enshrined in law. For example, through the introduction of the national curriculum, the Education Reform Act 1998 contributed to a reduction in gender differentiation in terms of the subjects girls and boys were taking to GCSE level (P. Orr, 2000). These rights are also enshrined in organisational policy documents that set out the rights of employees to promotion entitlement, maternity leave and so forth.

In arguing for sameness, liberal feminists have not only drawn on wider political discourses but have also taken up a particular view of the human subject. This is that of the rational, autonomous person that is found in humanist discourses. Such a view of personhood argues that a distinguishing feature of humanity is the ability to reason, where reason is taken to be logical, deductive thought. The self is viewed as an autonomous, unified, coherent identity that is organised around this reasoning core (Beasley, 1999). For these reasons also, liberal feminists have argued strongly for women's access to education. For example, Wollstonecraft's liberal feminism in the eighteenth century argued that the 'problem' of middle-class women lay in their lack of education. Such women were kept in idleness, were not permitted to make their own decisions and were left to indulge themselves, their children and their husbands. As a result, they had neither moral virtue nor powers to reason (Tong, 1989). Underlying Wollstonecraft's arguments that women should have the same education as men were two basic premises (Tong, 1989). The first was the utilitarian perspective that educated women would make better wives and mothers as they would no longer spend their time with frivolities. The second perspective took up the humanitarian position that education would facilitate autonomy of the subject through the development of logical reasoning abilities. As a result, women would cease to be slaves to their emotions and would be able to exercise sound judgement.

Beasley (1999) suggests that liberal feminism is the moderate face of feminism. Certainly, there is little in the foregoing that strikes one as unreasonable. As equal beings we should have equal rights, opportunities and choices. What is there to challenge or query? Liberal feminism appears as the voice of commonsense. Yet for this reason, and perhaps for this reason alone, we should stop to pause for a moment. How can we unravel this regime of truth? There are two points of cleavage I would like to note. The first relates to assumptions about the humanist subject at the centre of liberalist thought. The second is concerned with the operations of power assumed in liberal, and indeed other forms of, feminism. Overall, these features make several taken-for-granted assumptions about being in the world.

First, the view of the subject at the centre of liberal feminism operates across a binary of female–male, and in so doing continues to privilege the masculine. This subject is considered to be fixed, has a particular kind of rationality based on scientific, deductive thought, is independent and competitive. Each of these characteristics can be viewed as aspects of Western masculinity. To achieve equality it is necessary to achieve this form of subjectivity. It is to speak, think and act like a man.

For example, as we have seen, liberal feminism has paid particular attention to the role of education as a crucial site for creating more space for women in men's worlds. Education, as Wollstonecraft pointed out, was a place where the 'reasoned' mind could be trained. Here, social facts, such as statistics, are more reliable than feelings or emotions as ways of knowing. Deductive reasoning is privileged over intuition. Autonomy rather than interdependence is a desirable goal. Thus, while some liberal feminist positions argue not only for letting women in but also for letting women's values in (Eisenstein, 1991), liberal egalitarianism has mainly been about changing conceptions of how women might live their lives to fit more closely to the lives of men. Arguing that girls should have the same education as boys simply educates girls into existing male paradigmatic ways of knowing. The social change evoked is turning girls into boys or seeking a form of androgyny based on the male model.

Second, liberal feminism's attachment to the notion that power lies in the hands of those at the top glosses over the fragmented multiplicity of the ways in which power is enacted. For example, liberal feminism has focused on the need to remove the barriers and structures that inhibit women's progression up the ladder of male success. One aspect of this is the attention that has been paid to the operation of 'glass ceilings'. These are invisible barriers of culture and attitude that are operated through the existence of a closed male elite. A key liberal feminist solution to 'glass ceilings' has been to encourage networking and mentoring among women so that they form their own support networks or, indeed, their own closed elites. In seeing men as the problem, liberal feminism creates a monolithic view of power that insufficiently theorises the ways in which, for example, power and resistance coexist or how power is exercised rather than held. In these ways, 'glass ceiling' metaphors of organisational power create narratives of 'subjugated women and perpetrator men' (Luke, 1998: 261). In addition, 'glass ceiling' metaphors focus on particular cultural constructions of patriarchy that take no account of how power is exercised in culturally different ways or among groups. It is, as Luke (1998: 246) notes, a view of power that is focused 'exclusively on a generalised (usually white Euro-American) patriarchy as the sole source limiting women's career prospects'.

Similarly, the view of education as a site for building human capital and thus increasing life chances for all presents a rather neutralised picture of how power might operate in an 'equal opportunities' world. For example, liberal feminism suggests that, once the difficulties between women and men have been sorted out, we can all enter school as one and the same and will be treated as such. In this, liberal feminism overlooks the ways in which educational institutions constitute the subject through the operations of disciplinary power. In schools, children:

> are categorized as 'bright' or 'dull,' 'normal' or 'pathological,' and may come under surveillance by psychologists, psychiatrists, or criminal justice professionals. The examinations to which individuals are subjected result in case records, which 'fix' our identities in writing (on paper or in electronic databases), and these records may be passed from one disciplinary institution to another.
>
> (Middleton, 1998: 6)

As well as sifting and sorting children to take up their appropriate places in employment systems, educational institutions also contribute to the sifting and sorting of our subjectivities.

Finally, the world that this subject inhabits is one that is ordered alongside the values of competitive individualism, one in which, although we cannot all make it to the top, we should have an equal chance of doing so. In accepting these features of the social world, liberal feminism has not sought to overturn the hierarchical ordering of societies. As a result, the forms of equality that are being sought are those that leave unchallenged specific dominant ways of being in the world. Evans (1995: 30–1) indicates:

> Given that liberal feminists characteristically speak of equality of opportunity rather than condition, then it might be said that they uphold an unequal society and simply want to advance women within its ranks. To be more precise, they want to advance women to what is conventionally regarded as equality with men, within the various hierarchically ordered groups. This seems to me, on the whole, to be a true characterization of the school.

None of this is to say, of course, that the preponderance of liberal feminist discourses have not offered seductive promises in overcoming the material and subjective realities of women's lives. Nor is it to deny that many women have invested in these discourses. Indeed, it is to an exploration of the material and subjective realities of successful women's lives that I now turn.

Successful women: a contradiction in terms?

As travellers in male worlds (Marshall, 1984) women face a series of contradictions. Blackmore (1999) highlights the ways in which feminist women trouble organisations. They trouble the dominance of masculinist organisations and their positivist ways of knowing. Feminists are also troubled by organisations. How can they be changed to accord with a feminist agenda? What is feasible and doable in this way? Predominantly, feminist research highlights the ways in which women more generally do not fit into the cultures of organisations. Rather than changing organisations, many women mould their ways around the dominant model. Even so, they face a further contradiction. In the face of tangible success, women never feel 'good' enough.

In choosing traditional male career pathways, then, are we choosing traditional masculine ways of being? Or, in pursuing objectives that equate feminism's goals with male values, are we risking the creation of an 'overly rigid and stereotypic conception of what it is to act and speak "like a man" ' (Soper, 1994: 18)? Wajcman's (1996) research offers some interesting responses to these questions. Wajcman (1996) explores the dominant symbols of organisations through the ways in which managerial competence is linked to the qualities attached to men. In this her research is concerned with everyday talk and the taken-for-granted values and assumptions of managerialism. Wajcman illustrates how managerialism is naturalised as a sphere of action and doing, of 'firefighting' in retrenched and downsized organisations. Thus, managerialism is not a sphere for thinking and reflection. The natural world of high-flying managers includes total commitment to the organisation, demonstrated through long hours of work. It includes high levels of motivation, demonstrated through, for example, a desire for promotion and a sense of enjoyment from work. To be successful in such a world requires one to be committed and motivated in these ways. Moreover, for women, it requires some unique yet stark choices.

For her research Wajcman selected five multinational companies that were acknowledged to be at the forefront of equal opportunities policies. Her data indicate that those women who succeeded had similar backgrounds and attitudes to men. They worked similar hours, were equally motivated and had the same level of qualifications and experience. Indeed, 'women who have made it into senior positions are in most respects indistinguishable from men in equivalent positions' (Wajcman, 1996: 259). However, there was one key difference. The women at the top had forgone having children while the men had not. As Wajcman (1996: 276) comments ' what has emerged most strongly is that women have had to become more like men to pursue successful management careers.'

Wajcman acknowledges that this is a model of equality in which women are required to accommodate to pre-existing norms. As such, it is a fairly limited one. In addition, it is a form of equality based on stereotypes of male behaviour. This is a stereotype that reflects a dominant separation of the private from the public. Men, in their public lives, appear *as if* they have no family attachments because they are not the ones held responsible for the raising of their children or the care of their elders. Women at the top are not creating a fiction in terms of their family lives as those who make it tend not to have children.

This is not the only dissonance that women experience. Organisations reflect the splits of masculinity and femininity in the ways found more generally in society. For example, viewing organisations as spheres of male sexual dominance is central to Wajcman's analysis (see also Adkins, 1995). As a result, women have to negotiate their femininity and their sexuality. Thus, if women are perceived to be too sexual they are judged as not suitable for management positions. If they are not sexual enough, as older women testify, they lose the necessary male patronage to get on. If a woman is too feminine she is considered not tough enough for management but is seen to be Wollstonecraft's frivolous, silly woman. If she is too masculine then she is not a 'real' woman at all. Being a woman and being a manager are, in consequence, contradictory positions because management is so fully identified with masculinity.

Feminist research has illustrated how the male gaze acts as an appropriate regulatory force in shaping women's senses of self. For example, in the UK, New Labour has been congratulated on its policy of positive action in the recruitment of women Members of Parliament. A newspaper report on their experiences of life in Parliament carried the headline 'Blair Babes face barrage of sexual jibes from male MPs'(*Birmingham Post*, 10 December 1997: 1). The text reads:

> Midland women MPs have lifted the lid on the smutty comments and sexist behaviour they are subjected to at the hands of their male colleagues ... New Labour MP for Reading East, Ms Jane Griffiths, said she was interrupted with 'mocking laughter' from the Tory benches when she first spoke in the Commons. She said 'There are things that you half hear and you're not sure if you heard it right, and they use gesture and body language which gets missed by the cameras so they can't be caught at it.' Asked to give an example of the gestures, Ms Griffiths said 'The one where they put their hands out in front of them as if they are weighing melons.'

To be sexually objectified, as Bartky (1990: 27) puts it, 'is to be the object of a kind of perception, unwelcome and inappropriate, that takes the part for the whole.' This objectification selects woman's sexuality and applies it to the whole of her personhood. Other aspects of her identity are subsumed within her sexual identity and in consequence are negated. In the case of Blair's babes they are learning that, whilst they may think they have become MPs, in the eyes of (some of) the men they are primarily objects for masculine sexual amusement.

Bartky (1990: 27) notes how 'sexualisation is one way of fixing disadvantaged persons in their disadvantage'. There are other ways too, all of which continue to be far less noticed in this egalitarian age than men's sexual jibes. In a discussion of the gendered learning of shame, Bartky (1990: 89) offers the following description of the behaviour of mature women high-school teachers whom she taught on a post-experience professional development course:

> ... I was struck by the way many female students behaved as they handed me their papers. They would offer heartfelt apologies and copious expressions of regret for the poor quality of their work – work which turned out, most of the time, to be quite good. While apologizing, a student would often press the edges of her manuscript together so as to make it literally smaller, holding the paper uncertainly somewhere in the air as if unsure whether she wanted to relinquish it at all. Typically, she would deliver the apology with head bowed, chest hollowed, and shoulders hunched slightly forward. The male students would stride over to the desk and put down their papers without comment.

Bartky highlights the dissonance between these ways of behaving and their ascribed successes as high-achieving career women. To feel shame, Bartky notes, is to feel distressed and diminished by the gaze of another who is making a judgement about our inadequacy. However, it is not always necessary to have a audience to feel shame because shame also operates though internalised standards of judgement. In addition to these features, 'shame requires the recognition that I *am*, in some important sense, as I am seen to be.' (Bartky, 1990: 86). In the case of Blair's babes it is to feel that one *is* no more than a pair of breasts. Shame is inextricably linked to our senses of self. It is not simply a moral judgement exercised in a neutral way on a wrongdoer. It is a relationship of oppression. In learning shame, Bartky highlights how this shame is internalised through the social relations of everyday life that privilege the masculine.

Bartky lists a series of mundane and mostly unnoticed ways in which girls and women learn to know themselves as inferior to boys and men. This includes the ways through which girls are less often asked to speak in class and how their names are remembered less often than boys' names. In addition,

teachers interrupt girls more than boys and make more eye contact with
boys than girls. Further, Bartky notes how women are the object of sexist
jokes that are designed to 'spice' up a boring topic and they are patronised
through helpful gestures that suggest they need help with 'difficult' topics.
They are also viewed negatively when they display stereotypical male traits
such as assertiveness or ambition.

It is important to note, however, that these features of regulation operate
differentially among girls and women, as Walkerdine and Lucey (1989)
illustrate. Walkerdine and Lucey's research draws attention to the ways in
which the 'good' girl is constructed across class lines. Their starting point is
an analysis of a classic psychological study of the home lives of young children
(see Tizard and Hughes, 1984). This study suggested that, in contrast to
middle-class mothers, working-class mothers were not preparing their
children well for school success.

Walkerdine and Lucey followed up some of the children in the Tizard and
Hughes study. They found that when their school achievements were
compared with those of their classmates the working-class girls were doing
well. Moreover, their teachers thought well of their performance saying that
they 'worked hard'. The girls, similarly, thought that they were doing well.
However, Walkerdine and Lucy note that, in comparison with middle-class
pupils, the working-class girls were performing exceptionally badly. One of
them, Nicky, described by her teacher as an ideal pupil and ranked top in
maths in her class, scored only average on a wider scale that included test
results from pupils from middle-class and private schools. Dawn, a child from
another working-class school, was similarly ranked at the top of her class.
Yet, the top score in her class was lower than the bottom scores of two of the
private schools.

In contrast, Walkerdine and Lucey (1989: 20) offer the case of Angela, a
middle-class girl who is outstanding in her class and scoring top marks. She
too is thought of as a 'good girl' and an 'ideal pupil'. However, they note that
according to her teachers, Angela does not have 'that elusive gift, "brilliance"
– she must rely on hard work'. Thus:

> While almost all teachers in working-class schools also described
> high-achieving girls as hard-working, most of them viewed it as a
> positive phenomenon. In other words, for most of these teachers it
> did not have the pejorative connotations it had for the middle-class
> teachers. Hard work was highly valued. And it is noteworthy that
> the high-achieving working-class girls did not display the anxiety
> about the inadequacy of their performance present for the majority
> of the middle-class girls.
>
> Walkerdine and Lucey (1989: 195)

Walkerdine and Lucey illustrate how the same terms draw their meaning from different cultural contexts and practices. Working-class children will need to work 'hard' in their employment lives, as they are the ones most likely to be in manual and semiskilled occupations. As Walkerdine and Lucey's test score data illustrate, working-class pupils are unlikely to be successful in the senses outlined here in terms of education and career. Middle-class children, in contrast, are marked in different ways as hard work is eschewed. Middle-class girls need to be naturally (*sic*) brilliant.

Walkerdine (1994) further illustrates that, across both class groups, when girls were compared with boys it did not matter how well they were doing. Their performances were downgraded. Good performance was always considered to be the result of something else, such as rule following or hard work. Boys were often viewed as having 'potential', a term that was never applied to girls. Indeed, if 'a girl was performing well it was almost impossible for her to escape pejorative evaluations, whereas boys, it seemed, no matter how poorly they performed, were thought to have hidden qualities' (p. 58; see also Walkerdine and the Girls Mathematics Unit, 1989).

Yet the question remains, in becoming incorporated into masculinist cultures, as inferiors nonetheless, can we choose which aspects to select, which part of that whole we would like to take up? Is it likely that women politicians will learn to make sexual gestures off camera to assert their place? Luke (1998) offers some salutary remarks in relation to both the one-dimensional views of 'glass ceiling' metaphors dominant in liberal feminist analyses that solely regard men as the problem and the silence of feminist critiques on the conflicts that are enacted between women. She notes how 'senior women can misuse power and be just as divisive and unsupportive of women, as men' (p. 261). Hart (1992: 64) comments that when success is so thoroughly defined through a 'view of the model adult [as] a competitive, upwardly mobile individual [then] the characteristics of such a successful individual actually magnify prevailing stereotyped definitions of masculine qualities into exemplary social behaviour, significantly reducing the possible realm of meaning of "good work" and of "success".' Is this the female future that men fear?

Women are doing too well

The effect of 'women have made it' discourses, together with a broader sense of change in women's lives, has led to an important feminist interest not only in the 'truth' of such claims but also in deconstructing such discourses. If it is the case that women and men now have more or less equal life chances, expectations and experiences, then perhaps we have reached a post-feminist age in which we can live in harmony. Alternatively, such discourses may be read as representing contemporary counter-discourses that challenge feminism. For example, biological arguments of women's natural inferiority are being replaced by ideas that the growing dominance of women is creating legions of emasculated boys and men.

These discourses present both a political and an intellectual challenge for feminism. Such discourses can be understood as part of an inevitable backlash against the march of feminism in terms of feminism's threat to masculine power (Faludi, 1992). Here, masculinity is seen as reasserting itself in such a way that it seeks to squash or obliterate any opposition. In addition, such discourses can be understood in terms of the maintenance of masculine hegemony. They offer an opportunity to understand how hegemonic discourses sustain their predominance through, for example, incorporating aspects of counter-discourses within them. In making these distinctions, I am taking up Connell's (1987: 185–6) definition of hegemonic masculinity as follows:

> It does not imply that hegemonic masculinity means being particularly nasty to women. Women may feel as oppressed by non-hegemonic masculinities, may even find the hegemonic pattern more familiar and manageable. There is likely to be a kind of 'fit' between hegemonic masculinity and emphasized femininity. What is does imply is the maintenance of practices that institutionalize men's dominance over women. In this sense hegemonic masculinity must embody a successful collective strategy in relation to women. Given the complexity of gender relations no simple or uniform strategy is possible: a 'mix' is necessary. So hegemonic masculinity can contain at the same time, quite consistently, openings towards domesticity and openings towards violence, towards misogyny and towards heterosexual attraction.

To illuminate these issues, I draw on two studies that concerned with contesting 'women have made it' discourses. Wilson (1999) lists six discourses that suggest not only that women have made it, or are well on their way to doing so, but also that women have made it far too well. These are:

- Women's participation in the workforce has dramatically increased.
- Women have gained equality of opportunity at the expense of men.
- Women and men have greater equality, for example the law has ensured equality of pay for women.
- The absence of women at senior levels is simply the result of their lack of experience and seasoning. In time, women will increasingly find positions at the top of our organisations.
- Women and men increasingly have equal roles at home.
- The future is female.

These discourses draw on a range of social 'facts', predominantly in terms of statistics, to prove their truth. As 'facts', statistics can be difficult to contest except with another set of 'facts'. Indeed, it has been an important feminist strategy to use the techniques associated with dominant discourses to persuade (Hughes, 1996). For example, Stanley (1990) describes her use of statistics to influence approaches to social work practice. The data were drawn from her own and her parents' recent experiences of social work intervention. In presenting her material she did not let her audience know of the origins of her data. In an arena where faith in objectivity still reigns supreme, Stanley is clear about the politics of necessity. Thus, 'I felt that presenting "the case study" as my own still-recent experience of caring would disqualify both me and it from "research" and "papers"' in the eyes of those present' (p. 121).

This is the approach that Wilson (1999) takes in seeking to challenge any growing consensus that women have indeed made it. Although she acknowledges that there have been some changes in women's life experiences, predominantly she indicates that 'little real progress towards equality has been made' (p. 529). Wilson lists the facts of this inequality as follows:

- Women still retain primary responsibility for child care.
- Increasing participation in paid employment has not lessened the unpaid work women do in terms of family care.
- Employment sectors continue to be segregated both horizontally and vertically. Thus, men still dominate the tops of organisations in all sectors. Women remain at the lower levels of all organisations. They are also more likely to be employed in the lower-status caring professions such as nursing, teaching and social work than in the higher-status worlds of, for example, global financial capital.
- Many of the changes in labour market participation are due to the increase in part-time, flexible working. Such jobs are occupied predominantly by women, who, as a result, have fewer opportunities for work-related training and promotion.
- Despite legislation, sex discrimination continues in recruitment practices.
- Despite legislation, women's full-time earnings are, on average, only 80% of men's average full-time earnings.
- Gender stereotypes still prevent the promotion of women into top jobs. The 'softer' characteristics associated with womanhood are not deemed suitable for such jobs.
- Representations that girls are outperforming boys at school are misleading. Boys continue to outperform girls in science at GCSE. At 'A' level, the point at which, in this credentialist age, qualifications really matter, girls lose any educational lead they had.

There is, nonetheless, a danger in Wilson's approach. Henwood (1998) indicates how liberal discourses of equal opportunities and discourses of women's alienation in masculine cultures present an individual–society dualism that does little to create new discursive possibilities. Henwood's research illustrates how it is possible to 'accept and reinforce dominant assumptions about gender difference, whilst appearing to reject them' (p. 44). In seeking to prove that a woman is strong, not weak, and in saying 'treat me just like one of the boys' we are calling on existing gender dichotomies of the passive female and the assertive male. We are, paradoxically, reasserting the differences an equality of sameness seeks to deny.

It is to those discourses that masculinity-is-in-crisis (Blackmore, 1997) that Reed (1999) turns. While Reed does document the 'facts' of the case in her analysis of discourses of the 'underachieving boy', these are not her main concern. Rather, she illustrates how these discourses draw on contemporary psychological and sociological perspectives that are part of the scientism of society. In so doing, these statistics define the 'problem' in particular ways. The psychological dimensions focus on assumptions of innate differences between girls and boys. For example, the idea that the male brain operates differently from the female one is used to suggest that current teaching methods favour girls rather than boys. Men's brains, it is suggested, do not deal well with tasks that call for emotional reflexivity, whereas women's brains do. In consequence, classroom and assessment practices, such as those found in the coursework of GCSE syllabi, which require reflection and planned organisation are not suitable for boys. Calls for more structured teaching methods are made to prevent boys falling even further behind girls.

In sociological terms, male unemployment, particularly among Black and working-class men, is associated with boys' disaffection with schooling. Here, the symbiotic relationship between school and education is drawn into focus, as this suggests that there is no purpose in school unless there is a job at the end of it. In addition, the relationship between single parenthood and the lack of a male role model is particularly focused, stereotypically, on children from African–Caribbean backgrounds. Young African–Caribbean men and boys are assumed to be dominated by matriarchal cultures at home. Schools do little to readjust this as they are populated by too many (White) women teachers who cannot, as teachers should, provide the appropriate ways of being in the world that engage young men. The need for Black males to act as appropriate role models is asserted.

Reed outlines the effects of these discourses in the following ways. First:

> ... the overall effect is to force our gaze on the 'underachieving boy' as a subject constructed in need of our help. His 'existence' overly determines the interpretation of gender concern amongst teachers and schools, including the allocation of resources. His production is a consequence of teachers' failure (especially female teachers, predominant in the primary school, the English faculty or special educational needs provision) to meet his individual learning needs. His 'masculinity' is problematised by the changing world order post

feminism; it [masculinity] is not itself the problem. His crisis is always understood in relation to female independence and success.

(Reed, 1999: 102–3)

In these ways, discourses of the 'underachieving boy' deem feminism and socialism to be outmoded ways of achieving social justice. Rather, through the reassertion of competitive individualism, they reinforce the market as the arena for the achievement of this. Such discourses discipline women teachers in their failure to address the needs of boys. They reassert masculinity through privileging masculine ways of knowing and being and they legitimise the appropriation of resources to promote this agenda. Finally, such discourses blame mothers for their failure to provide appropriate male role models for their sons or for undermining the father's rule by being the main wage earner. And, because mothers are in paid employment, they are blamed for failing to care for their sons.

Summary

My aim in this chapter has not been to prove or disprove the facts of 'women have made it' discourses. My aim has been to deconstruct them in order to illustrate how they work to persuade. In doing so, I have identified four strands to 'women have made it' discourses that are, in themselves, dominant discourses. These are definitions of equality that are based on being the same as men; mainstream ideas that success can only be achieved through reaching the top of hierarchies; the idea of women as a universal category; and the legitimacy of statistics as a way of knowing the social world. I have suggested that 'women have made it' predominantly accords with a liberal feminist agenda that has focused on achieving equal rights, freedom of choice and equal opportunities for women and that liberal feminism is the most commonly held view of feminism.

My exploration of 'women have made it' has also sought to demonstrate critiques of this liberal feminist project. For example, I have indicated that the conceptualisation of success at the heart of this project is relatively limited as it encourages stereotypical conceptions of men's lives that women are expected to emulate. I have drawn attention to critiques of the humanist, choosing subject that is at the centre of liberalist discourses and I have indicated how liberalism leaves aspects of the hierarchical ordering of society untouched. I have also explored certain paradoxes that research indicates arise when women do *make it*. In particular, I have drawn attention to the gendered and classed processes of regulation that create shame and the 'good' girl. Finally, I have explored two ways in which feminist research has responded to refuting 'women have made it' discourses. The first, I have suggested, operates within the field of liberalism, and a danger of such an approach is that this may reinforce the very conditions that it seeks to undermine. The second piece of research was designed to illustrate how discourses impact on practices.

As a hierarchical discourse 'women have made it' cannot be a discourse for the majority. Most women take a 'best of both worlds' approach by seeking to combine employment with family life. It is to this that I now turn.

3

THE BEST OF BOTH WORLDS

... both men and women expressed concerns about whether it was possible to combine senior jobs with any real family life. Such views were widely held and, although not based on very specific knowledge of senior jobs, did seem at least superficially plausible on the basis of hours worked and work loads. This was an issue of particular concern for those women (at both levels of management) who currently had young children or were deciding whether to start a family in the near future. Their uncertainties about the possibility of combining a career and a family were reinforced by the very small number of visible senior women with children who could act as role models (or even as evidence that it was feasible). In this context it is perhaps not surprising that during the interviews women frequently expressed the concern that motherhood would spell the end of their career.

(Liff and Ward, 2001: 26)

British women still display a bi-modal pattern of workforce participation, with lower levels of participation in their middle years. Intervals of non-participation, or part-time employment, remain the norm, as mothers seek to reconcile their employment with their parental responsibilities in a country where there is a lower level of childcare provision than anywhere else in the European Union.

(Hatt, 1999: 102)

Statistics for the UK indicate how women's participation in the labour market grew during the twentieth century. For example, employer-based surveys indicate that in 1959 there were 7.9 million women in the labour force. By 1999 this figure had risen to 12.8 million (National Statistics, 2001a)). The National Statistics Office notes that this increase has come mainly from a strong rise in the participation rates of married women and arose particularly during and immediately following the Second World War (National Statistics, 2001b).

The figures for labour market participation of women with children also indicate how this is influenced by the age of the youngest dependent child. While their children are relatively young, the majority of women take part-time employment. As their children get older, women change from part-time to full-time work. Social Trends data from 1999 indicate that 38 per cent of married or cohabiting women with children under 5 were in part-time employment and 21 per cent were in full-time employment (National Statistics, 2001c). Of mothers of children aged between 5 and 10 years, 50 percent were working part-time compared with 25 percent working full-time (National Statistics, 2001c). When children reach 16 years of age or older, there is a change between the balance of those in part-time employment (38 per cent) and full-time employment (41 per cent) (National Statistics, 2001 c).

These changes in the economic activity status of women signify something of 'best of both worlds' discourses. As the findings from Liff and Ward (2001) illustrate, 'best of both worlds' can be seen as a resolution to opposing alternatives. For example, women who take up part-time employment can be seen to be making a choice between the needs of children for their mothers and the needs of mothers for independence and financial security. 'Best of both worlds' discourses also signify the hope that compromise is both possible and beneficial. In taking up part-time employment while their children are young and increasing their economic activity rates as children become less dependent, or remaining in full-time work, many women are hoping to maintain their place in employment markets. In this way we can see 'best of both worlds' as a discourse of balance that attempts to hold in place the desire to remain connected to one's child and the desire for the independence or the financial necessity of a wage that can come from being in employment.

Nevertheless, research into women's experiences of employment illustrates that, in career terms, this may not be a 'best of *both* worlds' tactic. This research has shown that women in both full and part-time paid work encounter significant difficulties in combining motherhood with employment. These do not solely arise through the logistical practicalities of fitting childcare into employment demands. They also arise from the intransigence of masculinised organisational cultures in competitive market societies. Walters and Dex (1992) illustrate how it is comparatively unusual for mothers of young children to be in continuous employment in Britain as only 3 per cent of women do so. Those that do are more likely to be in professional occupations. The most common pattern is for women to give up work on the birth of their first child and to return to a job of lower status and pay and to work intermittently (Arber and Gilbert, 1992). Explanations for women undertaking this pattern of working tend to blame the women themselves. For example, Blackwell (2001) observes that human capital theories suggest that women invest less in their education and training because they anticipate that they will leave the labour market to have children. In a brief review of the conflicting theories relating to women's participation as part-time employees, Lane (2000: 272) comments that there remains an enduring 'assumption that the female part-time worker is not committed to paid employment'. Despite its low pay and status, so far as employers are concerned mothers are seen to prefer part-time employment because they do not have to take on responsibilities that would conflict with their domestic commitments. In consequence, women face not only the glass ceiling in terms of their career prospects but also the 'bed-pan ceiling' (Lane, 2000).

Discourses of the good mother and discourses of competitive individualism can both be viewed as dominant discourses. The mother is seen as the symbol of all that is good in society. Market societies require the competitive individual. The 'best of both worlds' therefore marks a point of intersection. Yet it is one where we find that discourses of motherhood appear to have been subject to most change. Evetts (2000: 65) notes that, in terms of women's expectations in relation to employment, 'The biggest changes are perceived to have occurred in women's attachment to paid work and in their career ambitions. Women now expect to be in paid work for the large majority of their adult lives'. As a result, women delay childbirth or limit the number of their children or only take the minimum maternity leave break allowable in law. The 'best of both worlds' is therefore not simply a discourse of resolution. It is also a site of amelioration of the 'good mother'.

Nevertheless, the significance of mothers' increasing rates of economic activity can turn our gaze away from another important aspect of these statistics. The figures relating to mothers' employment patterns also indicate that 41 per cent of married or cohabiting mothers with children under 5 are not economically active. While this figure decreases to 25 per cent for those with children between 5 and 10 years, still around one-quarter of mothers with children over the age of 5 are economically inactive (National Statistics, 2001c). These statistics therefore indicate something further about 'best of both worlds' discourses. This is that, although there are many ways that women can 'do' motherhood in 2001, the Bowlbian notion that children come first and a mother's needs should be subsumed to the infant's has not disappeared (Bowlby, 1965).

This chapter is concerned with the discursive shifts and the constancies in the meanings of motherhood that 'best of both worlds' signifies. It is concerned with how these meanings of motherhood impact on women's relationship to employment and the market. In 'Feminist discourses on motherhood' I undertake a historical review of second-wave feminism. Early second-wave feminism is particularly noted for the ways in which it theorised motherhood as an oppressive institution. That this should be the dominant perception of this period suggests something of hegemonic discourses and the operations of power that demonised feminism in this way. Nevertheless, the effect has been that, when it comes to motherhood, feminism has since been on something of the defensive and has been determined to show its pro-natalist colours. As such, this review provides a useful case to illustrate the difficulties that women face in everyday life if they speak out against the sanctity of the mother–child bond.

In 'Varieties of motherhood' I set out the range of contemporary discourses on motherhood. The multiplicity of these is suggestive of the different ways in which women might now 'do' motherhood. These discourses also indicate how neoliberalist and market values are being incorporated into notions of the 'good' mother. In addition to responsibility, child-centredness and the importance of the two-parent heterosexual family that have always been present, these discourses extol the virtues of individualism and choice. Kaplan (1992) indicates that during a period of transition all discourses express anxiety. I suggest that absences of various kinds are common to each of these anxieties. These absences are both literal and metaphoric. I also suggest that the preservation of selflessness as the centre of how the 'good' mother is constituted is seen to offer a resolution to these anxieties.

In 'Resolving contradictions?' I consider the meanings of 'best of both worlds' in women's daily lives. I do this in two ways. I begin by exploring the claims to moral superiority that motherhood offers. This morality is based on selfless love. Here I explore research that has sought to explain the predominance of discourses of intensive mothering as a form of resistance to the individualistic and competitive ethics of capitalism. I question whether we can understand motherhood so absolutely as resistance because of the different class and 'race' meanings of motherhood as a moral domain. For middle-class women motherhood is confirmation of the already moral self. As already moral they may, both discursively and materially, be able to take up motherhood as a space of resistance. For working-class and Black women motherhood acts as a process of transformation to the moral self. This suggests quite a different positioning in relation to motherhood as resistance.

I then illustrate how 'best of both worlds' is a predominant motif in young women's lives. I suggest that the 'good' mother of contemporary discourses allows these young women to manage the contradictions of motherhood and employment because this 'good' mother incorporates the liberalist values of independence, individualism and self-sufficiency. In this sense we can see how 'hegemony does not mean total cultural dominance, the obliteration of alternatives. It means ascendancy achieved within a balance of forces' (Connell, 1987: 184).

In addition, I illustrate how the selfless mother is retained but is reconfigured. In Bowlbian discourses, the selfless mother evidenced her selflessness through attachment to her child. Yet this attachment came to be seen as overwhelming, and women were accused of engulfing their children with their own needs. In contemporary discourses, the selfless mother continues to put her child's needs first, but the needs that come first are those of independence. A 'good' mother must give her child space away from her to grow. I argue that these changing aspects of discourses of mothering have two implications. First, they represent an amelioration of motherhood towards the needs of the market. Second, they can act to reinforce 'best of both worlds' discourses because a mother's moral superiority can now be derived from the ways in which occasional absence instils the values of independence in her children.

Feminist discourses on motherhood

Most feminists support marriage and having children.
(Dornbusch and Strober, 1988: 5)

There are strong populist assumptions that feminism is antithetical to motherhood. The predominance of liberal discourses that equate feminism as mainly concerned with employment career success contribute to these assumptions. Feminism is viewed as anti-motherhood because the demands of motherhood restrict women's freedom to climb the career ladder. Feminists have also raised a series of further critiques of motherhood. These include analyses of the isolating conditions under which mothering is done and which lead to high rates of depression in women. They include an emphasis on the continuing existence of unequal divisions of domestic labour. And they include analyses of how imperatives to mother are dominant in the construction of feminine identity. To remain childless, whether through choice or not, is to forswear womanhood (see, for example, Letherby, 2001). Yet by challenging what for many is a sanctified and natural institution, feminists who raise the slightest critique of motherhood are also challenging many 'unscrutinized dimensions of people's fundamental self-conceptions' (Moody-Adams, 1997: 79). Accordingly, it is easier to 'demonize the theorist who demands scrutiny of institutions deemed immune from scrutiny, rather than examine the potential reasonableness of the disturbing substance of those demands' (ibid.).

An exploration of the development of second-wave feminist discourses on motherhood highlights several important features of the discursive terrain through which political struggle and change is enacted. First, it offers an example of struggle and resistance against dominant ideas and practices. Thus, some early second-wave discourses demonstrate resistance toward obligatory full-time motherhood and divisions of labour that rest on assumptions of women's 'natural' place. Second, such an exploration illustrates the amelioration of counter-hegemonic discourses as an inevitable part of the striving for political legitimacy and the resolution of internal divisions. The 'demon' texts of early second-wave feminist critiques of mothering have been transmuted into an emphasis on the diversity of the family (Snitow, 1992). And, when faced by attacks from Black women that second-wave feminism was a White affair, 'many theorists pushed motherhood to the fore as a powerful universalizing issue' (Umansky, 1996: 5). Third, despite being attacked as anti-mother, feminist discourses have opened up spaces for the articulation of alternative options in respect of how women 'do' mothering and, indeed, whether or not they will become mothers. We might therefore count this as a success for feminist politics.

Finally, an exploration of feminist discourses on motherhood provides a useful case study for understanding longstanding mores about motherhood and the dangers of transgression of those mores. If a movement that dared critique some aspect of the institution of motherhood was labelled 'baby-haters' why expect any less of a response at a more personal level? It is true that feminist discourses of motherhood have evolved in more complex ways than that summarised by negative and positive polarities. However, feminist writings have more fully moved towards a positive valorisation of motherhood than a negative one. For example, motherhood is taken in a range of writings to metaphorically express an idealization of the many relationships and experiences to which a feminist world could aspire (Umansky, 1996). An analysis of feminist discourses on motherhood offers some useful insights into how 'good' mother ideas persevere.

Focusing particularly on the USA, Snitow (1992) identifies three time lines in respect of feminist responses to motherhood. In so doing, she draws attention to key discursive shifts. She describes the first time line, from 1963 to about 1975, as the era of 'demon' texts. These texts are particularly those of Friedan (1963) and Firestone (1970). Writing from a liberal feminist perspective, Friedan named the dissatisfactions with housework and childcare of middle-class, educated, White married women as 'the problem with no name'. As much for their children's sake as their own, Friedan urged women to get out of the family and into paid work. Firestone, whose radical feminist politics locates sexual oppression as the most important source of coercive power (Beasley, 1999), sought an androgynous future in which reproductive technology and changes in traditional biological families would liberate women. For example, technology would shift the emphasis away from the biological mother being solely responsible for her child and the tasks of mothering would be undertaken in communal groups.

The second time line Snitow identifies is that of 1976–79. During this period, feminists began to open up and document two previously held taboos about motherhood: the joys of mothering and the pain. They were critical of the conditions under which mothering and housework were enacted yet hopeful about the potentiality of mothering as an alternative way of being. Writing from a radical feminist perspective, Rich (1977: 52) is a classic example of this, as the following indicates:

> The physical and psychic weight of responsibility on the woman with children is by far the heaviest of social burdens. It cannot be compared with slavery or sweated labor because the emotional bonds between a woman and her children make her vulnerable in ways which the forced laborer does not know; he can hate and fear his boss; the woman with children is a prey to far more complicated, subversive feelings. Love and anger can exist concurrently; anger at the conditions of motherhood can become translated into anger at the child, along with the fear that we are not 'loving'; grief at all we cannot do for our children in a society so inadequate to meet human needs becomes translated into guilt and self-laceration.

The third time line is 1980 to 1990. Feminism was on the defensive and the discussion moved from motherhood to families. In so doing, woman as an individual in her own right became once again invisible. The text by Dornbusch and Strober (1988) is an example of this. Anxious to demonstrate their mother-friendly perspective, Dornbusch and Strober argue for the need to focus on the diversity of family forms, on aspects of relationality and on the social rather than the individual and the personal (i.e. the mother).

Part of Snitow's concerns is that the 'demon' texts of the first period have been misread. She documents the ways in which they were anything but mother-hating despite the press they received. Nevertheless, the term 'misread' is misleading. In the context of their time these texts were understood in this way by some feminists, and certainly by non-feminists. In an era informed by the maternal deprivation thesis and the penis-envying woman of Freudian psychology, Friedan (1963) and Firestone (1970) said the unsayable when they challenged the taken-for-granted view that women have an innate desire to become mothers and that motherhood is a fulfilling experience of itself. Indeed, speaking out is always dangerous. Such was the public outrage at the time that 'Friedan's book made her a "leper" in her own suburban neighbourhood' (Oakley, 1981: 28).

It is hardly surprising that this era is marked by assumptions that feminists were mother-hating given that this is a useful counter-response from a threatened dominant position. It is important, then, to contextualise discourses in relation to their historicity and understand responses to them in terms of the then dominant discourses that they challenged or indeed stood in fear of. Reading back after twenty years of social, political, economic and discursive change the now relative tameness of Friedan and Firestone is suggestive of how much, or little, is different. For their time, as Snitow also notes, they were anything but non-controversial.

If we consider feminist discourses during the 1980s we can see how some feminists responded to this public outrage. Then, as Snitow has noted, feminists took up the position of being apologetic for daring to criticise the sanctity of motherhood. There are, of course, good reasons for this in terms of a feminist politics that wants its ideas to be legitimated and that also accepts the saliency of various critiques. The outrage that poured on to those feminists who spoke out against the tyranny of motherhood did not come only from right-wing pro-family groups which you might expect to respond in this way. Many women considered that such views devalued their lives and experiences. These, of course, are the very people that feminism purports to be liberating!

In seeking to be seen to be speaking *to* rather than *against* women, feminists were forced to think again. We can see this in the work of Rich (1977), who separates out motherhood as an institution from motherhood as experience. As such, she is able to speak to two different discourses simultaneously. On the one hand, she retains the positive terms of those dearly held values of love, selflessness and relationality enshrined in everyday conceptions of motherhood. On the other hand, she gives recognition to the ways in which motherhood can be experienced as drudgery, isolation and sheer hard work.

Responses to these particular feminist discourses on motherhood did not, of course, come solely from outside feminism. Within feminism, critiques were made of the classist and racist assumptions embedded in the labelling of mothering as oppressive. Intrinsically tied to issues of race, motherhood is always a political issue. While White women were focusing on alienating and oppressive aspects of motherhood, the Black liberation movements in the 1960s were more concerned about countering negative racial stereotypes with more positive images. In this they created the 'superstrong Black mother' through whose endeavour the Black race had survived (Collins, 1991: 116). The creation of counter-discourses of this kind opens up space for resistance. Nevertheless, they also give rise to their own oppressive elements.

Reviewing Black feminist responses to the imagery of the strong Black mother, Umansky (1996) notes how analyses were sought that were both feminist and anti-racist (see also Boris, 1993). The image of the strong Black mother is a controlling one. Like images of superwomen more generally the superstrong Black mother needs no support. There is no need to count the costs of her hardship and work. Accordingly, her poverty is rendered a romantic struggle that she always sees through. In recognition of this, some Black feminists took up a radical feminist approach that rested on the need to retain control of their own bodies. Black liberationists, for example, urged Black women to raise an army of children who would fight racism on 'women's behalf'. Black feminists focused on the dangers to women, and in consequence the broader Black struggle, of pro-natalist policies that left Black women unsupported in the home and therefore unable to be full participants in this.

Nevertheless, the imagery of the strong Black mother has been seen to have provided a strong affirmative base for Black feminism. Umansky demonstrates that this base drew on a longer verbal tradition in American Black culture that reveres the mother and reinforces the symbolism of maternal fortitude that is enshrined in imagery of the matriarch. Thus, while there was a brief period of criticism of motherhood in the 1960s, from the 1970s onwards mothering became 'a model for everything from ecological concern to revolution' (Umansky, 1996: 92). Umansky argues that it was this model that was taken up by the wider feminist movement.

In seeking to create an inclusive feminism, White feminists were concerned at the absence of Black women in the movement. Motherhood appeared to hold the potential to bring all women together. After all, we all had mothers and most women were likely to become mothers. Of course, the goal of creating a universal women's movement failed. 'Difference' politics provided a sufficient critique of motherhood to highlight that feminists could only speak of a unity between mothers in the most symbolic of ways.

Feminist concerns to incorporate discourses of difference together with a desire to address the critiques of feminism found in the right-wing pro-family discourses of the 1980s return us to Snitow's third time line of feminist responses to motherhood. This is the disappearance of the mother and the emergence of a focus on the diversity of families. Dornbusch and Strober (1988: 4) provide a classic example:

> Our continual concern with 'families' instead of 'the family' is a major part of the reconciliation between feminism and family rights and responsibilities. While the male/breadwinner–female/homemaker model is still present in millions of American homes and should not be omitted from our examination, it is the presence of numerous other forms of family life that has transformed the issues involved in the fulfillment of both genders and in the successful raising of the next generation.

In self-consciously seeking to reconcile feminism's attention to difference with right-wing discourses of family rights and responsibilities, Dornbusch and Strober's text can be viewed, as with the others mentioned here, as representative of their time. They speak to dominant discourses – of hegemonic masculinity, of neoliberalism, of feminist diversity – while at the same time being incorporated within them. Indeed, if the lasting effects of feminism's earlier foray into the effects of mothering on women's lives lead to a fear of being seen to be anti-mother, feminism's redemption can be found in the proliferation of pro-mother discourses.

Umansky notes how several strands of feminist discourses on motherhood came together during the late 1960s and early 1970s. From the cultural left there were concerns to create new family forms and new communal ways of living. These combined with a privileging of Nature and the body and led White feminists to a positive, often essentialist, view of motherhood. Similarly, within Black liberation movements, debates around matriarchy and male dominance led some Black feminists to reclaim motherhood in a positive way. Moving along similar trajectories Umansky notes (1996: 101):

> On the level of theory ... black feminist thought from the late 1960s and early 1970s influenced the focus and tenor of women's liberationist thought as a whole ... Black and white feminists moved simultaneously along the same trajectory as they positioned motherhood at the foreground of their theory and began to recast mothering in a positive, even romanticized, light.

This valorisation of the mother, and its symbolic power, continues to exert a strong influence on feminist thought as feminists working within psychoanalytic frameworks have also emphasised the goodness of motherhood and its nurturative qualities. For example Ruddick (1980) referred to 'maternal thought', which is concerned with the growth and development of the child. The reassertion of the importance of mothering has much to do with understanding motherhood as an aspect of identity. Crouch and Manderson (1993) note that a renewed interest in motherhood emerged during the 1980s. This interest was concerned not so much with an analysis of motherhood as the basis of women's social position as it had been earlier in the women's movement. It was a concern with motherhood as an aspect of identity and as a significant part of the feminine being. Discourses within feminism have, therefore, shifted towards an examination of the connections between motherhood, identity and self-actualisation. In so doing, they turn our attention away from the oppressive nature of discourses of motherhood in shaping identity. In this, feminism provides a useful case for examining how changing discourses give voice to a specific way of being and, at the same time, silence others. Thus:

> One can't speak blithely of wanting an abortion anymore nor sceptically about the importance of motherhood. In the 1980s we have apologized again and again for ever having uttered what we now often name a callow, classist, immature or narcissistic word against mothering. Instead, we have praised the heroism of women raising children alone, or poor, usually both ... Complaints now have a way of sounding monstrous, even perhaps to our own ears. For here the children are, and if we're angry, in backlash times like these it's easy for feminism's opponents to insist that anger at oppression is really anger at children or at mothers.
>
> (Snitow, 1992: 42)

As E. Kaplan (1992: 16) remarks 'women, like everybody else, can function only within the linguistic, semiotic constraints of their historical moment – within that is the discourses available to them'. Motherhood has not gone away. It has, however, transmuted into more pluralistic forms.

Varieties of motherhood

> Something that all the discourses have in common is anxiety – which is precisely what one would expect in a period of intense transition. In searching for a paradigm shift more specific than the global postmodern one – a shift that might encompass all the different forms of anxiety – I became aware that the overall change has to do with childbirth and child care no longer being viewed as an automatic, natural part of woman's life-cycle.
>
> (E. Kaplan, 1992: 181)

In charting changing representations of motherhood from 1930, Kaplan remarks that the late 1980s marks a time of transition. Through the incorporation of many subversive discourses this transition is one in which the clear polarisation between dominant and counter-cultures found in the 1960s has become blurred. In consequence, there is now a less distinctive sense of being outside the dominant culture. The multiple discourses of motherhood make space for many more ways of being, and these are not experienced as quite so oppositional. This is not to say that anything goes. Contemporary discourses do not sweep away the old world order. They come laden with its resonances. And, as with all such transitions, this transition is marked by anxiety. Previously taken-for-granted truths that a woman's main purpose is to reproduce have been effectively challenged. What is left is uncertainty and questioning as to whether or not women should become mothers. And, if they do, how should they do this?

To map this terrain I shall outline the range of contemporary discourses of motherhood that Kaplan has identified. In so doing, I shall draw out the ways in which they hold within them the values of individualism, responsibility, choice, child-centredness and the sanctity of the two-parent heterosexual family. Specifically, I want to illustrate that the selfless mother has not gone away. While she has been fractured, her pieces are at the centre of each of the discursive positions identified by Kaplan. Kaplan gives eight main discursive positions on motherhood. As she suggests, they all convey anxieties but these are, I suggest, anxieties in relation to various kinds of absences:

- Literally absent, the first discourse Kaplan cites is that of the absent mother who has left her children to fulfil her own needs. This mother has exercised her rights of choice, which are central to liberalist discourses, yet she has done so without its concomitant value of responsibility. Given that a mother's prime responsibility is to her children, this mother is considered selfish and wicked. In counterpoint, and supported through discourses of men's rights, this absent mother is replaced by the nurturative father. This is the 'new man' who finds parenting rewarding.

- The second discursive formation is that related to the mother in paid employment. Here we find the dependency of the full-time mother replaced by the more positive liberalist values of independence. Again, choice discourses are important here, as young women can now choose to combine motherhood with paid employment. Nonetheless, it is to a mother's peril should she refuse to retain her sense of being ultimately responsible for her family. In consequence this mother is both absent, through her independence from her family, and present, through the maintenance of responsibility.

- The third discursive formation compounds the child-centredness that lies at the heart of discourses of motherhood. These are discourses of childcare. These discourses build on fears that day care is a second-best option. They speak to those concerns that a mother's absence through employment will cause irreparable psychological or physical damage to her child. These discourses also have specific class-related meanings. For example, the middle-class mother's absence creates her vulnerability to exploitation by employed nannies, who are often working-class young women. In addition to fears of class contamination there are concerns about nannies who leave at a moment's notice or who are ill-trained and abuse children in their care.

- Kaplan's fourth discursive position speaks specifically to the absence of a mother's love, care and responsibility. Again, these discourses have specific class resonances as they are mainly addressed to poor working-class women, who always signify the fallen status of motherhood. These discourses are related to abusive and neglectful mothers who are poor or drug addicts or both.

- Discourses about lesbian mothers highlight the kind of absence that can be summarised through the phrase 'traditional families'. These are the absences of men and heterosexuality. Anti-lesbian discourses speak to the 'damaging' effects of raising children in a lesbian household. They are specifically concerned with the absence of a male role model for male children and with the maintenance of compulsory heterosexuality for both girls and boys. Male absence, of course, is also an important feature of a range of negative discourses related to lone mothers and Black 'matriarchs'.

- The woman-who-refuses-to-mother or the selfish non-mother is the woman who might create that most terrible of absences. This is the absence of the next generation. Selfish non-mother discourses speak also to an absence of selflessness in the character of such women. These women are portrayed as caring more for their own comforts than for those of others.

- What we find is absent in discourses of the self-fulfilled mother is coercion. Discourses of the self-fulfilled mother relate to those women who choose full-time motherhood. These discourses suggest that motherhood is intrinsically fulfilling. The evidence for this is the 'free choice' exercised by the women who decide against combining motherhood with paid work and become full-time mothers. In addition to coercion, other issues are also absent from these discourses. These are the messages of isolation and hard work that accompany motherhood. Discourses of the self-fulfilled mother transfigure selfless motherhood into an aspect of one's personal development. Through the care of others, for example, women can realise their caring potential. Moreover, in 'freely' choosing this option there are no grounds for complaint.

- The absence of a child is central to discourses of infertility and surrogacy. Pro-natalist discourses that support the search for new techniques in the fields of infertility speak to predominant discourses of natural desires. These natural desires arise from a biological imperative to reproduce and a psychologically based developmental view that having children represents the achievement of adulthood and the completion of the self. Discourses of reproductive technologies also set children's rights against mother's rights. In so doing they reinforce ideas of the selflessness of mother love. For example, discourses of the child-in-her-own-right are central to discussions of fetal consciousness. Here, the unborn child's rights are privileged over the mother's through discussions which suggest that it is only those women who are not 'true' mothers who do not put the needs of their unborn child first.

The anxieties that Kaplan identifies are anxieties about an absence of selflessness. Selflessness is, of course, a central aspect of symbolic meanings of motherhood. The only discourse that does not immediately signal anxiety is that of the self-fulfilled choosing mother. Yet it is a discourse rooted in anxiety nonetheless. This is the fear that women will cease to put their families before themselves. In its assertion of free choice, this discourse is both an updated version of the 1950s full-time mother role and a reiteration of it. In utilising choice, this discourse takes up an important tenet of liberal feminism that women should be free from patriarchal power to make their own decisions about how they live their lives. This choice may be in the direction of employment or family, or indeed both. It also finds its legitimacy in dominant neoliberalist discourses more generally. Choosing to be a full-time mother is simply the exercise of one's rights. Yet the linkage of selflessness to self-fulfilment also draws in a post-modern concern with the self and the individual. The 1950s mother is recast as the twenty-first-century woman who has found her 'true' and authentic nature.

Despite its moral superiority, the self-fulfilled choosing mother is, at the present time, a relatively minor discourse. More predominant are discourses associated with the mother in paid employment. These discourses, as I have indicated, draw on three values: that families are mainly women's responsibility, that waged work maintains independence, from a male partner as well as from state welfare, and that women have rights of choice. While maintaining ideas of women's family responsibilities, these discourses also draw on more generalised negative evaluations about women's work within the family. Unpaid, and part of the private sphere, housework and childcare have a long history of being denigrated as 'women's work'. Indeed, it could be said that it is no longer permissible to be 'just a mother'. As Sharpe's (1994) restudy of Ealing working-class White and Asian 14- to 15-year-old girls indicates, the full-time, stay-at-home, bread-baking mother of the 1950s is 'boring'. In these times of high divorce rates, to become a full-time mother is also a risky option. As Sharpe's study also demonstrates, young women are fully aware that there are no longer any guarantees that you will find a partner for life. A future that includes at least intermittent periods in paid employment is both a necessity and a desire.

This rejection of the full-time model of motherhood should not be viewed simply as one of the successes of feminism, as the messages that mothering is thankless, tiring, hard work and not necessarily fulfilling are being heard. The values of independence and individualism have also become the normative standards through which women's lives are judged. M. Kaplan's (1992) study of women who had established careers before embarking on motherhood highlights how negative evaluations of full-time motherhood enhance the more positive values associated with independence and individualism.

The women in Kaplan's Canadian study were highly educated, White, older mothers. These women grew up during the 1950s, when images of the ever-available and self-sacrificing mother were dominant. Most of these women's mothers were full-time wives and mothers. Yet their daughters' judgements of them are particularly negative. Kaplan's research respondents were especially concerned they that they would not replicate the kind of mothering that they had received. Kaplan uses object-relations analysis to explore how women make meaning of motherhood. She notes that the economic, social and discursive conditions of these women's lives are significantly different from those of their own mothers. It may come as no surprise, therefore, that they do not value 'old' ways of mothering. These women have different opportunities and choices to those of women in the 1950s. They, like the women in McMahon's (1995) study, were clear that they no longer had to be, nor should they be, a full-time, stay-at-home, mother. Nevertheless, Kaplan's research respondents were also critical of their mothers if they found them to be unsupportive or did not feel they could depend upon them. Fathers, on the other hand, were more than likely to be judged in far more sympathetic and positive ways whatever their behaviours.

E. Kaplan (1992) notes the mother in paid employment is presented with a host of competing and contradictory discourses. On the one hand, there are those discourses that say that it is beneficial for children to have a mother who is employed as it encourages greater independence. There are also those discourses that state that motherhood is good for employers as it creates a more stable employee. On the other hand, there are those discourses that say quite the opposite. For example, they suggest that being in paid work is detrimental to children's needs for security and consistency of good-quality care. Working mothers leave their children with naive babysitters or monster childminders or all day in the crèche without the 'real' care of their mother. Nor are mothers seen to be of great value to employers either. This is because they are more likely to take time off to look after sick children or require extensive leave during school holidays.

In attempting to manage this terrain it is no surprise that the majority of women take the 'best of both worlds' option. To make the 'wrong' choice and opt for full-time employment is likely to compound the extent to which one is subject to disciplining discourses of a socially negative kind. For example, discourses that speak to women's failure to fulfil the ideals of the selfless mother act as a powerful self-regulatory mechanism. This idealisation of authentic womanhood is immanent in the discursive formations outlined. Part-time paid employment has all the appearance of a rational compromise. As indeed it is. It enables the mother to negotiate a variety of discursive positions at less personal cost than might otherwise be the case. In return for being in a devalued occupational position of a part-time, temporary or casual worker, the mother retains some financial independence and also experiences less guilt and anxiety at leaving her children for extended periods. She also experiences less social disapproval.

This compromise can also be experienced as one of balance. Motherhood offers women access to a symbolic connectedness that contrasts with dominant masculinist discourses of the separated, individualised person who pursues his or her own interests within capitalist markets. In the binary of selfless and selfish, motherhood offers women access to a dominant discursive position. McMahon (1995), for example, notes how participants in her study represented motherhood in terms of connectedness, caring and inter-dependence. Motherhood offered an alternative, and superior, sense of self to that found in masculinist discourses of detachment, independence and competition. Similarly, Hays (1996: 125) comments that 'not only are children understood as distinct from participants in the larger corrupt world, but child rearing also stands in opposition to the self-interested, competitive pursuit of personal gain'.

Can motherhood be seen as purely an oppositional discourse? Are there not also accommodating elements to it? It is to these two questions that I now turn.

Resolving contradictions?

Given the demands and requirements of both spheres, motherhood and employment are somewhat contradictory. I discuss two ways in which we can understand this contradiction. The first is concerned with research which suggests that motherhood constitutes a space of resistance to competitive and individualist ethics that are associated with market societies. I raise a question mark against this because of the differential meanings and effects of motherhood that arise from class- and 'race'-based locations.

The second aspect of contradiction that I discuss explores how changing discourses and practices that surround motherhood can be seen as accommodation towards the market rather than an aspect of resistance.

Resistant spaces?

It's made me more responsible. It's changed the sort of person I am.
I used to be a trouble maker and get into fights all the time. People
have been amazed at the change in my personality.

(Young mother reported in Phoenix, 1991: 244)

Hays (1996) explores the contradictions between two dominant discourses
in North American society. These are the discourses of intensive mothering
and the discourses of capitalist individualism. Discourses of intensive
mothering place the child's welfare at the centre of the mother's role. They
draw on the unselfish and 'natural' nature of a mother's love and suggest
that mothers should spend a considerable amount of their time, money and
energy on their children. These discourses are part of child-rearing discourses
more generally. Marshall's (1991) analysis of child-rearing discourses, for
example, illustrates how the mother remains central to 'good' child-rearing
practices. The modern mother remains available twenty-fours a day and
should be actively engaged with her child in order to provide stimulating and
attentive company. Similarly, Hays' (1996) analysis of three best-selling
childcare manuals confirms how they place the child's needs first and assume
a deep natural commitment from the mother, who will dedicate herself to
fulfilling her child's needs.

Discourses of capitalist individualism are related to economic discourses
of the rational, utilitarian and profit-maximising man. These discourses draw
on assumptions that human nature is based in a natural self-interest and
that all social action is instrumentally based. One's actions are decided
through a series of calculations that weigh up one's preferences and
constraints. The point is to ensure that optimal satisfaction is achieved within
the parameters of those constraints. Discourses of capitalist individualism,
of course, fully subscribe to the notions of competition and survival of the
fittest that are endemic in market societies.

Hays argues that these discourses may be viewed as complementary when
viewed in terms of separate spheres. Discourses of intensive mothering are
relevant to the feminine sphere of the home. Discourses of capitalist
individualism are relevant to masculinist domains of paid employment. Yet
the rise in women's employment also renders these discourses contradictory.
Women will be operating within both discursive formations and will therefore
be experiencing the contradictions that this gives rise to. Moreover, given
the dominance of discourses of capitalist individualism 'Why', Hays asks, 'do
women continue to subscribe to discourses of intensive mothering?'. It is
certainly not rational to do so, in terms of the model of economic rationalism,
as discourses of intensive mothering clearly do not operate in women's self-
interest.

Hays argues that women's engagement in discourses of intensive mothering represents aspects of resistance to dominant capitalist and individualising ethics. In this way. the mothering relationship 'holds symbolic power as a form of opposition' (p. 173). Hays' argument is, of course, congruent with Umansky's (1996) analysis that contemporary feminist discourses take a metaphorical view of motherhood as representational of all that is good in the world. It should be no surprise, of course, that the moral worthiness of motherhood is also understood more generally in the wider society.

McMahon (1995) describes how the women in her study experienced motherhood as a moral transformation of the self. They called on the key themes of romantic love, which suggest that love transforms and reveals one's moral character. In so doing, motherhood enhanced their social commitment, their individual identity and their moral choices. Yet the particular class- and 'race'-based meanings of motherhood mean that both being a mother, as an identity position, and 'doing' motherhood, for example in terms of daily care regimes, is experienced in class- and 'raced'-based ways. While for middle-class White women becoming a mother can be experienced as confirmatory of the moral self one always knew one was, for Black/working-class women becoming a mother takes on an aspirational and redemptive quality.

McMahon explores these issues through an examination of the relationship between the identities of motherhood and adulthood. She argues that women's decisions to have children should not be understood simply in utilitarian terms, for example in terms of when the best age is to become pregnant or whether having a child will fit in with one's career plans. Instead, McMahon (1995) argues that the decision to have a child is essentially one related to identity. She illustrates that middle-class women's concerns about the 'biological clock' are not simply related to decisions as to when to have a child. They are also related to concerns about whether to have one. Time presents women with the option of two alternative and irrevocable identities. These are that of being mothers or that of being permanently childless.

Biological time is not the only factor middle-class women take into account when deciding when to have a child. In addition, it has to be the 'right' time. While the 'right' time includes being psychologically and financially ready, it is also understood in terms of being the 'right' sort of person who is fit to have children. As McMahon notes, women's adult achievements in respect of their employment careers, financial security and relationships with partners are viewed as preconditions for having children. 'Middle-class women had to *become* the sort of persons who could properly have children' (McMahon, 1995: 90, emphasis in text). For such women, this person was that of the mature adult.

Having already developed a sense of identity as a mature adult, becoming a mother, for middle class women, is experienced in terms of moral enhancement. Yet the relationship between becoming a mother and a mature adulthood was experienced differently by the working-class women in her study. For working-class women, having a child was a route to maturity. McMahon's findings confirm those of Phoenix (1991) in relation to young mothers. Phoenix notes that, while adolescents are encouraged to think of themselves as adults, the signifiers of adulthood are harder to achieve than they once were. Giving birth is, nonetheless, one such signifier. It is overwhelmingly perceived as an adult activity. As such, the status of motherhood is one of adulthood.

As adults, motherhood enables working-class women to claim for themselves some of those positive cultural meanings of being loving, caring and responsible. For the young women in the research conducted by both Phoenix (1991) and McMahon (1995), becoming a mother was a period of settling down. Motherhood gave a sense of purpose and meaning to their lives. As discourses of adolescence emphasise issues of irresponsibility, young people experience a sense of self that is other than moral. Similarly, 'breeding the next generation of thugs', 'young women only have babies to get a council house or live off the state', 'having children young ruins your life' are dominant in discourses about young mothers (Phoenix, 1991). And, the characterizations of Jezebel, Whore, Mammy and Matriarch juggle for dominance in representations of Black motherhood (Collins, 1991). For these women, becoming a mother is a route to moral redemption. Motherhood valorises women's identities. Accordingly, the discourses of essential womanhood and nurturative caring motherhood contribute to women's sense of respectability (Skeggs, 1997).

In addition, McMahon (1995) and Phoenix (1991) illustrate how the class-related symbolic meanings of motherhood are experienced in specific ways. For Black and working-class women, the experience of motherhood as moral redemption means that one has to live closer to the ideals of selfless motherhood. This is not necessarily the case for middle-class women, whose moral nature is less in question. Thus, working-class women are more likely to subscribe to the idea that they should stay at home for the first few years of their child's life. This is because these early years are viewed as crucial to a child's development. Can we say, then, that motherhood is a space of resistance to capitalism when it is viewed in terms of class and 'race'? Is it not more likely to also be a space of accommodation, both to middle-class views of the 'good' mother and, as I shall now explore, to the market?

Accommodating motherhood?

In seeking to maintain practices that would make them 'good' mothers, through, for example, part-time or homeworking, the young women in Phoenix's research bear much resemblance to the young women in the research conducted by Procter and Padfield (1998) and Sharpe (1994). These two studies were concerned with researching young women's future aspirations. In so doing, they tell us much about the ways in which contemporary discourses are framing these. Of course, it is impossible to predict whether or not these aspirations become lived practices. Writing in the early 1990s, E. Kaplan suggests that it is too early to know which of the emergent discourses she outlined will become dominant as this requires at least two or three decades to pass before an adequate analysis can be made. Nevertheless, studies of young women's aspirations in relation to motherhood and employment suggest that the realities of empirical changes we are witnessing in young women's lives are mapping with the discursive possibilities of combining career with motherhood.

Procter and Padfield's study of the relationships between family and employment in young women's lives comprised interviews with seventy-nine young adult women between the ages of 18 and 27. These young women were divided into two groups: the 'single' workers, who were childless, employed full-time and without partners, and the 'early mothers', who were in committed relationships and were mostly employed part-time. The women in the Procter and Padfield study, together with those in both Sharpe's and Phoenix's research, illustrate how 'best of both worlds' discourses are becoming dominant motifs in the framing of young women's expectations of their futures.

As I have indicated, these young women are fully aware that there are no certain futures. This relates to both marriage and employment. High divorce rates, lone motherhood and unemployment are everyday facts of life. These young women also view paid work as an important route to selfhood. The young women in Sharpe's study were unanimous that they would continue to work after having children. Procter and Padfield's 'single women' similarly expected to combine career and family. Sharpe's study further suggests that there is no longer a clear separation between working-class and middle-class girls' aspirations in terms of who can have a career. In its place we are more likely to find forms of individualistic pluralism that builds on ideas of choice. Thus, there was a recognition that, although not everyone would either desire or have a career, it remained a possibility for all regardless of one's class base. Moreover, Sharpe comments that, for Asian girls in particular, having a career was an important route to gaining self-respect and self-confidence. It was also a sign of their equality with men.

It is clear that having a career of some kind is a key aspect of young women's aspirations. However, becoming a mother remains a primary objective, as motherhood remains central to women's identity (Woollett, 1991). This remains the case despite the changes in employment opportunities for young women and despite the recognition that women now have to plan to become lifelong workers. Indeed, the centrality of motherhood to womanhood means that it is almost impossible to hear positive discourses related to voluntary childlessness. As Purdy (1997: 70) remarks 'where do girls and young women hear that life might be fully satisfying – or perhaps even more satisfying –

without children? Nowhere.' While there are now a variety of discourses around how one 'does' motherhood, not becoming a mother at all continues to remain less of an option.

In taking up 'best of both worlds' discourses, the young women in these studies were anxious that being in paid employment should not place them in jeopardy of being unable to fulfil their parenting responsibilities. The 'good' mother of contemporary discourses allows women to accomplish this contradiction. This is because the 'good' mother exhibits, albeit in a much more attenuated form, the values of independence, individualism and self-sufficiency which are also found in discourses of capitalist individualism. Rather than assuming that there are two diametrically opposed discourses, as Hays suggests, what we find is an amelioration of the intensive mother. Such an amelioration represents an accommodation *towards* the marketplace rather than an accommodation *of* the marketplace. It therefore marks a discursive shift arising from hegemonic relations of capitalism.

The research of M. Kaplan (1992) and McMahon (1995) illustrate key aspects of notions of the contemporary 'good' mother. 'Good' mothers can be in paid employment. 'Good' mothers do not live their lives through their children. 'Good' mothers no longer have to be selfless. They have their own needs and have the right to have these needs met. Yet they must meet these needs without expecting any support or help from anyone else. Nevertheless, while 'good' mothers no longer have to be physically available for their children twenty-four hours a day, they do have to be psychologically available. They need to maintain an emotional and psychological attachment even though they may be physically absent.

The 'good' mother is, therefore, someone who retains a strong sense of her own identity and who accepts that her child is, similarly, a unique person in her or his own right. As separate individuals, ideas of selflessness are also reconfigured. Within a relationship view, the mother's and child's interests could be assumed to be symbiotic. Yet assumptions that relate selflessness in women to a lack of self-regard have led to ideas that the mother is *too* selfless and therefore *too* lacking in self-regard. This has led to claims that mothers who live their lives through their children damage their individual development. As separate individuals, this can no longer hold true. While this conception of the 'good' mother holds that mothers have needs too, such a discourse of selflessness disciplines in a slightly different way from that of the older, 1950s 'good' mother discourse it has replaced. The mother's selflessness, for example, has to accept that, while she and her child have different needs, the child's needs come first. Without a sense of any symbiosis of needs the mother is even more disenfranchised in her relation to her child. Her only recourse is to ensure that she does maintain a sense of individuality. In consequence, such a response is likely to push her much more fully towards taking up the discourses that are associated with women's engagement in paid labour.

Balancing family and employment responsibilities, together with maintaining a sense of individuality and separation, is achieved through a series of possible options, as the young women in Procter and Padfield's and Sharpe's research demonstrate. These options include working from home, working as a 'freelance' professional, taking a career break and returning when the children are older, returning to education and taking evening shift work. In each of these ways, these young women could maintain their availability as primary carers while at the same time keeping their career options alive. Indeed, to ensure that mother and child retain a sense of their individual identities, 'good' mothers employ a range of strategies of separation even when this is not necessitated through employment. This means that 'good' mothers deliberately plan to leave a child with a grandparent or a childminder or a friend for limited periods of time while they pursue an interest or take some leisure. In this way, McMahon notes, 'good' mothers are able to demonstrate role commitment without role engulfment.

Nevertheless, the place of motherhood in these young women's lives is no longer viewed as a lifetime vocation. It is, rather, considered to be a stage in a much longer expectancy of a variety of life roles and experiences. This can be understood as much in terms of the ambivalent place that motherhood holds in Western societies as it can in terms of changes in employment markets or discourses of the 'good' mother. While, on the one hand, motherhood may be a metaphor for all that is worthy, on the other hand it remains 'women's work', and in consequence is denigrated. One might, for a short time, claim a moral superiority through motherhood. Such a claim is always set against the higher values associated with being in paid employment. Thus, although the 'young mothers' in Procter and Padfield's research were currently primary carers of their young children, they still considered that they were young enough to have a career at some point in the future. Indeed, for some young women, the morally redemptive qualities of becoming a mother are viewed as an encouragement to better things. It is too easy to be caught up by the negative discourses associated with young motherhood. As Phoenix (1991: 239) notes, 'It seems that some women may have done better if they had postponed childbearing, but early childbearing may equally have spurred some women on to get qualifications and be consistently employed.'

Finally, given the clash between the greedy institutions of home and paid employment, these young women know that having a career and caring for children are not easy options. As with the women in M. Kaplan's (1992) study, they also know that they will be the ones who will have to resolve the resultant tensions. Thus, Procter and Padfield confirm Hays' analysis that recent social changes have left women 'living a contradiction' with regard to employment and family roles. Principally, as later chapters explore, while the 'best of both worlds' option may appear a useful reconciliation, as women seek to 'have it all' they also find that they are left 'doing it all'.

Summary

This chapter has explored the 'best of both worlds' as a site of intersection between two dominant discourses. These discourses have been identified as those of the 'good' mother and those of neoliberalism and the market. The chapter began by outlining the strength of 'good' mother discourses through an analysis of second-wave feminism. This illustrated something of the hegemonic nature of motherhood as a symbol of goodness and moral superiority. It also illustrated how changing feminist discourses have been a response to wider discursive concerns in the social, political and culture order. This chapter also illustrated how, in contemporary society, the 'good' mother is no longer as fixed and secure a representation as she was depicted in the middle of the twentieth century. There are now a range of ways in which women can be good mothers. Nevertheless, this lack of fixity has given rise to discourses of anxiety that surround potential absences. These absences are seen to be both literal and symbolic.

This chapter has also explored the idea of motherhood as a site of resistance and as a site of accommodation. It has demonstrated that the discursive frameworks of class and 'race' place women in a different relation to motherhood as a moral domain, with consequent implications for how and whether we would see motherhood as a site of resistance to competitive individualism. In terms of motherhood as a site of accommodation to competitive individualism, research into young women's expectations coupled with the evidence of current statistics suggests that the mother represented by 'best of both worlds' discourses is likely to become the predominant model. Remaining at the centre of such a configuration is the idea that 'children come first'. Nonetheless, in order that a child's needs for independence are realised, a mother's selflessness can now be evidenced through intermittent separation rather than continuous attachment. In this way, I have argued that 'best of both worlds' is both an amelioration of discourses of the 'good' mother and an accommodation towards the market.

In seeking to explore the 'best of both worlds' I have illustrated how motherhood represents a powerful symbol of goodness in society. In the next chapter, 'Women are caring', I explore the implications of this further.

4

WOMEN ARE CARING

A democratic ethic of care starts from the idea that everybody needs care and is (in principle at least) capable of care-giving, and that democratic society should enable their members to give both these activities meaningful place in their lives if they so want. These conclusions can only be reached, however, when we acknowledge that caring should be integrated in the fullest possible manner in any vision of social life and social policies, and when we insert by consequence the care perspective in our everyday social and political theories.

(Sevenhuijsen, 1999: 17)

Some feminists celebrate the 'female' virtues of (a now sanitized) connection and care. Relatedness and connection are seen as relatively straightforward and positive virtues. Women are now praised for their greater immunity to 'bad' forms of individuality

(Flax, 1997: 317)

To care is to feel concern or interest. To care is to take responsibility. To care is to put others before oneself. To care can mean that one feels affection or love. To care can be an ethical stance. To care shows compassion. To care can be a worry.

The good woman, like the good mother, is caring. She shows concern and interest. She takes responsibility for the care of her family. She puts others before herself. She loves her child and the planet. She asserts that the world should be more caring. She shows compassion for those in distress. She worries. Overall, women *are* caring. Caring is seen to be an essential part of a woman's subjectivity. Thus, if a woman fails to care, if she fails to put others before herself, if she fails to take responsibility for others' needs, if she fails to show compassion, she is not a woman at all.

When care is judged in this way it is seen to be a higher-order trait. Caring is posited as a moral stance and as an important antidote in the face of fears of a predominantly unfeeling world. Do we care about the homeless on the streets or do we step over them? Do we care about our next-door neighbour whom we haven't seen for days? Do we care that the cheap goods in our shops are made by children in sweatshops?

The quotations at the beginning of this chapter say something of the nature of feminists' concerns around care. For Sevenhuijsen (op. cit.) care is such a universal need that it should be incorporated as fully as possible into political and ethical discourses. Sevenhuijsen's position would be described as falling within an 'ethics of care' feminism. Drawing on a combination of feminist psychoanalytic theory and philosophy, such feminists posit an ethics of care as an alternative to dominant hegemony. They point out that acts of care, and a caring disposition, are the hallmark of relationality and connection. Accordingly, care acts as an important counter or reverse discourse to individualism and atomism.

Flax (op. cit.) offers a rather more cautious view. She suggests that the turn to maternal fantasies that is the hallmark of such feminist concerns should be deconstructed. Flax notes how discourses of connection and relatedness are represented as relatively unproblematic. Connection and relatedness are seen as the basis of an alternative and superior subjectivity. Very simply, it assumes that it is nice to care. However, Flax argues that this can only occur when negative aspects of relationality, such as anger, hate and envy, have been repressed. Flax asks 'Who and what does this repression serve?' In addition, and alongside considerable feminist scholarship (see Chapter 6), Flax notes that the undertaking of care is not only women's work but is also marked by lines of 'race' and class, as working-class and Black women are paid to undertake the childcare and housework of middle-class women.

In discussing 'woman are caring' as a discursive position I explore the implications of an ethics of care as a counter or reverse discourse. Brine (1999) notes that reverse discourses represent clear sites of resistance to dominant discourses. Nevertheless, she indicates that any power that they have is necessarily precarious. As Chapter 3 indicated, the operations of hegemony mean that counter-discourses can be incorporated or appropriated by more dominant discourses. I would argue that this is the case here. In addition, there is such an intrinsic relationship between caring and concepts of the good woman that we have to ask 'For whom does an ethics of care represent a discourse of resistance?' As the research evidence I present here highlights, an ethics of care can also be viewed as a discourse of submission.

This chapter begins with 'Counter discourses: the case of an ethics of care', in which I set out the main tenets of ethics of care positions. I highlight how these are based on the centrality of relationality and connection as ways of knowing the social world. I also illustrate how care ethicists consider that ethical and political systems that are based on care will provide a superior, and alternative, mode for social organisation. In this way, they seek to challenge more dominant liberalist and rights-based ethical discourses. Ultimately, the hope is that in place of aggressive, competitive individualism we will have a society based on care and concern for others.

The origins of an ethics of care discourse are based on work undertaken by Gilligan (1982). Gilligan argued that women resolve moral questions in terms of their impact on others. This was contrasted with a greater focus on rights issues that is the mark of masculinist-based ethical reasoning. Because of its attention to how women resolve moral questions in a different way to men, Gilligan and those who follow her have been accused of essentialism (see, however, Gilligan, 1998). Thus, they have been accused of conflating women's essential nature with the conditions through which they live their lives. And they have ignored the differences that exist among women. This concern has been reinforced through further developments of an ethics of care that have drawn on mothering as an exemplary moral relationship (see, for example, Noddings,1984).

There are two problems with care as a counter-discourse. First, it carries the danger of essentialism, as I have just outlined. Second, in using the moral value of mothering and relationality as the basis of an alternative position it seeks to reverse margins and centres. In place of arrogant individualism we find connected relationality. As a consequence, we might simply be changing one oppressive discourse for another. Ethics of care feminists are, of course, aware of these dangers and have responded to them, as I shall illustrate.

Having set out the context for an ethics of care, my purpose in the next three sections is to explore empirical research that can serve to illuminate some of the attendant issues. In 'The desire to care' I explore the processes of subjectification that occur through engagement in formal education. Education is, of course, an important site of disciplinary power in which bodies are categorised and classified. And, although it is a site of submission to the technologies of discipline, such as timetables, examinations and course evaluations, it is also a site of mastery of those disciplines as some become skilled at punctuality, passing examinations, scoring high marks in coursework and so forth. This simultaneity of submission and mastery is an important aspect of subjectification. Butler (1995: 45–6) notes in this regard that:

> The more a practice is mastered, the more fully subjection is achieved. Submission and mastery take place simultaneously, and it is this paradoxical simultaneity that constitutes the ambivalence of subjection. Where one might expect submission to consist in a yielding to an externally imposed dominant order, and to be marked by a loss of control and mastery, it is paradoxically marked by mastery itself ... the simultaneity of submission as mastery, and mastery as submission, is the condition of possibility for the subject itself.

I explore these simultaneous processes through research into young women who were taking health and social care courses at a further education college (Skeggs, 1997). Skeggs' research highlights the connections that are made between *doing* and *being* in the construction of identities based on care. Her work also illustrates how submission and mastery of the curricula of these courses was enacted and how it shaped emergent identities. The significance of this research is that, as working-class women, these students invested in the discourses of care not simply to gain employment, but also as a route to moral superiority and respectability. Yet, as working-class women, such claims are never secure. Skeggs' research demonstrates how these students had to overinvest in the discourses of caring to maintain their place in the moral order.

In 'Appropriating care' I explore the emergence of 'soft' discourses of human resource management and I note how these have combined with the 'hard' discourses of marketisation in the field of education management . It has been argued that the combination of these 'soft' and 'hard' discourses has provided opportunities for women to gain promotion and climb management hierarchies. I explore research into the changing management of the further education sector as a space where it would appear that some credence could be given to this view. In so doing, I note how women have taken up the discourses of new managerialism and marketisation to place themselves at the vanguard of a newly organised sector.

Nevertheless, I also highlight that one of the rewards for this has been that of unremitting work, tiredness and guilt. Accordingly, these women's experiences mirror those found in early feminist research into domestic labour. As the title of this section indicates, my position here is to emphasise that, while these 'opportunities' may benefit individual women, the harnessing of 'women's skills' is much more concerned with facilitating the workings of the market. Although corporate organisations have discovered only relatively recently the competitive advantages that accrue from women's emotional and caring labour, those concerned with the management of schools and the regulation of the urban poor did so in the nineteenth century.

In an exploration of the genealogy of the urban teacher, Jones (1990) notes how it was recognised that pedagogies based on fear only hardened the spirit. However, pedagogies based on love would be an instrument of moral training. Teachers were therefore instructed to encourage children to love them so that their love would be for the teacher and the school rather than the backstreets. This was reinforced through the shame that was collectively brought on those who failed to love school. In this way 'The object of the exercise was to create an ethical regime that stimulated morality from the shame of offending rather than a "fear of the rod" ' (p. 64). Jones notes that it was but a step from the notion of the humble and virtuous teacher to the notion of the teacher as a good parent. In addition, this linkage of love and the model family as the basis of regulation of working-class children also opened up the teaching profession for specific curricula for girls and its supervision by women teachers. Of course, this similarly provided opportunities for individual women, but we have yet to see these translated either into a new moral order or into the collective advancement of a feminist project in school education.

The issue of political social change is taken up in 'Caring for social justice'. However, rather than looking more broadly at issues of social justice and leadership, my purpose here is to explore the implications of including an ethics of care in conceptualisations of feminist leadership. Here, I note how much research into leadership conflates the notion of women's leadership styles with enactments of feminism. I illustrate how an ethics of care produces a new regime of truth that needs interrogating. In particular, I highlight how it produces discourses around strong women leaders that replicate, rather than disrupt, leadership as autonomy, instrumentalism and control.

Counter discourses: the case of an ethics of care

> Women's construction of the moral problem as a problem of care and responsibility in relationships rather than as one of rights and rules ties the development of their moral thinking to changes in their understanding of responsibility and relationships, just as the conception of morality as justice ties development to the logic of equality and reciprocity. Thus the logic underlying an ethic of care is a psychological logic of relationships, which contrasts with the formal logic of fairness that informs the justice approach.
>
> (Gilligan, 1982: 73)

In listening to the voices of women making decisions about abortion, Gilligan (1982) argued that women's patterns of moral reasoning did not fit into existing male-as-norm theories of human development. In particular, she argued that the women in her research stressed issues of connection and personal relationships when making moral decisions. This was contrasted with the ways in which dominant moral theory held that moral dilemmas can be resolved by an abstract view of formal rights. Gilligan argued that this different pattern of reasoning was associated with a different sense of self. Whereas men have a sense of self as autonomous and separate, women have a sense of self as interdependent and relational.

Gilligan's aim was to illustrate that the philosophical and psychological literature on moral development was systematically biased (Tong, 1989). Not only were men the primary producers of these systems of thought, but also these theories were based on research into the lives of men. Their predominance meant that when women failed to live out these normative theories they were perceived to be morally underdeveloped. Gilligan argued for an expanded view of moral development that included women's ways of reasoning.

This counter- or reverse-discourse to masculinist ethical paradigms was taken up by Noddings (1984), who set out the dimensions of an ethics of care. Overall, Noddings offers an ethics of care as an alternative vision for society. This does not simply seek to ameliorate the competitive individualism that lies at the heart of market-based economies. It seeks to replace this with caring. An ethics of care paradigm begins by placing interrelationship at its centre. In addition, it draws on motherhood as the epitome of a caring relationship.

An ethics of care contains five aspects (Diller, 1996):

- In contrast to humanist ideas of the separated individual, an ethics of care assumes that we live in necessary relation to each other. In this way the basic ontological position of an ethics of care is that of relationality.
- An ethics of care demands that we take up the other's position as our own. This act of engrossment, as Noddings calls it, is not the same as putting oneself in another's shoes. It is not one projecting how one would feel and act but accepting the other's views and feelings as one's own.
- An ethics of care focuses on the particular not the general. Thus, an ethics of care does not seek resolution through some universal set of rules or principles.
- An ethics of care requires the one who cares to act. It is a commitment that one follows through from engrossment to action on behalf of the cared for.
- Caring comes first. Caring is an elementary and primary aspect of the human condition. An ethics of care requires that ethical justifications shift away from rights issues to how we can live within relations of caring.

Diller (1996) divides the critical responses to advocates of an ethics of care into two groups. The first relates to those who see the saliency of an ethics of care as applicable only to specific domains. Noddings' exposition of an ethics of care draws on the mother–child relationship as the epitome of what is involved in caring and being cared for. Those who argue that an ethics of care is a domain ethic suggest that it is an inappropriate mode of conduct in areas such as economics, business, national and international politics. Diller notes that those who take a domain approach argue that different moral priorities and procedures are needed for different contexts. For example, what may be suitable for education may not suit law.

The second critique levelled against an ethics of care is that, from a feminist perspective, it leads to essentialism for two reasons. First, an ethics of care is strongly associated with motherhood in particular and with women's relational ways of being more generally. These associations lead to assumptions that because caring is what women do caring is an innate aspect of womanhood. In consequence, an ethics of care can trap women back into the labour of caring that so much of feminist politics has been at pains to expose. Second, because of its linkage to ethical systems, an ethics of care is seen to romanticise caring labour. In seeking to make care a positive value in society it overlooks the ways that caring for others can be burdensome and onerous.

Feminists working in this area have responded to these critiques by acknowledging that simply to equate an ethics of care with an essential notion of womanhood is flawed. Yet they reject both the notion that an ethics of care is relevant only to certain domains and the idea that caring can be understood only in terms of its association with women's traditional spheres. Rather, they argue that, to facilitate transformative social change towards a more just society, it is necessary to place an ethics of care at the centre of moral and political discourses. In addition, it is necessary to broaden our understanding of the meanings of care. In this way we will be able to understand more fully the operations of hegemonic systems of masculinity and capitalism.

In developing this agenda Tronto (1993) argues that it is necessary to understand how current moral and political theories work to preserve inequalities of power and privilege and in so doing degrade those who do caring work. Tronto illustrates how the complex interrelations of the discourses of individualism, autonomy and self-made man shape taken-for-granted understandings of care as a devalued activity. In consequence, dominant moral and political discourses about care ensure that care is contained within the realm of the private, the personal and the trivial.

Tronto illustrates this through a deconstruction of care into four phases. These are: caring about; taking care of; care giving; and care receiving. Within each phase, Tronto highlights how the values we place on care are structured in such a way that the types of care undertaken by the most powerful are those that are most highly valued. In contrast, the types of care undertaken by the least powerful are those that have the lowest value.

Tronto describes 'caring about' as the first stage in caring. This involves an initial recognition that care is necessary. We may, for example, care about the world's poor or the homeless. We may care about what happens to our children or our partner. Tronto notes that it is often perceived that what we *care about* is defined in individualistic terms and so defines the sort of person we are. Yet the division between what we care about and who has the responsibility for this initial recognition is crucial. Caring about the public issues of state and economy, for example, are the spheres of the most powerful. Caring about these issues is accorded high value. Caring about one's children or one's partner are primarily the spheres of the least powerful. Caring about these issues is, in consequence, of low value.

'Taking care of' is the second stage in the phases of care. This involves notions of agency and responsibility. 'Taking care of' means that one has taken responsibility for a need and has decided how to respond to it. We may, for example, decide that to take care of the needs of the homeless we need to build more housing. We may decide that to take care of our children we need to buy healthy foods. And we find the same divisions in terms of value and power. When 'taking care of' is associated with the public spheres of life it is viewed as prestigious. When it is associated with the private realm it is viewed as trivial. Moreover, the form through which we 'take care of' influences our judgement of its importance. Men take care of their families through being in paid employment. Women take care of their families through housework.

The third phase in the process of care is that of 'care giving'. This is the direct meeting of care needs and involves physical work and coming into contact with those who need care. We may, for example, feed the homeless or provide them with shelter. We may do the cleaning, dusting and cooking in the home. Tronto notes that the giving of care is primarily the work of slaves, servants and women. When men do undertake this work we find a pattern of exceptionalism. Doctors have higher status than nurses, and men who enter the caring professions, such as social work and teaching, are more likely to reach the top of them.

The final phase is that of 'care receiving'. This is the assessment that care needs have been met. The homeless are now housed. The child has a healthy diet. Nonetheless, the acknowledgement that one has care needs is a threat to one's sense of autonomy. To receive care is to place oneself in a position of dependency, and those with most needs are perceived to be the most dependent. In addition, we are either pitying or disdainful of those who need care. We may, for example, feel sorry for the homeless or we may blame them for their plight. Yet those with most power are able to define their needs in ways that maintain rather than undermine their privilege. In these ways the identification that to have care needs is to be less autonomous, to be disdained or to be pitied is avoided. This is accomplished in two main ways: first, by having care needs met by those who are in positions of greater dependency; and, second, through defining care needs in terms of freedom to pursue higher-order activities. Thus, men's needs for care of themselves and their children are primarily met through the invisible and unpaid work of women. In the sphere of paid work, managers delegate care needs to others to free up more time to manage and senior hospital consultants delegate the lower-care needs of patients to junior staff. Indeed, in paid work environments, such work is conceptualised not as care but as 'service', 'support' and 'assistance'.

Tronto argues that we need an expanded conceptualisation of care that shifts conceptions of human nature away from dominant binaries of autonomy/ dependency into conceptions of interdependence. This has four main features:

- Care is not restricted to interactions between people but includes objects and the environment.
- We cannot presume care to be a dyadic or individualistic activity. Care functions socially and politically.
- Caring is culturally defined and varies among cultures. This allows us to see that the motherhood paradigm of care that has informed so much of feminist theorising is culturally specific.
- Care can be both a single activity and ongoing.

Sevenhuijsen (1998, 1999) draws attention to the universal nature of care by commenting that we all need care and are capable of giving care. She remarks that the problem of care is no longer confined to a question of balance between motherhood and employment as adults are confronted with issues of care in their workplaces, their friendships and in their relations with older relatives. In this way, the concerns that surround care have gone beyond the traditional dividing line between public and private spheres of life. It is, therefore, a timely moment to take feminist concerns for an ethics of care beyond its essentialist assumptions.

With some similarity to Tronto's agenda, Sevenhuijsen seeks to illustrate how an ethics of care should, and can, be built into democratic systems of government. Sevenhuijsen argues that it would be a mistake to dismiss the potential of an ethics of care for feminism simply because of post-modern fears of fixed identities. She comments that much of the debate that surrounds an ethics of care has focused too much on issues of identity and far less on issues of agency and morality. She therefore seeks to combine issues of identity, agency and morality in her analysis of policies that surround care.

In terms of her aim of drawing attention to the moral nature of ethics of care discourses, Sevenhuijsen seeks to illustrate how an ethics of care offers a radical alternative to more predominant ethical discourses that are based on liberalism. In particular, she aims to foreground the relational image of human life rather than the atomistic and individualistic image that is the mark of rights discourses that surround care. For example, she comments that:

> In contrast to an atomistic view of human nature, the ethics of care posits the image of a 'relational self', a moral agent who is embedded in concrete relationships with other people and who acquires an individual moral identity through interactive patterns of behaviour, perceptions and interpretations.
>
> (Sevenhuijsen 1998: 55)

Thus, in a critique of 'third-way' policies, Sevenhuijsen (1999) highlights how debates that suggest that fathers should have greater parenting rights position women and men in an antagonistic relation. Such debates become construed in terms of who has the greatest rights as individuals. This focus on individual rights detracts from the ways in which caring relations are practised within a wider context of social arrangements. In particular:

> It might, after all, be the case that the one-sidedness of caring between mothers and fathers has more origins in the hegemony of the work ethic and in the dominant social arrangements of labour and care, than in an uneven division of rights between single fathers and single mothers.
>
> (Sevenhuijsen 1999: 24)

Accordingly, rather than speaking of parenting rights, it would be better to conceptualise the concerns for childcare in terms of labour rights. This, in turn, would mean that the focus of the debate is centred around employment law rather than social welfare.

In addition, Sevenhuijsen considers that a post-structural concept of identity formation offers much to ethics of care debates. This is because the idea of a self that is continually in the process of being formed means that moral identity is also being continually revised and developed. This marks a radical break with the notion of the presocial self that is found in liberal ethics and enables feminists to explore how moral identity is a social practice that arises within the narrative conventions of specific social and political contexts.

Finally, Sevenhuijsen argues that because care ethicists refuse a separation between the self and the other this means that they are more able to see the meanings of care in their own lives. Thus, 'The stable, complete and unlimited self of universal ethics makes place for a multiple and ambiguous moral self, who is aware of his or her own limitations, dependencies, vulnerability and finiteness, and who is prepared to accept responsibility for these things' (Sevenhuijsen, 1998: 57). In this, therefore, an ethics of care requires that we acknowledge our own care needs as an act of responsibility as well as those of others.

The desire to care

> The seduction of caring may be that it offers a means to feel good, even morally superior. This is a powerful incentive when set against the prospect of unemployment. Their [research respondents] experiences of being worthwhile and externally valued give them an authority from which to speak.
>
> (Skeggs, 1997: 62)

Skeggs' (1997) research is based on an extensive ethnography of women she first met when they were students taking a variety of 'care' courses at a further education college where she was employed. With its focus on class as a key analytic category, her study draws on post-structural perspectives, Bourdieu's concepts of capitals and Black feminist theorising. Of interest here is Skeggs' analysis of the technological practices through which the caring self is produced. Through this analysis, Skeggs illustrates how working-class women are already positioned and position themselves in relation to caring.

The women in Skegg's research had few, if any, formal educational qualifications. Combined with this lack of human capital, as working-class women they also had little cultural capital upon which to trade. At a time of high unemployment, these women had little option but to go to college. Skeggs demonstrates their decision to take a course on caring represented an investment in becoming a respectable and respected person. To be working class is to be deemed pathological, dangerous and threatening. To be working class is to desire respectability. To be working class is to live with unease. Skeggs' analysis illustrates how the women in her research refused to be fixed or measured by class. One way of trying to escape negative class identifications was by taking up the discourses of improvement.

Skeggs notes the predispositions that facilitated these young women's choice of a 'caring' course and being positioned within the discourses of caring. These women had not achieved high levels of academic qualifications, but they had enjoyed the social side of school and so they were not averse to continuing their education. They had previous experience, mainly babysitting, upon which to build. And caring was something that they felt able to do and at which they were unlikely to fail. They also knew that, as 'non-academic' courses, the health and social care courses were located at the bottom of the college hierarchy. These young women therefore entered further education as an 'attempt to gain some status and value for themselves ... in the face of negation' (p. 59).

One way of dealing with this negation was to identify fully with the vocational and practical aspects of the course and to disidentify with its academic content. The vocationally relevant practical activities and their associated placements in community homes and hospitals were therefore seen as being of most value. This value was not solely because work experience is a requirement of a competitive labour market. It was also because placements were the sites that legitimated the developing caring subject.

In successfully undertaking taxing and challenging placements, these young women began to receive validations from those they cared for and from their teachers that they had the essential qualities and competences of the caring person. For example, one young woman commented that the warden at the home where she was on placement had told her that she was a 'natural' (p. 61). The experiences of placement also reinforced the distinctions between practical and academic knowledge. Thus, helping clients in need was viewed as a far more socially worthwhile activity than studying for 'A' levels.

The development of the caring self was further enhanced through the ways in which the courses classified the caring person and used this classification as the basis of coursework. In this way, the students were assessed to determine if they had the qualities and disposition necessary to be an expert carer and, if not, to shape them in that direction. For example, the courses presented a range of techniques of the 'correct' ways in which caring should be undertaken. All of these were based on a model of the 'family' as the site of care. Students had to conduct projects on 'the family' that included presenting photographs of their own family and classifying 'problem' families. The courses presented information on child development and 'remedies' for bad behaviour. The students studied topics such as maternal deprivation and undertook courses that developed skills in constructing children's toys and clothes. They were taught about 'bad' practices through case studies and videos and were expected to list the faults of 'non-caring' others. These aspects of the curriculum, and its linkage to the idea of the family, created frameworks through which these young women evaluated their own and their family's caring practices. One young woman, for example, wondered whether her father would have stayed with them if her mother had been more 'caring'.

In addition, Skeggs notes that the caring person is defined through the conflation of *caring about* and *caring for*. Thus, the caring person both exhibits a social disposition that expresses concern for others and undertakes the practices of caring. Skeggs demonstrates this point through a table derived from her data that sets out the essential qualities of a caring person. This table illustrates that these include being: kind and loving; considerate about others; understanding; warm and friendly, reliable; sympathetic; tactful; never selfish; never cruel and nasty; never unkind; never sharp-tempered; never unpleasant; never impolite. Skeggs also asked the women in her research to rank the qualities that they believed they had themselves. She notes that in most cases they considered that these were their attributes. This combination of *being* caring and *doing* care was also reinforced through examinations. For example, one examination question asked students whether they would choose to babysit for a friend who asked them unexpectedly or whether they would choose to go to the cinema with another friend. Of course, those who chose the former course of action received the highest marks!

In each of these ways, the caring self is monitored, enhanced and shaped. Drawing on discourses of motherhood, femininity and familialism, the placements, coursework and evaluations that form part of formal technologies of surveillance embed an ideology of caring that is based on self-denial as an enactment of responsibility. This caring self is honed and reinforced through mechanisms of self-surveillance such as self-reflection and self-examination as the women question their own upbringing and their qualities as caring people. Indeed, the extent to which these processes of subjectification were mastered and taken up as their own can be seen through the ways in which these young women formed judgements of others. For example, they were very critical of middle-class women who 'farmed' their children out, as this was seen as indicating that such women were uncaring and unnatural.

Nevertheless, the divide between being a respectable caring person and a non-respectable working-class woman is always tenuous. While there is pleasure and a sense of well-being to be obtained from achieving the status of a caring person, 'At the same time, the abject other, who does not gain such a pleasurable sense of well-being, is always present, not only as other, but always, potentially, as herself' (Davies *et al.*, 2001: 178). As members of the working class, the young women's sense of being caring was always subject to scrutiny and always required external validation. Although it risked exploitation, maintaining an identity of respect and value predisposed them to undertake voluntary and unpaid caring. Although it induced guilt, the ideals of caring led them to evaluate their own practices continuously. And although it reinforced inequitable divisions of labour and high domestic workloads, the linkage between *being* caring and *doing* caring meant that they undertook all the childcare themselves.

As part of a dialogic relation, Skeggs' research demonstrates that the investments these women make in caring allows them to develop for themselves some status and moral authority. To develop the caring self through both paid and unpaid care work may reinforce existing social and sexual divisions. It may produce subordination, guilt and the constant monitoring and evaluation of that caring self. Yet it also offers the chance of respectability. Within class relations, working-class women's access to the cultural capital of femininity is always under scrutiny and is never guaranteed. For women more generally, moral superiority is profoundly nested within the 'natural' realm of motherhood. It is similarly precariously based, as the line between the 'good' and the 'bad' mother is a fine one. Paradoxically, therefore, 'while self-regulation is the condition of possibility for the subject itself, the mastery of self-regulation is at the same time an act of submission' (Davies *et al.*, 2001).

Appropriating caring

So-called 'female' attributes, such as interpersonal skills, consensus, teamworking, negotiation and being able to handle several projects at a time, were beginning to be acknowledged within organisations in the late 1980s as comprising the missing components of a newly discovered 'soft' leadership style. It was predicted that these 'female' ways of organising and managing would be more appropriate to organisations by the millennium.

(Colgan and Ledwith, 1996: 2)

In the mid-1980s a noticeable discursive shift was taking place in the corporate boardrooms of Western capitalism. This shift is commonly termed the movement from 'hard' to 'soft' management practices. The most evident marker of this changing discourse was the renaming of personnel and training departments as 'human resources' departments. The shift from 'hard' to 'soft' discourses has been seen as a move away from the view that employees are the passive repositories of the orders of their superiors or 'empty shells' with nothing to offer except the skills for which they were employed. It is one suggestive of a people-centred philosophy that views employees as 'resourceful humans to be developed by humanistic policies' (Legge, 1995: 35).

Within 'soft' management discourses employees are seen to be worthy of being educated, trained and developed. Managers work in a dialogic relation with employees rather than a dictatorial one. They are encouraged to listen to the views and suggestions of their subordinates and to involve them in the planning processes of managerial work. The discourses of 'soft' human resource management use terms such as 'empowerment' and 'teamwork' to convey a liberatory and egalitarian backdrop to these new management techniques. Managers and subordinates are viewed as co-workers with a commitment to producing high-quality goods and services. These 'soft' discourses suggest that it is important to release the inner creativity or latent talents of all employees. This is seen to be good not only for the company but, in times of global recession and organisational downsizing, for employees also. They will have new skills and experiences to trade in a competitive job market when they are no longer needed by their current employers.

Suffice to say that the conditions that facilitated this shift were not those of a new moral order informed by ethics of care debates. Rather, as Legge (1995) demonstrates, they were the result of changes in the economic, product and labour markets of both the USA and the UK, the competitive threat of Japanese industry yet the iconic status of Japanese working practices, the mediation of new technologies and the swing to right-wing political ideologies. Thus, the shift to valuing the human 'resource' was prompted not by the development of a greater sense of responsibility towards workers but by the search for economic advantage in a global market. Accordingly, such discourses argue that paying attention to the 'human' side of business practices will increase productivity and competitiveness.

The phrase 'your employees are your most valuable resource', which is central to human resource discourses, derives from the idea that in a global market all other resources, whether natural, such as iron, tin or coal, or manufactured, such as machinery and plant, are available to any competitor. The mark of competitive difference is the quality of the people you employ in the manufacture or servicing of these products. The organisation that wins in a global market is the one that develops employee skills and knowledge and creates collective, rather than time-consuming and energy-sapping competitive, internal working practices. Accordingly, 'soft' human resource management develops discourses about internal customers, quality systems and human resource *development*.

The core skills at the centre of human resource discourses are those associated with relationality. Often termed 'people management skills', they include listening, discussing, taking an interest in and facilitating. As a discourse that is designed to fit with flatter organisational structures and so to some extent challenge traditional hierarchical relations between managers and workers, further skills that are required are those of subordinating your ego and needs to those of others. These are important in order to facilitate the teamworking that has formed part of more recent managerial responses to gaining competitive advantage. It is perhaps no surprise that this was viewed, as Colgan and Ledwith (op. cit.) note, as an opportunity for women's advancement (see also Wyatt with Langridge, 1996). These are seen as the core skills of womanhood.

In a parallel, yet separate, trajectory, Thatcherite politics in Britain encouraged the public sector to embrace the values of the market. This was a move away from the egalitarian and collective principles of state provision and towards standards, freedom and choice. In part, this embrasure of the market can be seen as a move in the opposite direction from that occurring in the private sector, i.e. it can be viewed as a move from 'soft' to 'hard' principles of organisation. For example, Exworthy and Halford (1999) note how the individualist policies of the New Right have promoted business ethics as central to new managerialism in order to reduce state involvement and facilitate new forms of public welfare provision. The more collectivised concerns of the New Left, who held power in many urban authorities, have sought closer connections between service users and service providers and greater professional accountability. Entrepreneurialism, customer care, a community focus and individual responsibility all jostle together in a series of discursive formations.

Nevertheless, the changing nature of managerial practice in the public sector in the UK is linked to the changing nature of professional practice. This is because new management discourses have meant 'a shakedown of old managerial and professional privileges' (Exworthy and Halford, 1999: 8). Moreover, the discourses associated with new managerialism replicate the enabling and 'softer' discourses of human resource management that have been promoted within corporate cultures in the business world but simultaneously draw in the discourses of individualism. New managers are:

> policy 'entrepreneurs', highly motivated, resourceful, and able to shift the frame of reference beyond established norms and procedures ... [they] enable staff to make their own contributions and, in doing so, to generate greater identification with, and commitment to, the corporate success of the organization.
>
> (Exworthy and Halford, 1999: 6)

The discourses of new managerialism promote a sense that career success is no longer reliant on knowledge of rules and procedures in order to climb the bureaucratic ladder. Rather, it lies within an individual's ability to manage and create new projects and to 'grow people beneath them'. In addition, the meritocratic emphasis on the creative individual implies that the 'old boy' networks that have been central to career success will no longer hold their power. Women will be able to 'make it' on their ability.

As Arnot et al. (1999: 95) reflect 'Notions of equality of opportunity, whether on grounds of social class, gender or race, began to give way to notions of individualism, the ideals of competition and the reward for performance'. Although for different reasons, with some similarity to Colgan and Ledwith (op. cit.) Arnot *et al.* have suggested that these aspects of individualism and competition have opened up spaces for young women to succeed. This is partly because the resulting shift in educational values towards academic performance is close to liberal feminism's concerns to 'de-gender the public sphere' (p. 101).

One sector of education in which Arnot *et al.*'s suggestion of greater opportunities for women would appear to have been achieved is that of further education. In 1992, the Further and Higher Education Act established a new 'incorporated' sector, with colleges of further education becoming autonomous and self-governing. Combined with a change in the funding regime, the effect of incorporation was to push colleges towards greater competitiveness. Incorporation encouraged colleges to see themselves as operating within a market (Hughes, Taylor and Tight, 1996). Corporate identities shifted to those of an entrepreneurial public service approach of 'real- world' 'can do' flexibility that is a mark of the 'hard' organisation (Hughes, 2000). Yet, despite this embrace of the market, or perhaps because of it, it would appear that this sector has provided space for women managers to colonise and to be colonised.

As we have seen, Skeggs' analysis focused on how the educational curricula of further education enhanced the development of the caring subject. Research in the sphere of further education management has noted how perceptions of women's relational and caring skills have been a significant reason for the increasing opportunities for women in management. Prichard and Deem's (1999) analysis of this sector illustrates that, although men continue to hold the majority of senior posts in further education, in total women constitute 44% of those in management posts. Moreover, their data suggest that women are more heavily represented in younger age groups, in those posts that have been newly created and as recent recruits. Overall, this would suggest that developments in this sector are facilitating women's access. Should this continue the thesis would be that over time there will be a 'trickle-up' effect, with more women reaching senior management.

In seeking to explain this take-up by women of management opportunities, Prichard and Deem suggest that what we are witnessing is not women's advancement but a feminisation of the management of further education. Feminisation refers to the processes whereby women are brought into occupations at low levels where the status and rewards are limited. Prichard and Deem's explanation for this draws on both labour process theory and post-structural approaches. Labour process theory focuses on the ways in which feminisation of the labour force reduces labour costs and facilitates the intensification of labour. Women's appointments in further education replace higher paid bureaucrats and require them to double-shift by undertaking both teaching and management work.

Within a post-structural approach Prichard and Deem's analysis, together with that of Leonard (1998), illustrates how the 'soft' discourses of new management, in terms of their emphasis on people skills and empowerment, are drawn on by women managers. Women managers contrast their managing techniques with those of their male colleagues to signal how they are more effective because they are able to develop more conciliatory and facilitative working relationships. Thus:

> whereas the (male) college management was perceived as using their gender to 'ram home' their initiatives ... [A] 'feminine style' was invoked as providing ... a way forward which would carry the staff along with it.
>
> (Leonard, 1998: 80)

Similarly, Prichard and Deem note how one woman respondent who was promoted to a senior management post took up the identity of one who was 'constantly valuing people' and 'increasing the confidence and self-esteem of people' (p. 332). She rejected the old further education management model as one of 'all drawbridge and defences' (p. 331). It was 'a complete waste of time, as it neglected the client and strategic direction' (p. 331). Instead, she embraced the new model of further education management that is characterised by 'flexibility and reconstruction' (p. 334).

The 'flexible' manager is one who has to bend to fit herself, and her subordinates, within the requirements of this greedy new corporatism and 'can do' culture (Hughes, 2000; see also Clarke and Newman, 1997). Occupying the middle and lower ends of the (much reduced) managerial levels of incorporated colleges of further education, women managers are much closer to the concerns, worries and anger of those that are required to deliver the more-for-less products of this ever-changing world of further education (Hughes et al., 1996). The emotional and physical labour that is required to accomplish this is well practised by women. As Tamboukou (2000: 472) remarks in relation to school teaching 'what seems to emerge as a "truth" is that, however "independent" women have come to be, they have never stopped caring for others'. Through what can only be expressed as managerial gymnastics, women managers in further education have sought to ameliorate the worst excesses of a greedy corporatism through tactics that include the 'creative' management of staff workloads and working conditions. They have, therefore, sought to manage timetables and contractual conditions in ways that 'give back' something to their subordinates.

In intensified organisational cultures the costs of these new practices are those of exhaustion, stress and self-blame. Sachs and Blackmore (1998: 271–2) comment in relation to school leadership that:

> Principals are being positioned as 'emotional managers' in schools which are under increased financial constraints, accountability and social pressure for easy solutions ... Women principals can be trapped

as they are expected to provide the positive and nourishing emotions of care, warmth, patience and calm which maintain the 'greedy organisations'.

Yet, ethics of care feminists lay great stress on the importance of caring for self as well as others. However, in research that I conducted with colleagues Malcolm Tight and Paul Taylor, middle managers considered that they were already asking too much of their staff and therefore the only person left to ask too much of was themselves. This intensification of their own workloads led to a feeling that they were failing their staff. As one respondent commented, 'Possibly I could argue better for my staff if I didn't have 55-hour responsibility' (Hughes, 2000: 259). And it led to a feeling of being overwhelmed by it all. Thus:

> I've got a marvellous team. They really are second to none in the college and they do adapt very well to change. Even the older people, myself included. What we can't do is the constant more work and more work. There is no way now. There is no slack and it still keeps coming. It still keeps coming.
>
> (Curriculum manager reported in Hughes, 2000: 259)

What appears less disturbed in the creation of new management discourses is the relation between management and masculinity. Leonard (1998: 82) describes new managerialism in the further education sector as the reinforcement of masculinity whereby the 'highly charged, competitive culture has legitimated an authoritarian, task-oriented style of management'. The data from all the research in this area highlight how women are uncomfortable with these aspects of managerial work in further education. One way forward would appear to be a management approach that is based on a feminist concern for social justice that is located within an ethics of care. It is to this that I now turn.

Caring for social justice

> ... the literature suggests that there are four main defining characteristics of feminist educational leadership. Women whose leadership is informed by a feminist agenda work for improved school justice and equity for staff and students in their schools, challenge and resist injustices, are committed to empowering those they work with, and work to establish a caring school community.
>
> (Strachan, 1999: 311)

The literature relating to women and management asks several questions about the connections between gender and the enactment of managerial responsibilities. Do women manage differently to men? Do women have a distinctive style of management? What are women's attitudes to power? There has, in consequence, been a good deal of research on the attributes of women as leaders. As much of this work rests on a comparison with men it always suggests a deficit model of women managing. Research has focused on women's personalities in a 'Do they have what it takes to manage?' vein. It has focused on women's motivation by asking 'Do women *really* want to manage?' It has focused on women's skills. For example, 'Are they bright enough to manage?' And it has focused on women's styles of leadership through a 'Women don't manage properly' perspective.

Feminist writings on women managers do suggest that there are key differences between women's styles and those of men. This is thought to be largely because of women's rejection of masculine management approaches. These particularly relate to aggressive, competitive and controlling behaviours. Indeed, the association of management with masculinist traits is sufficient to deter women from applying for promotion (Bloot and Browne, 1996). Thus, research that indicates that women's preferred and actual management styles are built around relational ways of being resonate in the literature on woman and management. For example, research by Palmer (1996) on the managerial approaches of women working for HM Customs and Excise indicates the desire for more collaborative styles of working. This study found that women managers prefer to persuade and encourage rather than order and impose. Similarly, research into school leadership has indicated that women 'run more closely knit schools than do men, and communicate better with teachers. They use different, less dominating body language. They seem to be more flexible and sensitive' (Ozga and Walker, 1995: 37).

Nevertheless, it is easy to assume that women managers are also feminist managers. Strachan's (op. cit.) research examined the connections between values and style, and she suggests that there are two aspects that distinguish women managers from feminist managers. One of these is a commitment to social justice. The other is the development of one's own and others' practices of caring. In this framework, feminist management is considered to be the *doing* of feminism 'in such a way that it challenges and changes hegemonic institutional practices. This emancipatory practice is also imbued with an ethic of care in order that a sense of belonging, of being cared for, is built into organisational practices' (Tanton and Hughes, 1999: 248). Ozga and Walker (1995) suggest that it is feminism's rejection of authoritarian and hierarchical organisation, its recognition of the masculine inherent in such structures and its politics of emancipation that create the value context for this.

Although Strachan (1999) highlights the diversity of ways in which feminist leadership is enacted, her findings also illustrate how an ethics of care is combined with a social justice perspective in the practices of feminist school leaders in New Zealand. In many ways, these replicate the general literature on women's management styles. For example, through including parents and colleagues, the organisational practices of the school are those that emphasise collaborative and consensual decision-making processes. However, in seeking to develop a 'caring' culture in their schools, the principals in Strachan's research can be seen to be following Noddings' (1994: 176) solicitation to teachers that 'like mothers, [they] want to produce acceptable persons – persons who will support worthy institutions, live compassionately, work productively but not obsessively, care for older and younger generations, be admired, trusted, and respected.'

One of the ways through which this was set in place was through the development of anti-sexism, anti-racism and anti-violence policies. This valuing of diversity was viewed as caring in action through which respect, nurturance and compassion would not only be enacted but would be instilled in children and colleagues. In addition, Strachan illustrates how an ethic of care was seen to address the needs of the oppressed through a stress on the importance of education in improving children's life chances and a commitment to improving the academic achievement of the school.

Strachan's research illustrates how some feminist leaders take up very positive views of caring and view caring as an altruistic act that can bring about a change in the relations of domination. Yet, like women managers in the English further education sector and the women students in Skeggs' (1997) study, the costs of being 'caring' were high. Strachan (1997: 320) notes that:

> These women worked very long hours, including many evenings and weekends ... For Jill and Marie their reluctance to delegate compounded their workloads. Both had sought ways of reducing their workloads, not only because of the stress involved but because it also isolated them from friends and family more than they were prepared to accommodate.

Flax (1997) reflects on the ways in which feminist theory often perceives connection and care as unproblematically good. She notes how the negative emotions associated with care, such as aggression and abuse, are rarely acknowledged. Thus, although it might be argued by some that an ethics of care is a significant feature of feminist leadership, this in itself is highly problematic. Blackmore (1999) comments that feminist leadership based on an ethics of care is potentially troubling for feminism because it produces a new regime of truth. In particular, Blackmore notes that 'the problem is that discourses about women's styles of leadership, in reifying care, can position women as self-sacrificing, and are prone to idealize women's oppression' (pp. 58–9). As the research that has been discussed here indicates, what is produced is a discourse of the strong woman leader who has no needs for care herself. Such a discourse serves only to reinforce, rather than challenge, masculinist leadership discourses that seek 'to control the uncertainty that might be generated by emotional intimacy' (Kerfoot, 1999: 187).

The expression of needs for care represents a threat to ideas of leadership that have been constituted through sets of discourses around instrumental rationality, objectivity and control. In this regard, Kerfoot (1999: 187–8) notes how:

> Ever concerned with their own and others' judgements of themselves as to their competence at being 'on top of' situations, masculine subjects must at all times labour at being masculine and to conceal or downplay personal fears and weaknesses that stimulate a questioning of this competence.

These are, of course, not the only discourses that position leaders. Women in managerial and leadership roles are also positioned by discourses of femininity that place them as being either too masculine or too feminine. For example, the expression of anger is seen as unfeminine, as, indeed, is not expressing emotion at all. Crying, on the other hand, locates women leaders within 'wimpish femininity' (Blackmore, 1999: 164) with a consequent loss of credibility.

In striving for social justice, feminist leaders may draw on the current legitimacy of the 'softer' discourses of management, and they may map these on to certain stereotypical feminine traits of relationality and 'people skills'. They may indeed recognise the need for the care of self and they may prescribe it to their colleagues and friends. Nevertheless, the expression of their own needs for care continues to be an inadmissible space in organisational politics when time is always at a premium. The overwhelming view of care as women's business means that women continue to be viewed, and view themselves, primarily as care-givers rather than care-receivers.

Summary

This chapter has explored an ethics of care as a counter- or a reverse-discourse. In doing so, it has sought to highlight the centrality of relationality as an important aspect of feminist theorising. The empirical research that has been presented here has explored some of the dilemmas and dangers that are contingent within ethics of care debates. There is no doubt that an ethics of care can be a seductive concept. As the young women in Skeggs' research demonstrate, investment in caring discourses can create a higher moral sense of self. In addition, as an oppositional discourse it posits an alternative vision of society that is indeed welcome. Nonetheless, as a purely counter-discourse it remains problematic. Ethics of care debates can distract attention from a range of issues. These include the differences between women, the differences between different forms of feminism, issues of masculinity and the gender/ power relations in social life. In addition, it produces a new regime of truth that would be as regulatory and oppressive as that which it seeks to replace.

Moreover, we need to be cautious in assuming that an ethics of care functions solely as a counter-discourse. An ethics of care can also be viewed as a discourse of submission to the hegemony that caring is women's work. Certainly there is pleasure, bliss and reward in such submission and in the mastery [sic] of becoming a good, caring subject. Nonetheless, the assumption that caring is women's work confirms essentialist views that can work to fix women into caring roles. In addition, its appropriation by managerialist discourses may herald opportunities for individual women but it also means that, as women *try* to relinquish their primary responsibilities for domestic care, they take on the primary responsibilities for the care and nurturance of employment-based relations at a time of widespread change.

As I indicated in the introduction, care ethicists are fully aware of these critiques. The need to deconstruct liberal and justice-based ethical discourses is one course of action that has been proposed (Sevenhuijsen, 1998). Paying consistent attention to the political nature of moral concerns that posit 'is' and 'ought' in the binary set-up, whereby 'the 'good woman' becomes caring by becoming selfless and disappears from relationships and the 'real man' becomes independent by using justice to rationalise violence' (Gilligan, 1998: 138), is another. I discuss these issues more fully in the final chapter.

5

HAVING IT ALL

... having it all is not having all of everything, but finding out what is most important and learning to lift these things of importance out of their usual leaden trappings. Having it all involves crafting new things from what is already there.

(Apter, 1993: 115)

Linda Kelsey resigned from her post as editor of *She* in late 1995 ... her own individual departure was heralded as the failure of mothers to achieve success and certainly to 'have it all'.

(Woodward, 1997: 272)

With some similarity to 'women have made it', 'having it all' is a discourse of success. 'Having it all' is a celebratory statement of achievement. Yet there are some important differences. As I have noted, 'women have made it' discourses specifically exclude any reference to the family. Women cannot 'make it' solely by building their careers as housewives and mothers. They have to be engaged in some kind of paid work or educational project. Yet family life and motherhood can be incorporated into 'having it all' discourses. For example, Woodward's (op. cit.) analysis of *She* magazine illustrates how the independent mother is depicted as someone who does 'have it all'. This is achieved through evoking images of autonomy and self-determination to create powerful identificatory positions. In this age of high divorce rates, serial relationships, smaller families and growing numbers of women in employment, the contradictory natures of motherhood and independence are overlooked in *She* magazine's celebration of a woman's lessening need, in economic, emotional and social terms, for a permanent man in her life.

The notion of some kind of freedom is resonant in another depiction of 'having it all'. This freedom, however, is a freedom from the work associated with childcare and paid employment. In May 1999, the *Independent on Sunday* (23 May 1999) carried an article with the headline 'Having it all – the housewife makes a comeback'. The article suggested that we are witnessing the birth of a new breed of woman: the 'born-again housewife'. This woman is young and childless. She is married to a wealthy man and has given up her own high-powered career because she wishes to support her husband's career and she wants to spend more of her time in leisure activities. The article stated that 'having it all' means having time and someone else's wealth to buy the freedom of that time.

These two similar yet different conceptualisations of 'having it all' illustrate something of the range and ambiguity of meanings that can be attributed to specific discourses. In one case, 'having it all' means motherhood and the freeing up of the ties between women and men. In another case 'having it all' means childlessness, the purchase of time and economic dependency. There is no single way in which 'having it all' is taken up as a discursive position. Thus, the ambiguities of meaning allow for multiplicity and difference. 'Having it all' for one person is not necessarily 'having it all' to another.

This very individuation implicit in the discourses of 'having it all' contributes to another aspect that marks it out as different from 'women have made it'. 'Women have made it' is a hierarchically competitive discourse as 'making it' requires you to be beating others and climbing higher. These features are not absolute requirements to 'having it all'. Rather, the competitive elements are more latent. Clearly, in market societies, to achieve the status of 'having it all' suggests something of winners and losers. Yet this discourse is suggestive of finding something that is more personally important, and this means that the notion of hierarchical ordering is far more muted. The trend towards downshifting, for example, whereby individuals give up high-powered jobs for more 'quality' time is indicative of this. Such individuals may justly claim that they 'have it all' in terms of their own values and aspirations.

Finally, there is an aspect to 'having it all' that is highly significant for the analysis that is presented here. 'Having it all' is a discourse of symbiosis that promises full realisation. It is a discourse for utopia. Women who want to 'make it' in the world have to choose to some extent between career and children. 'Caring' women are selfless, not selfish. Certainly, women who seek 'the best of both worlds' endeavour to hold employment and family in a form of synchronic balance, but this is imperfectly achieved. In consequence, women often feel that they are fully fulfilling neither one role nor the other. In contrast, 'having it all' implies perfect harmony. One can have children *and* career *and* husband *and* independence. Indeed, despite Apter's (op. cit.) claim, 'having it all' does imply that one can have all of these things, though not necessarily all at once.

The main empirical literature that is drawn upon here to explore 'having it all' as a discursive position is that related to women 'returning' to education. Education provides the promise of transformation: either economic and/or the retrieval of one's latent potential. Those women who do return to education are often wives and mothers. They are in many respects the role models, and the future, for the young mothers in Procter and Padfield's (1998) study who expect to return to education or employment as their children grow up. These women expect to enjoy their children while young *and* believe that there will be sufficient time in later life to have an employment career. Through their life course, therefore, they expect to 'have it all' – partner, children, education and career.

This sequential form of 'having it all' is also significant for the analysis presented here because it draws attention to how educational participation is conceived of as a process of transition. Such a theme is common in the literature on adult education, where it has become 'part of popular educational mythology' (Blaxter and Tight, 1995: 235). For example, education can be seen as a route to the realisation of a new identity and a new way of life. Higher levels of education promise the opportunity to be no longer 'just' a housewife or to be trapped in low-paid part-time jobs (Pascall and Cox, 1993).

The concept of transition suggests movement from one place to another or from one set of circumstances to another. Transition implies a momentary experience from one point of fixity to another. Within the literature on educational transitions journeying metaphors are resplendent (Blaxter and Tight, 1995) as learners follow paths, get lost, seek direction and, finally, reach their destinations. And so one might assume that women who take up study as adults do indeed manage to move from one set of circumstances or one sense of self to another to achieve their 'all'. And, even if the journey was a little bumpy along the way, once they have arrived this achievement will be experienced symbiotically and harmoniously.

The danger of the journeying metaphor, and ideas associated with transitions, is that they can belie the impact of the past in the present. Giles (1990) notes that the model of women returning to education has often been understood in terms of a straightforward progression. Women are seen to enter higher education with a wealth of life experience but with a lack of confidence. They are seen to leave as confident and materially independent. Feminist research has strongly critiqued this unproblematic conception of transition from one state of being to another. As Giles (1990: 358, emphasis in text) comments 'Higher education *has* enriched my life materially and psychologically, yet the woman of nine years ago co-exists (not always amicably) with the woman of the present'.

The simultaneous nature of the past/present means that, rather than experiencing education as a process of relocation, it can be experienced as a process of dislocation.

It is a location that is described in literature of migration, exile and diasporas as 'not quite' and 'in-between' (Boehmer, 1995: 232) because a key feature of such analyses is that of simultaneously belonging to, and being outside of, one's country of origin and the host nation (Beasley, 1999). As I hope to indicate, women 'returners' share these diasporic experiences.

The concepts of transition and metaphors of journeying are, of course, not confined to the field of adult education. They are also resonant in other literatures that I have drawn on to frame the analysis for this chapter. In particular, it is the work of the philosophers Benhabib (1992) and Braidotti (1994) that I explore here. Benhabib and Braidotti have made important contributions to feminist debates that surround women in transition and the associated processes of border crossing and migration (Davis and Lutz, 2000).

Drawing on aspects of migration, their respective metaphors of 'exile' and 'nomad' have enabled feminists to think critically and creatively about the potential of dis/location. This chapter begins, therefore, with an examination of these writings in order to provide the context for what follows.

Notwithstanding, these metaphors have been controversial, and the two sections that follow apply the metaphors of 'exile' and 'nomad' to research on women 'returners'. The purposes of these sections are to explore and illuminate some of the implications and associated critiques of these metaphors. In 'The woman "returner" as "exile" ' I undertake a symbolic form of 'exiling' as I leave my 'home' discipline of education and journey through the fields of post-colonialism. Specifically, I place my analysis of the empirical literature on women 'returners' alongside that of empirical understandings of migration and exile. I do so because both literatures resonate with ideas of leaving and return and because, as academic fields, they also constitute separated spaces. Such a process of 'exiling' is, of course, not an uncommon intellectual act. As Benhabib aims to make clear through her metaphor, it is undertaken because of strong beliefs that such travel will enable us to see the taken-for-granted in new ways and that it will heighten levels of critical understanding.

Through the juxtaposition of the woman 'returner' and the 'exile' I highlight two issues. The first relates to the 'myth of return'. Brah (1996) points out that the 'myth of return' is not a feature of all diasporas yet it is an important conceptualisation in this field. Myth and myth making are significant discursive practices. While we commonly understand the concept of myth as meaning some kind of falsehood, the grand and minor stories of myth shape everyday practices in important ways (see, for example, Hughes, 1991; Hughes and Tight, 1995). The 'myth of return' is seen to have an economic, psychic and social presence in the lives of migrants and exiles. This can be through the importance of sending financial, and other, aid home, of being anxious to retain one's 'native' way of being in the host culture and how the 'myth of return' lends a sense of transience to the experience of being in a foreign culture.

Although they are not conceptualised in terms of 'myth', these features are resonant in the women 'returner' literature. Students speak of a desire to return to their families or class of origin with the prizes of their 'exile' in education (Pascall and Cox, 1993). They speak of wanting to retain aspects of a past self in a new milieu (Tett, 2000). And they experience further and higher education as momentary and transient in terms of the life course (Adams, 1996). While the notion of 'exile' foregrounds the idea of separation, the 'myth of return' foregrounds the relational aspects of the 'exile's' location. A focus on the 'myth of return' therefore keeps our attention on the implications of simultaneously being located and dislocated within the culture of origin and the host culture.

A second, and related, aspect I take from the post-colonial literatures is the attention paid to ideas of 'home' that are embedded within the concept of 'return'. These literatures highlight how 'home' is itself a problematic conception given that it can simultaneously mean a place of origin *and* the 'Mother Country' (Chamberlain, 1997) *and* the site of everyday experience (Brah, 1996). For the woman 'returner' 'home' may, of course, be her class/ ethnic origins *and* education *and* her place of residence *and* her family. This problematisation of 'home' brings into focus how there are multiple sources of identification and desire. It allows us to interrogate ideas of assimilation, colonisation and resistance that are significant to the conceptualisation of 'exile' and the notion of 'return' that it encompasses.

In the section 'Nomadic moments' I draw attention to the joy and pleasure in this transition to 'having it all'. The length of this part of the discussion also signifies the amount of attention that has been paid to these aspects of women's experiences of further and higher education and confirms Braidotti's contention that the 'nomad' is a minority position figuratively, empirically and theoretically. One of the main critiques of Braidotti's conceptualisation of 'nomad' is that it is a metaphor for the privileged who are not required to 'name an identity' (Brah, 1996: 3) as they cross the borders between nation states in both a literal and metaphoric sense. As the border post that has to be crossed, education may be perceived to be a transitional process to a new state of being. However, the literature on 'returners' demonstrates how students' engagement within education requires them to name their identities as classed, 'raced', sexualised and aged bodies. Once they have 'passed' through the borders they also find that these aspects operate to 'return' them to their places of origin.

Exiles and nomads: metaphors for transition

For some, a central feature of the political significance of diaspora is the creation of a ' "nonnormative" intellectual community' (Barkan and Shelton, 1998: 5). Such a community is considered able to provide a critical, though ambivalent and fragmented, voice that may contribute to dismantling the relations of colonialism. Wisker (2000: 16) refers to this as colonisation in reverse and she makes the point that 'Post-colonial migrants both unsettle and enrich what was thought of as the centre of imperial powers'.

This idea of the development of criticality is central to Benhabib's (1992) conceptualisation of 'exile'. In a critique of 'feminist friends of post-modernism' (p. 211) one of Benhabib's concerns is to put the case against a wholesale rejection of the metanarratives of philosophy and a wholesale retreat to local narratives.

The critique of metanarratives rests in part on the ways in which they act as forms of social legitimation. As Norris (2000: 28, emphasis in text) notes 'A metanarrative is a story that wants to be *more* than just a story, that is to say, one which claims to have achieved an omniscient standpoint above and beyond all the other stories that people have told so far'. Femininism and Marxism are regarded as metanarratives because they claim to have the 'truth' about egalitarian relations and because they offer, in a 'modernist' way, the hope of a better world. They are, as Barrett (2000) puts it, grand stories we tell ourselves. Post-modern critiques note that there are as many claims to truth as there are different language games and discourses. For example, in seeking to speak for all women, early feminist claims to knowing the truth about women's experiences have been shown to be the truth of White, middle-class, Western feminists. The naming of 'Black' and 'White' similarly occludes issues of difference and in so doing represents universal ways of naming and knowing diverse groups of people. Ifekwunigwe (1997: 129) comments in this respect that 'the prevailing and inconsistent social and political stance that anyone who does not look White is seen as Black impinges on identity construction for many multiethnic metis(se) people'.

The retreat to local narratives is a response or a resolution to the ethical, and epistemological, issues that arise from these forms of critique. For example, post-modern theory highlights how each local narrative contains its own belief system, values and criteria for what counts as the truth. In consequence, social critics cannot, and ethically should not, claim to offer a superior discourse by using their own criteria to judge the practices of others. All the social critic can do is to note the differences that occur and 'not make the error – the typical 'Enlightenment' error – of believing any one such story to possess superior truth-telling warrant' (Norris, 2000: 29).

Clearly, these ideas are controversial and have been subject to much debate. Benhabib (1992) offers one example of this. Benhabib notes that philosophy has been critiqued as providing a metadiscourse of legitimation because it claims to provide superior tools of epistemological judgement. One of the debates that has arisen from this critique has focused on the future role of philosophy as providing a framework for social critique. Benhabib also notes that generally feminists have sought to avoid these debates by not taking sides. Benhabib's case is that feminists must take sides, and the side they must take is to argue for the retention of the superiority of (some) philosophical methods.

There are four aspects of Benhabib's case that are relevant here. First, she notes that the retreat to local narratives is itself a metanarrative in that it claims to be a superior truth or way of knowing the social world. Second, she argues that everyday practices and traditions are not value neutral and contain within them their own processes of legitimation. Third, she questions whether local narratives are sufficiently reflexive and self-critical to critique themselves. Finally, she notes that the social critic is 'never "the view from nowhere," but always the view of the one situated somewhere, in some culture, society and tradition' (p. 225).

Behabib argues strongly both for the need to retain universal categories and for the critical potential of being outside one's culture of origin. She argues that, at minimum, and when faced with conflicting and irreconcilable narratives, philosophy provides a framework for the ordering of one's normative statements. It provides a statement of methodological assumptions and helps clarify principles of judgement.

The case for being located outside one's own culture is based on the idea that this can provide a necessary epistemological distance from everyday certitudes. Distance can facilitate social critique. Benhabib uses the metaphor of 'exile' to describe this critical social analyst who locates herself 'beyond the walls'. Thus, Benhabib (1992: 226–7) comments:

> There certainly may be times when one's own culture, society and tradition are so reified, dominated by such brutal forces, when debate and conversation are so dried up or simply made impossible that the social critic becomes the social exile. Not only social critics in modernity from Thoreau to the Frankfurt School, from Albert Camus to the dissidents of Eastern Europe have exemplified this gesture. Antiquity as well as the Middle Ages have had philosophers in exile, chiliastic sets, mystical brotherhoods and sisterhoods, and Prophets who have abandoned their cities. Certainly the social critic need not be the social exile; however, insofar as criticism presupposes a necessary distantiation of oneself from one's everyday certitudes, maybe eventually to return to them and to reaffirm them at a higher level of analysis and justification, to this extent the vocation of the social critic is more like the vocation of the social exile and the expatriate than the vocation of the one who never left home, who never had to challenge the certitude of her own way of life. And to leave home is not to end up nowhere; it is to occupy a space outside the walls of the city, in a host country, in a different social reality.

Davis and Lutz (2000: 375) indicate that Benhabib describes exile as the distance between the place of origin and the contemporary context in which one is spending one's life. It is never a view from 'nowhere' but is a view located outside or beyond. In using the metaphor 'exile', Benhabib draws on historical images of the intellectual to convey its political imperative as a critique of post-modern tendencies that celebrate the loss of boundaries and a withdrawal from the political (Braidotti, 1994). Given that we do not have a place of 'nowhere', this point of location provides the best vantage point we have at the moment from which to judge the everyday and taken-for-granted of one's native culture and may indeed provide better or more superior knowledge.

In taking up a place 'beyond the walls', the 'exile' aims to gain a critical perspective on the cultural milieu left behind. The political reasons for exile are associated with the ways in which such knowledge will contribute to social change. Though she might not necessarily do so physically, in a metaphoric sense the exile 'returns' or revisits her culture of origin with this new knowledge to work for change from within.

There are three related critiques that surround Benhabib's metaphor of exile that are important to the analysis in this chapter. The first concerns Brah's (1996) point that locating oneself outside the city gates or crossing borders is not, of itself, sufficient to raise critical consciousness or provide a vantage point from which privileged insight can be gained. This is because such places remain sites of multiple intersections of identification and disidentification and 'the probability of certain forms of consciousness emerging are subject to the play of political power and psychic investments in the maintenance or erosion of the status quo' (Brah, 1996: 208).

The second critique concerns the idea that the exile can sufficiently distance herself from her everyday certitudes to return with a higher level of analysis. This underplays the difficulties involved in discarding aspects of one's past in terms of the identifications and investments that one has made with it. M. Lewis (1993) illustrates how these are evidenced through the resistance that women display towards feminist ideas because feminism threatens established ways of being and knowing. The 'myth of return' similarly highlights the thread of connection that exists between 'exile' and 'home' .

The third critique relates to the implications for social change that would form the political project of those who seek 'exile'. While post-colonial migrants may act as colonisation in reverse, as Wisker (2000: 16) also points out 'Some critics see post-colonialism as not always resistant but collusive; a state of being and thinking which involves siding with the forces of imperialism'. With resonances of Lorde's (1994) contention that 'The master's tools will never dismantle the master's house', Braidotti comments (1994: 32):

> Whereas for Benhabib the normativity of the phallogocentric regime is negotiable and reparable, for me it is beyond repair. Nomadism is therefore also a gesture of nonconfidence in the capacity of the *polis* to undo the power foundations on which it rests.

It is, of course, an open question as to whether the 'nomad' would accomplish such a task.

Braidotti offers the metaphor of 'nomad' as a way of conceiving a post-humanist utopian feminist subjectivity that is located within language and geopolitical contexts but has given up all desire for fixity. In comparison with the 'exile', who always has a 'home' and who might indeed return to it when she chooses, the 'nomad' desires a subjectivity composed of transitions. The purpose of these transitions is not the progressive acquisition of the ultimate 'truth'. Nomadic transitions are transgressive. They are enacted as a way of resisting assimilation and seek to embrace the multiplicity of the post-humanist subject. Thus (Braidotti, 1994: 22):

> The nomad does not stand for homelessness, or compulsive displacement; it is rather a figuration for the kind of subject who has relinquished all idea, desire, or nostalgia for fixity. This figuration expresses the desire for an identity made of transitions, successive shifts, and coordinated changes, without and against an essential unity. The nomadic subject, however, is not altogether devoid of unity; his/her mode is one of definite, seasonal patterns of movement through rather fixed routes. It is a cohesion engendered by repetitions, cyclical moves, rhythmical displacement.

Braidotti's depiction of the 'nomad' as a metaphoric way of understanding the potential of feminist subjectivity is designed to disrupt the idea, predominant within feminist theorising, that women's lives can only be understood in terms of victimisation and oppression. As Davis and Lutz (2000: 374) comment:

> ... the 'nomad' provides a playful and empowering image for the feminist critic. It breaks definitively with the link between feminism, victimization and oppression. The feminist 'nomad' is the agent par excellence, always in transit and constantly transgressing boundaries.

This empowering image is based upon two aspects. One of these is that being nomadic is enacted as a positive choice and with purpose. It recognises women's sense of agency and autonomy. The second aspect is the idea that, because it is a repetitive process, being uprooted can be seen as a point of fixity in itself. Repeated transitions are viewed as beginnings or openings and as regular patterns in the tapestry of life. They provide for a renewal of the self that does not grieve for a lost homeland:

> 'Nomadism' is a metaphor ... which allows women in transit to reformulate their experiences of migration in a way which provides an optimal sense of agency. It enables a kind of situatedness which takes the realization of being uprooted as a starting point, without resorting to an idealisation of the community of origin.
> (An interview with Braidotti, in Davis and Lutz , 2000: 376)

Braidotti's metaphor of nomad has, like Benhabib's metaphor of exile, been subject to criticism. Gedalof (2000) argues that nomad is a fitting metaphor only for those with privilege, i.e. those White Western feminists whose racial/ethnic identity is not constantly called to account. For such women:

A nomadism in which 'all that counts is the going' is an option for us. Yet for black, diasporic and postcolonial feminists (and, I would venture, for the white western women of Kosovo or Bosnia) this option is not really available.

(Gedalof, 2000: 344)

In an interview with Davis and Lutz (2000: 374) Benhabib makes the same point:

Nomadism requires having many passports. As a metaphor it does not deal with the power and complexities of the nation-state systems within which we still operate. We still need to have identity cards at border crossings. And we still need to be able to negotiate the different spaces in which we are. Unlike the nomad who does not seem to have a particular home and whose home is in different places at different times, exile suggests the loss of an origin and a home space.

To explore these issues further I now apply aspects of 'exile' and 'nomad' to an analysis of the women 'returner' literature.

The woman 'returner' as 'exile'

In [Benhabib's view] feminism is still in need of a (utopian) model in order to provide itself with a raison d'etre ... she [also] dismisses the 'celebration of fragmentation' as a concept which conflates fragments with fluidity: 'Fragmentation has its downside. It has a psychic as well as a moral cost. When the fragments are in contradiction to each other, they are pulling in different directions.' As an alternative she prefers Jessica Benjamin's concept of 'synthesis' which enables the construction of coherence by discarding what does not make sense from the life story. This concept appeals to Benhabib, both in terms of her work and her biography.

(Davis and Lutz, 2000: 373)

As 'exiles', the 'returner' literature is replete with examples of women metaphorically, and literally, seeking to leave aspects of their lives behind in order to have a better view on the future. This might be in terms of leaving behind their identities as housewives and mothers (see, for example, Pascall and Cox, 1993), the oppression of the working class (Jackson, 1998), their current jobs (see, for example, Blaxter and Tight, 1995) or their partners (see, for example, Edwards, 1993). In terms of 'return', the most basic understanding is that of a return to the unfinished business of education. In the more recent literature on identity, this can be understood as a form of retrieval by returning to the 'potential' self that was left behind on early cessation of education (see, for example, Green and Webb, 1997; Britton and Baxter, 1999). And, because of the impact of age, class and gender, it is also understood in terms of being 'returned' in a rather forcible sense to the roles and duties of a prestudent personhood (see, for example, Edwards, 1993; Pascall and Cox, 1993; Adams, 1996).

In exploring aspects of leaving and return that are part of the formulation of 'exile', I provide a reading of a study by Tett (2000). My reading of Tett's study is juxtaposed with the empirical literature on migration. My aim has been to use these literary counterpoints for illumination and explication. In particular, there are two aspects that are resonant in the migration literature that I use as the basis of my reading of Tett's study. These are the 'myth of return' and the multiple locations of 'home'. Through the ways that these concepts contain the cross-cutting, multiaxial nature of location, I hope to illustrate something of Benhabib's 'exile' and point up some the difficulties for the achievement of utopian visions and the 'discarding of what does not make sense' (Davis and Lutz, op. cit.). I begin by illustrating how Tett's data can be read in terms of the 'myth of return' and 'home', which constitute aspects of 'exile'. Through a series of projections, I then pose questions for reflection.

Tett (2000) explores the experiences of working-class community activists taking a part-time accelerated degree in community education. As 'exiles' these students were seeking to 'go beyond the walls' of their communities in order to return with something of value to contribute. They were entering a space that they already perceived to be alien in terms of its middle-class nature and where they would be designated as outsiders. They also entered this space as critical beings in the sense that their own personal memories and the collective memories of their class have taught them to be wary of the colonising effects of middle-class higher education. These students defined themselves as 'working class and proud of it', and any middle-class pretensions were subject to derision and control. In many ways, these students were seeking to 'have it all' in the sense that they wanted to take from education necessary skills and knowledge while at the same time they sought to return to their communities with their working-class subjectivities intact.

Summerfield (1993) gives three examples of how the 'myth of return' becomes lived practice in the lives of Bangladeshi migrants living in England. In consequence, she highlights how the exile is located as simultaneously connected and disconnected in relation to the host and the home society as neither fully part of nor fully separate from. Thus, Bangladeshi men give the place where they would like to be buried as their country of origin. Children are returned to Bangladesh for their education. Parents choose spouses from Bangladesh for their children.

For the community activists in Tett's study the 'myth of return' is evidenced in terms of its gendered meanings of employment and family. Thus, the men in Tett's study indicated that they would return with 'a permanent full-time job back in my own community' (p. 190). For women, the contribution was in terms of 'giving a better life to the kids' or 'putting something back into the community' (p. 191, passim).

'Home' is a 'symbol of both place and belonging, features in the narratives, and in their transmission and plays a key role in the construction of … identities' (Chamberlain, 1997: 70). Brah (1996: 24) notes that in the early post-war period in Britain Asians were secure in the sense of themselves as rooted in the social milieu of their origin. However, continued experiences of racial abuse and a collective concern about the undermining influences of living in British society drew concern around the importance of fostering positive cultural identities. Recreating aspects of the culture of origin is one approach to this. Eastmond (1993: 40) demonstrates that in the lives of Chilean exiles 'Chile attained an almost physical presence … aspects of life, such as language, forms of address, food and dress, which at home had been rather unreflected aspects of everyday life, now became conscious values as symbols and markers of Chileanness'.

For the community activists in Tett's study these aspects of home and resistance to the middle-class ways of higher education were witnessed in statements such as 'I don't want to be seen as a wee swot', 'I'm working class and proud of it' and 'My life is richer where I am so I'm not intimidated by all these middle-class people' (p. 189, passim).

'Home' is both 'a mechanism for social control, and a metaphor of imperial loyalty' (Chamberlain, 1997: 70). The home country should not be solely understood as the country of birth but also as the site of imperialist power. In Chamberlain's research this is evidenced through the ways in which, prior to arrival, Caribbean migrants' images of England and the English way of life were informed through radio broadcasts of cricket at Lords and the Oxford–Cambridge boat race, the Festival of Britain and the Coronation. It was also informed by the fact that the educational system in the Caribbean required public examination scripts to be sent to England for assessment, hence both symbolically, and actually, marking the recipient as a member of the British Empire. The images that built up gave the 'Mother Country' a mythological and sacred status to the extent that, despite experiencing racism, coldness and an alienating urban landscape, this was never spoken of in letters and messages home. As a result 'the imperial mythology, the "sacred geography" of empire, remained unpunctured within the Caribbean' (Chamberlain, 1997: 72).

We do not know what messages the respondents in Tett's study gave about higher education to their children, partners, family and friends. We do know that, in common with other research into the experiences of women 'returners' (see, for example, Giles, 1990; Pascall and Cox, 1993; Edwards, 1993), these students experienced considerable difficulties in terms of continuing to meet the needs of their children and partners while undertaking academic study. As one Black female respondent commented in Tett's study, 'I'm always spinning plates so whenever the kids are ill then everything falls apart' (p. 189).

We also know that the respondents in Tett's research experienced higher education as working-class aliens in a predominantly middle-class landscape. Did they speak of classism to their friends and families or were they like the women and men in Chamberlain's study, who never spoke of racism but evidenced a 'collective, pervasive muteness which characterised the primary years of migration' (p. 74)? Chamberlain illustrates how to have spoken out would have caused worry and concern for those left behind. She notes that many migrants thought it was not necessary as they believed that their stay in Britain would be temporary or that it was a peculiar idiosyncrasy of Britishness. To have spoken out would also have given lie to the mythology of migration as improvement that is itself part of the mythology of the 'Mother Country'.

Indeed, despite their difficulties, Tett reports that, as the students progressed through the course, their attitudes to higher education changed as they could see the positive benefits that it could bring to their lives. However, there is evidence that the discourses of derision of middle-class ways were called upon to restrict and control pretentious behaviour in gender-specific ways. Thus, one woman commented 'my mother and my husband can't see why I'm doing this. They just see me as neglecting the kids and not doing the things I used to do in the community' (p. 191).

Can someone in this position speak of classism and oppression without contributing to her family's view that she should not be getting herself 'educated'? Yet not to speak out only serves to maintain the 'imperial mythology' of higher education.

I noted above that there are aspects in the lives of these community education students that resemble aspects of Benhabib's concept of exile. In particular, these people took up a place outside their communities in order to return with some benefits for their community. Certainly, this was perceived in terms of economic benefits and the use of professional skills and knowledge that their participation in higher education would bring to their communities. Yet these students wanted to return with their class-based subjectivities intact. Is this possible?

Reay (1998) reflects on the colonising aspects of British higher education and the ways in which it operates in various subtle ways to negate rather than validate working-class identities. She comments 'Through British higher education, including Women's Studies programmes, learning for working-class students is simultaneously about learning to be middle class' (p. 12). In recognising that there is never a view from 'nowhere', Benhabib is conscious of these colonising and assimilationist effects. Her argument is, however, that the ethical project of feminism is to offer a 'better vision' (Benhabib 1992: 230) as this will provide guidance for its future realisation.

There is evidence in Tett's paper that structural explanations for inequality were replacing more individualist ones, and this again confirms other research in this field (see, for example, Adams, 1996; Green and Webb, 1997). This may be suggestive of a criticality that Benhabib argues can be developed from outside one's 'home' community. We might also want to argue that these forms of criticality do provide 'better' knowledge. Yet can we state this so unambiguously?

The students in Tett's study wanted to return with useful knowledge and skills in order to work from within to improve the lives of their communities of origin. Nonetheless, what might engagement in higher education mean for these students on their return?

Working-class derision of middle-classness highlights how 'better' knowledge is not only contestable but contested. In a discussion of the colonialist nature of Western knowledge and the place of indigenous peoples, Smith (1999: 69) comments that 'the position within their own societies of "native" intellectuals who have been trained in the West has been regarded by those involved in nationalist movements as very problematic.' She notes how such intellectuals are seen as closely aligned to the colonisers in terms of class interests, values and ways of thinking (see also Tsolidis, 2001). She also notes that indigenous communities continue to view Western education as antithetical to self-determination. This leads to struggles over leadership and representation. Is this the future for Tett's respondents?

Smith comments that, despite these concerns, many indigenous communities have an ambivalent relationship to Western education as they struggle to send their children to university. Brah (1996: 25) similarly notes that because Western countries continue to play a dominant international role 'Western education remains a coveted possession in the "Third World" '. We also know from other research into women 'returners' that such students see their participation in education as a benefit for their children through the ways that they can help with homework tasks and act as role models (see, for example, Edwards, 1993; Pascall and Cox, 1993).

Is it not likely that the respondents in Tett's research will encourage their own children to continue into further and higher education and so continue this working class transformation?

Nomadic moments

Braidotti explains that her migration experience is both the most painful and the best part of her life:

> It rescued me from a fate worse than death, but it has meant that I have had to deal with the pain of leaving my parents behind. I don't want to minimize the problems of migration. I know them only too

well. But if you write books, you have to give people hope. In that way, I guess I really am a migrant. Always wearing my best clothes.
(Davis and Lutz, 2000: 377)

The 'nomad' is offered as a figuration of what feminism might achieve. For example, 'Nomadic consciousness is akin to what Foucault called countermemory: it is a form of resisting assimilation of homologation into dominant ways of representing the self' (p. 25); 'The nomad is only passing through' (p. 33); 'nomadism [is] an acute awareness of the nonfixity of boundaries. It is the intense desire to go on trespassing, transgressing.' (p. 36). Braidotti's vision of feminist subjectivity is one that does not take any kind of identity as permanent but rather has 'too many' (p. 33) passports. In comparison with the exile who is pausing to return, Braidotti argues that the nomad is an active subject who stops to take a rest before continuing her journey.

Braidotti (1994) comments that, just like real nomads, who are an endangered species, the nomad is a minority position. With the demise of the intellectual left in Europe and the rise of neoconservativism and 'lukewarm' neoliberalism, Braidotti offers 'nomad' as a discursive escape route for preserving the radical and subversive. Through the idea of 'nomad' she also conveys a sense of hopefulness and a desire to move 'beyond the early feminist lament about women as victims without falling into a postmodern cynicism with its dissolution of identity' (Davis and Lutz, 2000: 376). Nomadic discourses can therefore be perceived as an antidote to the messages of victimisation and oppression that are predominant in feminist research.

To explore the hopefulness of feminism, and the pleasure that is conveyed through 'having it all', I focus here on what I have called 'nomadic moments'. These are moments of joy and excitement that arise from intellectual endeavour. Such moments can be envisaged as spaces of constant and repeated transitions to many and varied forms of knowledge. They are moments of pleasure in just 'being' and 'becoming'. 'Nomadic moments' are incorporeal as material existence is fleetingly suspended. Their inclusion allows us to give recognition to their significance.

Davis and Lutz (2000: 374) describe Braidotti as the 'prototypical nomad', having moved from Italy to Australia and then to France and then to The Netherlands. They also note that Braidotti migrated to Australia when she was 14 and, as is somewhat typical of girls of her class background, used education as a way of moving on. As their interview with Braidotti indicates, there is evidence of real pleasure in the intellectual work of the academic:

Being an intellectual is the closest thing to my true identity, [Braidotti] notes ... Whilst most Australian philosophers went to Oxford for their doctorate, Rosi headed straight for France. The next phase of her life – my 'highpoint' – was spent in Paris. It was a time of real intellectual excitement: Foucault, Irigaray, Derrida, Deleuze and Guattari.

Davis and Lutz (2000: 375)

Other feminists' autobiographical reflections also signify something of the potential of nomadic thinking. Alberti's (1997) narrative contains an imminent nomadism that she says arises from the intellectual freedom of the academy. In deciding that she does not want to be fixed by any one identity and in seeking to go beyond a state of 'exile' she says (p. 153):

> … I could have combined becoming a headmistress in a private school for girls with marriage and motherhood. I struggled with these identities and sought others: historian, feminist, lesbian and writer. I have found a home in none of these and remain an exile, an outsider. But there is perhaps an identity, and certainly there is much pleasure, in embracing wholeheartedly absorption in the temporary, the ephemeral. There is an agency and power in the ability and the willingness to visit.

Stanley (1997: 176) offers celebration as an antidote to the discourses of difficulty that are most commonly associated with being working class:

> I come to revel in what we do well, not to grieve over all the places where we fail. To exult in some of the fleeting paradisical moments … when I see I fit my world, and it fits me beautifully – me as working-class – oh-so-critical feminist. A moment of being spiritually *and* socially 'at home'.

In the literature on women 'returners' there is also evidence of the pleasure of academic life. Blaxter and Tight (1993, 1995) note the enjoyment that adults take in education and how this contributes to a sustained engagement in study. Adams (1996) notes how women responded that they found that it was only while they were at university that they felt they could be themselves rather than somebody's mother or partner. Jackson (1998: 207) reported that the requirement for women to keep a journal during their studies was 'intellectually and emotionally stimulating'.

The incorporeality of 'nomadic moments' is, of course, its point of critique. Life 'in the mind' is a life of privilege and, for most, its momentary nature makes it privileged time. Indeed, Braidotti is clear that she is speaking to feminist intellectuals who can choose nomadism as a way of thinking (Davis and Lutz, 2000). In consequence, Brah's (1996: 3, emphasis in text) reflections on being asked whether she was African or Indian during an interview are salutary when she says:

But, of course, he could not *see* that I could be both. The body in front of him was already inscribed within the gendered social relations of the colonial sandwich. I could not just 'be'. I had to *name an identity*, no matter that this naming rendered invisible all the other identities – of gender, caste, religion, linguistic group, generation.

Gedalof (2000) notes that Brah's attention to 'naming an identity' highlights how racialised and minoritised groups are always called on to explain where they fit in a hierarchical grid that never accords them the status of the norm and never allows them just to 'be'. In her critique of Braidotti's metaphor, Gedalof argues that the nomadic aspect of just passing through 'has only ever been really available to white western feminists, and only under conditions where our 'whiteness' and our 'westernness' continue to function as the invisible, unmarked norms that do not seem to fix our identities at all' (p. 343).

'Naming an identity' is both an everyday process and an institutionalised practice. Pattanaik (1999) conveys something of the daily nature of 'naming' when she relates an experience that occurred while travelling on a tram in Melbourne, where she was undertaking doctoral study. The woman sitting next to her asked whether she was Sri Lankan or Indian. As she says, ' "Indian woman" is the new marker of my identity' (p. 185). In their study of older women returning to higher education to become teachers, George and Maguire (1998: 428) comment that 'all the women in this study reported experiences of being excluded because they were "othered" as older women in school and in college'.

In higher education the discourses of access and selectivity have been taken up and have created the institutionalised naming of 'normal', 'abnormal' and 'alternative' students (Williams, 1997). Green and Webb's (1997: 151) study demonstrates how students take up such institutionalised designations as markers of their difference:

> … In their acknowledgement of differences between themselves as alternative entrants and other students, they used the categories with which they have become familiarized through the discursive practices of admissions tutors and those of institutions which have required them to complete forms in particular ways to produce monitoring and research data. Such practices have legitimized the divisions between students using the categories of age, gender, 'race' and class as well as types of qualifications. In some cases the students in some of these categories have been idealized in the attempts to widen entry, for example, mature women, or ethnic minority groups.

The experience of being 'other' or 'alien' in higher education is, nonetheless, also experienced in other aspects of returners' lives. The simultaneous location of being fully part of neither one culture nor another means that such students experience the more general feeling of dis/location that, as I indicated earlier, Boehmer (1995: 232) refers to as 'not quite' and 'in between'. Edwards (1993: 144) conveys this in the following way:

> ... all the women felt a sense of doing something unusual, perhaps even deviant. The women felt this within the higher education institution and they felt it outside of it; they were out on a limb on all sides. Within higher education they were not proper full-time students; students are not people with family responsibilities. Outside of the higher education institutions the women were different as well. Other mothers did not do the sort of thing they were doing.

Visweswaran (1994: 106) uses the phrase 'negotiating privilege as loss' for those on the receiving end of this dis/location and illustrates this through an account written by one of her students, Lara Angel:

> My bitter sense of never being able to be fully accepted in my community after I achieved a certain sense of upward mobility tells me how I relate to my privilege. How embarrassed I am to talk to my grandparents and find myself using words that they never heard of, and yet knowing that I am not truly a product of privilege.

Finally, despite hopes that education would be a transition to a sequential 'having it all', aspects of difference work to 'return' the student to her former life as mother and part-time worker. Given the diversity of the higher education sector and the diversity of those who constitute the group 'returners', Skucha (1999: 81) is rightly cautious about making universal assumptions regarding employment outcomes for all women. Nevertheless, she does note that 'Otherness in HE ... tends to extend through to graduate life in relation to the employment outcomes of the transition'. Adams (1996: 216) notes that for older working class women in particular:

> With their 'mature student' social identity now a thing of the past, women had to renegotiate the meanings placed on their more permanent social identities, and came to see representations of their new sense of self and changed attitudes as inappropriate. Many thus felt it necessary to revert to 'pre-university' representations of self, and conduct their negotiations in relationships in ways that were consistent with their restored dependent, caring identities.

Summary

I have been concerned in this chapter to explore 'having it all' as a utopian vision. In so doing, I have focused on aspects of transition that might take us to that 'utopia'. To enable me to do this I have explored the metaphors of 'exile' and 'nomad' in terms of their philosophical principles and through their application to the case of women 'returners'. In particular, I have argued that the woman 'returner' represents a sequential form of 'having it all' in that through her life she might experience family, higher education and an employment career. I have therefore focused on her experiences of higher education as a transition to 'having it all' in terms of the life course.

Both the metaphors of 'exile' and 'nomad' as depicted by Benhabib and Braidotti emphasise the agentic nature of transition. As discursive devices they are important in that they foreground the idea that women are not simply passive victims. For the development of her critical consciousness, the 'exile' chooses to take up a space 'beyond the walls'. For the purposes of constant renewal and to avoid assimilation, the 'nomad' chooses to keep moving.

However, through an analysis of the women 'returner' literature I have sought to illustrate the material and subjective conditions in which the 'exile' and the 'nomad' operate. Specifically, I have sought to show something of the multiaxial nature of location with its cross-cutting points of identification and resistance. I hope that this has conveyed something of the difficulties of transition, the politics of locatedness and the 'fixity' and 'fixing' of aspects of difference. Evidence from the 'returner' literature illustrates how the desire to 'have it all', whether in terms of maintaining class and gendered identities or indeed in leaving aspects of the self behind, is complicated by the multiple meanings of 'home' and the 'myth of return'. I have also sought to portray something of the joy and fun of 'having it all' through those nomadic, and indeed privileged, moments of just being or becoming. These are, nonetheless, fleeting and precarious because of the ways in which class, 'race' and gender identities continue to both fix and unfix the subject.

In the concluding chapter I take up these issues more fully through Brah's (1996: 181) discussion of 'diaspora space' as a location that 'includes the entanglement of genealogies of dispersion with those of 'staying put'. Meanwhile, I now turn to a further issue that the women 'returner' literature confirms. In seeking to 'have it all' many women find they are 'doing it all'.

6

DOING IT ALL

Recent British governments have declared, first, that the gendered division of work is a matter for private decision-making and choice, while taking steps in public policy to limit public provision and hence increase the amount of unpaid work to be done; and, second that women should be free to compete in the labour market. ... Somehow 'families' – usually women – must meet what is acknowledged to be a growing responsibility for informal care and juggle their paid work, which in the post-war years has made an increasingly significant contribution to the family income.

(J. Lewis, 1993: 5)

If equality and an egalitarian sharing of domestic tasks exist between men and women within a household before the arrival of children, and we will explore the extent of this below, it is almost always the case that once children have arrived the allocation of tasks reverts to what comes 'naturally'. That is, it reverts to what is defined as natural within familial ideology; women take on the household and child-care tasks and men assume the mantle of breadwinner.

(Charles and Kerr, 1999: 191)

It has long been thought that women's greater engagement in paid work and education would contribute to the achievement of equality. What women have found is that in their endeavour to have this 'all' they end up 'doing it all'. Paid work and education become additions to the seemingly intransigent nature of women's responsibilities for domestic care. Women who return to education experience pressure to 'maintain their overall performance in all of their roles' (Blaxter and Tight, 1994: 167). In consequence, they 'juggle' their commitments to fit studying into an already full life. They read while ironing, answer the door while correcting an essay draft and keep a book behind the till during the evening shift (Blaxter and Tight, 1994). In addition, Blaxter and Tight (1994) note that 'juggling' easily becomes 'struggling' given the major responsibilities that women have to manage.

As both Lewis (op. cit.) and Charles and Kerr (op. cit.) indicate, it should not be considered that 'doing it all' occurs only when women are engaged in education and in consequence have a triple load. Although one might assume that when both partners are in full-time work household responsibilities become more equitable, research indicates that heterosexual women in dual-income families continue to retain the major responsibilities for childcare (Lewis *et al.*, 1992). This point can be extended to the field of community politics, where research also illustrates how women take on the triple roles of reproduction, production and community management (Moser, 1996). The result may be that women are key producers of social capital (Blaxter and Hughes, 2000), but at what cost?

'Doing it all' speaks of some harsh realities. These are the oppressive and tyrannical nature of responsibilities and the injustice that they should fall inequitably on one person. 'Doing it all' says that some things are simply unfair. 'Doing it all' is often spoken in a rueful tone as if the speaker, now sadder and wiser, realises that the promise of a utopian 'having it all' was but an illusion. At its worst 'doing it all' marks the end of resistance and the beginnings of a resigned acceptance that, despite the struggle, some things will never change. At its best 'doing it all' represents a cautionary tale.

In terms of feminist politics 'doing it all' draws attention to the political difficulties inherent in ideas of equality. The struggle for equality has been a major issue for feminism. This struggle has been not only in terms of its achievement but, more significantly, in terms of how equality is to be conceptualised. As Chapter 2 demonstrated, the predominant understandings of equality draw on the idea of sameness. The assumption is that as humans we are all born equal and it is only the impact of inequalities in society that create differences in outcomes.

Chapter 2 made clear that one of the most common expressions of equality as sameness can be found in discourses of equal opportunities. Equal opportunity discourses challenge those men who occupy top positions in organisations. They are a call to make way for less represented groups. But, importantly ,they also argue 'that if women are to obtain equal opportunities, men will have to step out of their ivory towers and take ... equal responsibility for housework and child care' (Lees and Scott, 1990: 334).

The idea of equality as sameness has come under considerable scrutiny through two key debates. Through identity politics feminists have given due recognition to the differences between women, in terms of age, 'race', class, *dis*ability, religion and sexuality. This has been a radical challenge to more conventional views that equality is concerned with achieving levels of sameness in all spheres of social life between women and men because it breaks down the idea that there is some kind of unity between women. For example, Black feminist critiques have illustrated how 'The desire for equality, the struggle for social justice, and the vision of universal sisterhood' (Mirza, 1997: 9) is the project of an imperialist White, middle-class feminism.

Post-structural perspectives have also challenged the idea of sameness. Such perspectives have argued that these forms of equality rest on a notion of the unified, rational, choosing self. Drawing on Derrida's delineation of *différance*, post-structuralism argues for the fragmented, contradictory and discursive self. This form of difference is conceived as the difference within.

In its strongest form, the implication of différance is that there is no category 'woman' at all. Given her 'disappearance', on what basis would feminism achieve equality?

To the extent that Felski (1997) refers to it as a doxa or an orthodoxy, difference, in all its varieties, has been highly significant in the development of feminist politics. In particular, a feminist goal of equality as sameness has been seen by many to be flawed because the basis on which that sameness is predicated assumes a false unity of experience. As Evans (1995: 17) points out, this means that ' "woman' or "women" or "we" [are] not terms that [can] be used without caution'. Nevertheless, political action requires some basis of unity upon which to rally. If we cannot speak for 'all', however small that collectivity, can we speak at all? With some similarity to women who find that they are 'doing it all', the result of these debates has meant that feminism has faced something of a crisis of faith.

The political implications of equality, sameness and difference provide the framework for the analysis of 'doing it all' that I present here. I explore the materiality and politics of 'doing it all' through research that has focused on the divisions of responsibilities within households. In the section 'Equality: feminism's discourses on sameness and difference' I begin with a discussion of the concepts of sameness and difference to give a more detailed understanding of their relation to equality than can be found in Chapter 2. I also illustrate some key problems in the use of concepts of sameness and difference for feminist politics. In respect of sameness, I explore these problems in terms of the ways that they can lead to an essentialising of women's identity. With respect to concepts of difference I focus on the problems that arise because of the implications for division and disunity within feminism.

The subsequent two sections are designed to illuminate the meanings of sameness and difference in relation to empirical research. In the section 'Discourses of parity and fairness' I consider research in relation to heterosexual relationships. Here difference, in terms of the sexual differences between women and men, is examined in order to assess whether equality in terms of sameness has been achieved. I illustrate how some of feminism's hopes that women's greater engagement in paid labour would contribute to more equitable divisions of household labour have not been fulfilled. Whatever their employment circumstances, women continue to undertake the majority of tasks associated with household domestic labour. I explore these issues by drawing attention to the discourses of parity and fairness that inform discussions, and outcomes, of household divisions of labour.

In 'Egalitarian relationships?' I turn to research that does suggest that women need not be 'doing it all' when it comes to achieving forms of equality in their personal relationships. This is research that has focused on the lives of lesbian couples. This research explores the spaces and possibilities for radical action within contemporary societies (Gordon, 1990). My main concerns here are to focus on sameness in terms of the potential of same sex solidarity. Specifically, I take up Dunne's (1997, 1999) argument that sameness, in terms of same-sex relationships, can offer the potential for more egalitarian ways of living. Dunne argues that if we take out of the relationship one of the axes of difference, that of heterosexuality, gender loses much of its power to structure relationships in terms of inequality.

Equality: feminism's discourses on sameness and difference

> The problem of reading 'equality' in a way which does not automatically imply 'the same' is one which has consistently dogged feminists, and indeed all students of gender ... Equality, in the light of what feminists now assume about the gendered construction of apparently gender-neutral terms, is one in the considerable line of concepts which are regarded with some suspicion.
>
> (Evans, 1994: 4)

Evans (op. cit.) highlights how we are taken up by dominant discourses of equality. It is tremendously difficult to move beyond the idea that equity means 'the same'. Moreover, although difference is commonly used as the antithesis of equality, strictly speaking this is in fact false. Felski (1997: 15) notes that the opposite of equality is inequality, 'a principle to which presumably no feminist would subscribe'. In consequence, equality and difference are commonly employed terms, leaving 'sameness' more imminent, less visible. This hegemony of 'same' is, moreover, evident in the discussion that follows. The tyranny of binaries means that it is impossible to talk about difference without referring to sameness and vice versa.

On sameness

> Liberal equality feminism ... asks for equality in the sense of sameness of attainment, and therefore treatment, and justifies it via sameness, 'androgyny'. It says: we deserve to be equal with you, for we are in fact the same. We possess the same capabilities; but this fact has been hidden, or these abilities have, while still potentially ours, been socialized, educated, 'out'.
>
> (Evans, 1995: 13)

As Chapter 2 detailed, the most common understanding of equality as sameness is that found within liberal feminism. This is perhaps not surprising given that 'most feminist national strategy today remains liberal feminist' (Eisenstein, 1993: xv). Phillips (1987) illustrates that some of the main achievements of feminism have been through equal rights legislation, such as equal pay and sex discrimination acts. She defines these as 'formal equalities' (p. 5).

On the face of it, this idea of equality appears to be the most commonsensical because it builds on the idea that as humans we are all the same. It also appears to be the most fair because it suggests that as we are the same we should have the same opportunities. Nevertheless, there are three aspects of sameness that make it an important issue within feminist politics. First, feminist theory has highlighted the essentialising characteristics of sameness. This has given rise to some major concerns in terms of the goals of feminist politics. If feminists argue that all women are the same in some main respects, such as they are more relational or more caring, this takes us down the path of essentialism. These traits become seen as, or this argument can maintain ideas that, these are natural characteristics of women. The result is a fixing of identity and a restriction of choices in how women might lead their lives.

If we argue that women and men are all human beings and this is the basis of our sameness, we are presented with a second problem. This is the problem of the normative subject. This is the subject position that we count as a guide to appropriate behaviour. Given the dominance of masculinity, the problem is that what is defined by the masculine is most often the norm. This means that when we argue that women and men are the same we are led to the question 'The same as what?'. These problems are evident within liberal feminism, which assumes that women and men are essentially the same: they are both humans. In consequence. women should have the same rights, opportunities, resources and positions that men have. In such a discourse, the normative subject is clearly man. He is the yardstick through which women's lives can be measured.

Although the normative subject shifts, the same problems arise within identity politics. Here, the normative category may be other women with the addition of other differences or the more dominant masculine subject, again of course differentially marked. For example, Young (1996: 179) comments in relation to Black feminist perspectives that:

> The study and analysis of racial and cultural identity has come to revolve around 'Blackness' as the object of fascination (desire?) leaving unspoken issues of 'white' ethnicity, 'Whiteness' as the unarticulated norm.

Such reasoning contributes to the maintenance of the very hegemonies of masculinity and Whiteness that feminism seeks to subvert.

In addition, arguments for building a system of social justice on the basis of sameness can be critiqued in terms of their underlying logic. Sevenhuijsen (1998) highlights three that we should take into account. First, arguments that call for distributive justice on the basis of sameness are circular and speculative. We assume, for example, that if all people are born equal that they should be treated equally. We assume that if they are treated equally that there will be equality in the results. Yet it is hard to prove a natural or original equality. The reason we think people are equal is because we use the evidence of inequalities of treatment. We assume women are innately equal to men but that, because they are treated differently, this equality is hidden. Thus, the proof of innate equality lies in differences of outcome. Such an argument keeps turning around the same circle.

Second, Sevenhuijsen argues that the result is a conflation of principle with objective. The principle of equality is nested within the objective of equality of outcome. In political terms, the problem with this is that when equal treatment does not realise equal results it is too easy to fall back on biological explanations, such as women are innately poor at science or maths. Alternatively, should the objectives be realised, this may not necessarily change women's lives. This was one of the concerns within the wages for housework debates, when Marxist feminists argued that women's unpaid work in the home was productive for capitalism. In consequence, this should be paid for. Paying for housework was seen to be one way that the status of this hidden sphere of work could be raised. However, the receipt of payment might also become a reason why women should be kept in the home. They would have no reason to enter the paid labour force (for a fuller discussion, see Tong, 1989: 54–61).

Third, dominant assumptions of sameness are based on androgynous views of equality. This suggests that that there is a mid-point between women and men. The task is for women to discover their masculine side and for men to discover their feminine side. Yet this not only returns us to the male, autonomous and self-constituted normative subject, but also suggests the choosing subject that can be free of ideology, discourse, the unconscious and language (Rothfield, 1990). As Rothfield notes, concepts of androgyny are suggestive that the differences between women and men are external to their identity. They suggest that these differences could be peeled off to leave the neutral subject behind.

Nevertheless, political unity implicates sameness. To be drawn together for a cause is suggestive of at least some interests or values in common. Without this, or with divisions within, the success of a social movement is jeopardised. 'Difference' feminism is indeed seen to be problematic in this respect.

On difference

The women's movement and the structures which have grown out of it are struggling with the politics of 'difference'. Today in the 1990s, any taken-for-granted notion of 'woman' is up for scrutiny and subject to change.

(Jarrett-Macauley, 1996: xiii)

This focus on sameness cannot be fully appreciated without a similar consideration of its opposite term, that of difference. Both Barrett (1987) and Evans (1995) note feminism's ubiquitous use of the term 'difference'. Endlessly invoked, it carries a range of meanings that can lead to an inevitable confusion. As it is commonly understood, 'difference' signifies a boundary 'between those who can and those who cannot belong to a particular construction of a collectivity or population' (Anthias and Yuval-Davis with Cain, 1992: 2). As such, it is a marker of inclusion and exclusion. Because of the emphasis on the non-fixity of the subject, for *différance* feminists even the notion of some kind of bounded collectivity is problematic.

Evans indicates that there are three main ways in which difference has been conceptualised in feminist writing. The first two, differences between women and men and differences among women in terms of class, 'race' and so forth, are again the most commonsensical and familiar uses of this term. This is because they rest on notions of the unitary, agentic, human subject, and this form of difference has confidence in empirical methods and an ontological reality (Barrett, 1987).

The first, and most basic, difference that Evans (1995) identifies is that of women's difference from men. There are two forms of this. As we have seen above, liberal feminists argue that any differences between the sexes are due to differences in treatment. Essentially, women and men are the same. If women and men were treated identically then any major differences would be eradicated.

Alternatively, we find those who argue that women are indeed different from men. However, their difference is one of superiority rather than inferiority. Tong (1989) defines such feminists as 'celebratory'. Their basic position is that, whatever the ways in which women differ from men, this does not make them unequal. Rather, it is the ways in which the operations of patriarchy work to devalue women's ways of being that is the problem. Such a position would argue, for example, that women's work is attributed a low value because of the low value given to women in systems of male sexual domination. One example of the associated political action is provided by radical feminism, which argues for the need for separatist politics. Separatist politics advocates non-cooperation with entrenched systems of power on the grounds that our continued participation in them contributes to their maintenance (Tong, 1989). All-women groups, such as rape crisis centres and some forms of women's adult education, are examples of this approach. The political imperative is to work towards a revaluing of women's differences and to create women-only spaces where this can happen.

The second difference is that which is found within identity politics. This difference arises through the key social divisions of 'race', class, sexuality and disability. Black women have illustrated how feminism has assumed Whiteness as a normative category (Carby, 1982). Feminism, therefore, is imbued with racism. Similar points are made in relation to the other axes of difference. Overall, feminism is charged with being White, middle-class, ableist and heterosexual. As Beasley (1999) notes in relation to issues of 'race', there is not a single feminist framework that defines the positions that are taken here. Reminiscent of separatist politics, these positions include debates in relation to the relative significance of 'race' or gender as oppressive systems. For example, should Black women work with Black men for the end of racial oppression or should they work with other women to end sex-based oppression?

However, it cannot be assumed that identity politics simply breaks up the categories of womanhood into prominent social divisions. As many feminists have noted (see, for example, Spelman, 1988), within the groupings of Black, White and so forth there will be many other axes of difference. The implications of this are that markers of identity have different meanings in different contexts. Patel (1997) discusses how, in the name of God, the militant right-wing Hindu nationalists in India had begun a course of annihilation of minorities. Yet, as a Black woman in Britain, she is a minority. She comments how this gives rise to a recognition that at one and the same time she belongs to an oppressive majority and an oppressed minority that leads on to a more critical assessment of 'white majority/black minority' dichotomies.

The third difference is that of *'différance'*. *'Différance'* is the term used by Derrida and is derived from the French verb *différer*, which means to defer or to put off. Johnson (2000) notes that, although the closest English translation is 'deferment', this loses the complexity of associations that arise in the French. These are particularly those of temporality, movement and process, which institute difference 'while at the same time holding it in reserve, deferring its presentation or operation' (p. 41). Thus:

> The suffix '-ance', which in French is more precisely a substantivization of the present continuous tense ('different', deferring), connotes a sense of temporal extension impossible to render in English. Moreover, in French the term is phonetically indistinguishable from the word 'difference'. It is therefore through the essentially untranslatable linguistic device of homophony that Derrida establishes a conceptual link between the notion of writing as (spatial) difference and writing as (temporal) deferment: writing **is** difference **is** deferment (différence).
>
> (Johnson, 2000: 42, emphasis in text)

Différance feminists argue that the universality of the humanist subject is constituted around the subjectivity characterised by White bourgeois men (Barrett, 1987). In addition, the contribution that Foucault has made is to have given recognition that the sites of difference of class, 'race' and so forth are also sites of power (Barrett, 1987). *Différance* theorists do not simply emphasise that woman has many sources of identity. *Différance* feminists challenge the idea of identity being fixed altogether. They believe that identity is, rather, a process formed through engagement with the discursive order. The political task is that of deconstruction. This is because one of the central issues for *différance* feminists is that of the linguistic order. As I discussed in Chapter 1, such a position focuses on the ways in which language is ordered in terms of hierarchical binaries. The political task is to focus on the discursive level and to unravel these binaries so that they no longer exert the power that they do.

In political terms, the problem for feminism is that once we move from the most basic form of difference, that between women and men, we are, step by step, diminishing the basis upon which to build collective action. What we have left is either a series of factional groupings within feminism, for example Black versus White, middle-class versus working-class, able-bodied versus disabled, lesbian versus heterosexual, or the total disappearance of any grouping at all. While the first form of difference I outlined above positions women and men in antagonistic relations, more widespread factional groupings are the implications of the second form of difference outlined above, that of identity politics. Here, the idea that women will come together through shared experiences of male-based oppression is challenged by the idea that women are themselves divided by key social divisions. Such a view acknowledges that women can exercise power over other women and that it will be in some women's interests to maintain, rather than subvert, other forms of domination. This does not necessarily have to be on an individual level. As post-colonial politics have illustrated, feminism in a more wholesale way is also charged with being another form of Western global imperialism.

Yet, as I have noted, the notion of a collectivity of interests is further reduced by the recognition that axes of difference operate within different axes of power. The political task, as Patel (1997: 256) illustrates in relation to some of the campaigns of Southall Black Sisters and their sister organisation, Brent Asian Women's Refuge, is to 'situate our practice within wider anti-racist and socialist movements, involving alliances and coalitions within and across the minority and majority divides'. As Patel notes, working in these ways is not easy.

This is a point that Ang (1995) develops in her stress on the difficulties of dealing with difference. She notes that, despite the diversity of feminist politics in relation to issues of difference, overall feminists always attempt to resolve the contradictions that the difficulties of difference give rise to. In this way, feminist politics is always predicated on notions of inclusion. Thus, the goal has become a plural feminist sisterhood that will accommodate the differences and inequalities that exist between women. Ang argues for the necessity of a politics of partiality. This means that feminism must self-consciously place limits on its spheres of intervention. It has to acknowledge that feminism:

can never ever be an encompassing home for all women, not just because different groups of women have different and sometimes conflicting interests, but, more radically, because for many groups of 'other' women other interests, other identifications are sometimes more important and politically pressing than, or even incompatible with, those related to their being women.

(Ang 1995: 73)

Ang's points bring us to the local, episodic and fragmentary focus that is seen to be a key marker of post-modern politics. Within post-modernism the hopes for grand changes that are in accord with grand narratives are challenged. Feminism's grand-narrative of the subordination of all women has become a series of petit-narratives in which varied intersections of power and difference give rise to more local and more specific bases for feminist politics. Nonetheless, it is the notion of *différance* that has particularly vexed feminism. This is because the basis for solidarity is even more problematic. *Différance* assumes that woman is an internally divided category. This means that the basic unit upon which to build collective action, that of woman, no longer exists. The disappearing woman is taken to mean a disappearing feminism. As Barrett (1987: 29) notes *différance* deconstructs 'the very historical identity on which feminist politics has traditionally been based'.

There are, of course, many responses to this issue, some of which have been outlined above. More generally, there are two main concerns. One of these relates to the relevancy of both post-modern and post-structural approaches for feminist politics. As Maynard and Purvis (1994) note, for some feminists there are forms of post-modernism that are so far removed from the practical concerns of everyday politics that they can suggest that research is pointless. Another concern relates to the politics of unity for social movements. How can feminists deal with the problem of the disappearing woman? As Francis (1999) notes, in response to this question we find either outright rejection or strategic recognition. One of the reasons for rejection relates to methods of deconstruction that lie at the heart of post-structuralism. The problem arises that, because post-structuralism preaches that all 'truths' are relative, the processes of deconstruction leave all ethical positions paralysed. In consequence, any injustices lose their power to be political or moral injustices. Those who take a more strategic view argue that, although theoretically we can acknowledge issues of *différance*, it is important for reasons of political solidarity to retain the categories 'woman' and 'girl' (see, for example, Jones, 1993).

This discussion has focused on the discourses of sameness and difference in relation to theories of the subject and the politics of feminism. I now turn to feminist research that has taken up these varied discourses of sameness and difference in respect of the politics of women's personal relationships. I begin with research that has focused on feminism's first difference, that of the difference between women and men. I highlight here how issues of difference and sameness become formed into discourses of parity and fairness.

Discourses of parity and fairness

In a review of British research conducted in the last fifty years Pilcher (1999) remarks that there is little evidence to suggest that there have been any significant changes in respect of women's responsibilities for household work. Despite a greater egalitarian consciousness, and despite women's increasing participation in paid labour, women still undertake the majority of caring tasks associated with family life. Press and Townsley (1998) come to a similar conclusion in respect of an analysis of North American data. They comment that there is no evidence to suggest that husbands are doing any more housework than they were a quarter of a century ago.

The extent to which housework is a woman's sphere is illustrated by the number of feminist sociological studies of caring and family life from which Pilcher and Press and Townsley draw their conclusions. In British sociology these are seen to stem from the classic studies of Gavron (1966) and Oakley (1974). Both Gavron and Oakley documented the scale and unending nature of the caring and servicing tasks of household labour that are undertaken by women. These feminist critiques highlighted the fallacious assumptions underpinning much malestream sociology. This assumed a symbiosis of equal but different in relation to women's and men's places in the separate spheres of home and paid work. As these early studies indicated, not only did women work longer hours in the home than men worked in paid labour, but household work was devalued, invisible, isolating and an intensification of responsibility.

The development of the household divisions of labour literature since this early research illustrates a key feature of notions of androgyny in relation to egalitarian goals. This is the assumption that as women and men are the same they are equally capable of undertaking the main tasks in relation to household labour. Working within this view, the research in this area seeks to measure aspects of both quantity and form in relation to the achievement of equality between the sexes. This gives rise to some tensions in respect of a notion of equality based on sameness. Does sameness mean identical or is it a more diffuse notion of parity?

Considerable attention is given to measuring the overall quantity of household work undertaken by women and men in daily and lifetime terms. This research certainly does indicate that there has been little movement away from women having lifetime commitments for care. Such commitments are also evidenced across a range of changing family situations. For example, research into responsibilities for care has shown that women undertake the majority of childcare tasks in first and subsequent families (Hughes, 1991). It has demonstrated women's caring roles in lone-parent families (Graham,

1993) and in the care of older parents (Corti *et al.* 1994). Research also indicates that even in families in which the husbands are unemployed and wives are in paid employment women continue to undertake the majority of household labour (Morris, 1990).

In terms of differences in relation to feminist identity politics, the research literature highlights that being predominantly responsible for care is a universal experience for women. Graham (1993) argues that women's role as primary carers transcends any differences that arise from issues of class or ethnicity. While Ferri and Smith (1996) report that the care of children is more equitably shared in working-class families, Gregson and Lowe (1994) suggest that social class makes little difference to the distribution of household tasks. Graham's view of the universality of women's responsibilities for care is also supported by the work of Bhopal (1997), who found that British women of South Asian ethnicity perform the majority of household tasks.

This attention to sameness in terms of quantification inevitably leads to some critical debates that focus on the 'truth' or accuracy of research. This is both because quantification is viewed as an objective measure and also because the idea of equality is suffused with notions of 'identical.' Introducing an aspect of difference that has, until recently, been more neglected in feminism, Arber and Gilbert (1989) sought to illustrate how research ignored the fact that men formed a large proportion of those who care for others in the family. The implication was that feminist research in this field was at best inaccurate and at worst biased. The truth games of this academic discourse rest on the underlying assumption that when we use identical as our measure of equality we are comparing like with like. The resulting flurry of research has sought to demonstrate that, although men may form a proportion of carers, women continue to form the majority (Blaxter and Hughes, 2000).

Research in this field has not simply focused on quantifying the amount of household work that women and men undertake. It has also illustrated how there are differences in the types of work undertaken. Caring does not mean only physical care. Women's responsibilities include the emotional needs of others as well as the practical (Cotterill, 1994). For example, although British law may construct parental responsibility as joint, Piper (1993) indicates how post-divorce mothers are viewed in mediation and conciliation services as responsible for the maintenance of good relationships between themselves and their ex-partners. In respect of the differences between women and men, research reveals that men may now be taking a greater, though not equivalent, role in childcare.

This recognition of the different forms of household labour brings us to a concern that equality can be understood in terms of parity, in which there is exchange between equivalences. Parity continues the theme of separate spheres though it brings this to a more refined focus on household relations. It can be seen in terms of the trade between different forms of household labour. For example, does spending time caring for children equal the time spent cleaning the toilet? Parity can, of course, be understood in quantified terms. Parity can be found when the trade between time spent in household labour and paid labour is not identical but is viewed as being of equal worth. For example, women may 'trade' the extra hours they spend in household labour with the perceived more 'alienating' conditions that their partners experience in paid work.

Parity adds to equality the issue of values and status to the worth of household labour. These values are predominantly those related to gender. Bornat et al. (1999) suggest that there is evidence from the ways in which women talk about caring of the impact of a feminist language of independence. This language of independence and equality was found in relation to finance, role sharing, cohabitation, women's authority, family violence, fertility and employment. Nevertheless, the gendered nature of household tasks was also evident. Bornat et al.'s research illustrates that gender continues to form part of the assessment in relation to who should undertake which tasks. This was particularly the case in respect of intergenerational care between parents and children.

Bornat et al. illustrate how women's sense of obligation and responsibility towards the care of their children and their elderly parents remains strong. They argue that, despite expectations that rising divorce may be weakening 'traditional' family ties and would lead to a more egalitarian division of labour, this is not the case. Rather, the 'new family is a feminized family in which the traditional expectations of caring responsibilities and the emotions which underpin and sustain them are described and explained in terms of the quality and strength of matrilineal ties' (p. 127).

This combination of quantity and equivalence is subsumed within discourses of fairness in which exchange based in reciprocity is a key form of judgement. Fairness is, of course, a more diffuse notion than equality. It allows for parity, in the sense of equal but different, and identical, in the sense of equal and the same, to become combined in a range of taken-for-granted judgements. A useful example of this can be found in Pilcher's (1999) comments. Pilcher's (1999) analysis of data in relation to household divisions of labour illustrates that, overall, women spend less time than men in paid labour. However, they spend longer hours undertaking household labour. When the differences between these different forms of labour are calculated, they illustrate that 'women spend 39 minutes more per day working than men' (p. 60). Bringing together the meanings of equality in terms of identical through this quantification, and the gendering of parity through the term 'even', Pilcher notes that 'the fact that women do more household work than men (even allowing for differences in their hours in paid work) is unfair' (p. 60).

Discourses of fairness were explored in research undertaken by Dryden (1999). Dryden highlights how they operate in the everyday of heterosexual marriage. It is clear from her research that the majority of women she interviewed were less than satisfied with existing divisions of labour.

Nevertheless, they were anxious to minimise any challenges to the status quo, partly because this would reveal deep-seated problems in their marriages and partly because of their economic and personal circumstances. All the couples in the study, except one, had children. Dryden suggests that one way of managing feelings of inequity was to take a 'balancing the books' approach to fairness. In her research she found four forms of this:

- Traditional claims of fairness: These were primarily related to a division of labour that was based on separate spheres or were based on personal 'choice'. Thus, because women were at home and men were in paid labour, it was 'practical' that women did most of the household work. Alternatively, it was women's 'choice' to take on the majority of responsibility because men 'hate' housework.
- Stretching traditional claims of fairness: In stretching traditional claims of fairness women were willing to overlook inequities because they were in paid labour part-time rather than full-time or because they employed paid help in the home. These features 'balanced the books' to some extent.
- Taking the blame: Here women would make comments such as 'I take things too personally' or they only had 'little niggles'.
- Making positive comparisons: Positive comparisons were made in relation to the quality of the man in their life. In terms of household divisions of labour, husbands were described as 'much better than most' or 'there's a lot worse'.

These practices accord with Connell's (1987) analysis of compliance as a form of emphasised femininity. Emphasised femininity is 'femininity organized as an adaptation to men's power, and emphasizing compliance, nurturance and empathy as womanly virtues' (Connell, 1987: 188). As Connell notes, emphasised femininity is maintained through practices that prevent any other models of femininity from gaining cultural articulation. What we find in Dryden's analysis is how women's structural dependency is reinforced through their husbands' engagement in pervasive conversational practices that seek to blame their wives for any perceived inequalities. These practices of woman-blame were achieved by constructing their wives as personally inadequate, by constructing a wife's role as biologically given or by constructing themselves as more superior.

In addition, Dryden's research highlights the problematic nature of the impact of equity discourses in relation to women's and men's roles. Dryden illustrates that women are caught up within a 'guilty secret'. Whilst contemporary personal relationships should be egalitarian, their own personal experiences do not match this. She suggests that women experiencing deep-seated problems in relation to equality may find it increasingly difficult to speak about these publicly.

Overall, Dryden argues that heterosexual marriage acts as a barrier to the achievement of women's equality. She comments (p. 150):

> This is because the institution frames the relationship at the outset
> in terms of women's dependency and makes it hard for a woman to
> retain an independent sense of identity in the eyes of family, friends
> and society at large. I think it is a necessary but not sufficient
> condition of a long-term swing towards gender equality that
> heterosexual women resist the contract and allow themselves some
> space to define gender and personal identity in more liberating and
> non-traditional ways.

Dunne (1997, 1999) echoes such points in her analysis of the greater
egalitarian nature of lesbian relationships. It is to these issues of sameness
that we now turn.

Egalitarian relationships?

Lesbian women may in many ways represent the vanguard of change…
(Dunne, 1997: 231)

Dunne (1999: 71) suggests that 'something much greater than "fairness"
is at stake' when it comes to the threats that arise in the creation of egalitarian
relationships. What is at stake is one's identity as a woman or a man. Dunne's
analysis illustrates how gender is affirmed in everyday routines. The division
of spheres of responsibility into gendered categories contributes to the
maintenance of inequality because these spheres simultaneously contribute
to what it means to be a woman or man. Dunne notes how these boundaries
are fiercely policed so that, for example, when men take on childcare they
are often viewed as 'honorary women'. These boundaries reflect the idea that
there are only two genders, women and men, and that these are oppositional
categories. In consequence, the extent to which there is sameness between
women and men is overlooked in this logic of difference.

In arguing for more attention to be given to sameness, Dunne focuses on
the doing of gender as a socially constructed accomplishment. In the everyday
of doing household tasks we are enacting, reinforcing or undermining parts
of our gendered identity. As we have seen in Dryden's research, women were
able to accomplish their sense of womanliness by being compliant or taking
an ameliorative rather than a challenging approach to the unequal divisions
of household labour they experienced. Conversely, when women say that they
feel guilty because their paid work commitments limit the attention they
can give to their children, this guilt can be seen as a reflection of a failure to
accomplish a sense of womanliness. In these terms, changing notions of
fairness can be understood in terms of changing notions of what it is to be a

woman or a man. The 'guilty secret' that Dryden discovered is, of course, a metaphor for these issues. It highlights changing senses of identity that are not matched with practices.

Dunne argues that the enactment of gender implies an audience. If we change the sex of the audience then the meanings of gender simultaneously change. Dunne illustrates this in respect of lesbian relationships. A defining feature of many of the lesbian relationships in Dunne's (1997) research is that they are structured around individual autonomy. With some similarity to Gordon's (1990) feminist mothers, these women had a heightened sense of power inequalities between women and men. These understandings of power were linked to greater political activism, the processes of 'coming out' and the women's experiences of previous 'unequal' heterosexual relationships.

Dunne (1997) argues that, in seeking to create personal lives that are different from the norm of heterosexuality, lesbian women cannot take for granted many day-to-day issues. This is particularly the case in relation to gendered role play, in which in heterosexual relationships gender inequalities are translated, whether intentionally or not, into everyday actions and outcomes. As Dunne's (1997) research illustrates, trying to live life differently does not necessarily lead to egalitarian relationships in every case. Dunne's findings illustrate three main ways in which lesbian couples organise the division of household labour. These replicate in some ways the idea of equality being either identical or managed within some sense of parity. Where relationships were unequal this was predominantly in terms of the quantity of household tasks each partner was undertaking. These categories are:

- The symmetric shared approach to household tasks: In this case, household tasks were either performed together or by each partner in turn. The main concern was to avoid specialisation so that both women felt competent to undertake both 'male' and 'female' tasks. In this way, both partners sought a relationship of no differences in this regard.
- The symmetric specialised approach to household tasks: In this scenario, household tasks were divided according to likes and dislikes. Other tasks were shared. In these ways equality could be achieved through the trade of parity.
- The asymmetric approach to household tasks: Inequalities in respect of divisions of household labour could be developed in a range of ways: through the replication of traditional gendered 'butch/femme' roles; through 'mother–daughter' relationships, in which one partner, by virtue of greater experience related to age or different standards of household cleanliness, did more than the other; or because one partner suffered from long-term illness or was unemployed. Overall, it was the quantity of tasks that one partner undertook in relation to the other that was the issue.

Dunne (1997) suggests that lesbian women's greater emphasising on avoiding relations of domination means that unequal relationships are either relatively short-lived or change into more egalitarian forms. She notes that in her research lesbians under 30 typically did not desire a 'butch/femme' relationship and had not experienced one.

These points in relation to younger women highlight the nature of changes at the discursive level that Dryden's 'guilty secret' conveys. As research into attitude change suggests, changing discourses about women's and men's roles have clearly had an impact on expectations in terms of what are deemed to be appropriate divisions of household labour between women and men. Kiernan's (1992) research suggests that there has been a shift in attitudes between women and men in terms of the division of household responsibilities. Kiernan, analysing data from two survey points, found that, in 1987, 72 per cent of households in which both partners worked full-time reported that women were primarily responsible for housework, whereas in 1991 this figure had dropped to 67 per cent. Survey evidence also suggests that it is among women, younger people and those with more education that the greatest attitudinal changes can be found (Kiernan, 1992). Goldscheider and Waite's (1991) North American research suggests that well-educated men assume almost a third more responsibility for household tasks than men with little education.

Nevertheless, at the level of lived practice, at least in relation to heterosexual couples, very little has changed to shift the overall division of household labour into more egalitarian arrangements. For sociologists this is perceived to be a problem of 'lagged adaptation' (Pilcher, 1999), the hope being that men will eventually catch up and change their ways. For Dunne (1999) the feminist task is to develop a 'passion for sameness', with difference losing its power.

In this, Dunne is focusing on how, as an attraction of opposites, heterosexual relations are assured through the suppression of similarities between women and men. This is because heterosexual desire is located in female/male difference. While Dunne notes that in many ways the concept of sameness in relation to sexuality is paradoxical given the many other ways that women are different, she also argues that lesbianism is a preference for same-sex solidarity. Accordingly, this solidarity provides the basis through which the identities available to women can become expanded towards a more self-conscious sense of self. As Connell (1987: 182) notes, 'there are many more possibilities than the standard dichotomy'.

Summary

My purpose in this chapter has been to recognise that the phrase 'doing it all' is one of lament for the continuing oppression that women face in their everyday responsibilities. This lament is also evident within feminism as the project for emancipation has been critiqued as being imperialist and modernist. In doing so I have sought to illustrate how sameness and difference are meshed within ideas of equality. I explored this in relation to feminist theory and feminist politics.

I have also explored the theme of 'doing it all' through feminist research that has focused on women's personal relationships. In so doing I have sought to show how each of the three concepts of equality, sameness and difference has a range of meanings and an associated range of practices. In particular, I illustrated how notions of equality become transfigured into discourses of sameness, parity and fairness. These discourses inform the everyday of women's lives in their negotiation of household divisions of labour. Yet, despite growing discourses of equality, little has changed for the majority of women.

How does feminist post-structuralism respond to this? Evans (1995) suggests that sameness, difference and equality form the three corners of a triangle. She argues that we might view them as continua along which we will find different feminist positions. To configure feminist theory in such a way is useful as it enables us to envisage the complexity of the debates. It also enables us to recognise the contradictory nature of different positions and the minute shades of difference that simultaneously exist. But the triangle does not move us beyond the categories of sameness and difference that already shape ideas of equality. It does not deconstruct these very binaries and unravel them to such a degree that they no longer hold such power over the ways in which we seek to place order on the social world. As the concluding chapter indicates, deconstructing binaries *is* a significant post-structuralist response.

7

WITHIN AND BEYOND THE MIRROR

Orlando looked himself up and down in a long looking-glass, without showing any signs of discomposure, and went, presumably, to his bath. ... Orlando had become a woman – there is no denying it. But in every other respect, Orlando remained precisely as he had been. The change of sex, though it altered their future, did nothing whatever to alter their identity. ... Orlando was a man till the age of thirty when he became a woman and has remained so ever since.

(Woolf, 2000: 87–8)

Alice's eyes are blue. And red. She opened them while going through the mirror. Except for that, she still seems to be exempt from violence. She lives alone, in her house. She prefers it that way, her mother says. She only goes out to play her role as mistress. School-mistress naturally. Where unalterable facts are written down whatever the weather. In white and black, or black and white, depending on whether they're put on the blackboard or in the notebook. Without colour changes, in any case. Those are saved for the times when Alice is alone. Behind the screen of representation. In the house or garden.

(Irigaray, 1997: 217)

The opening quotations to this chapter illustrate something of the politics of feminism. Through Orlando's change of sex Woolf brings 'to the surface our false associations ... [S]he de-natures our assumptions about gender, about nature and the natural' (Beer, 1997: 90). Her resolution is one of androgyny in which the identities of Orlando as man and woman are encompassed together. Indeed, it is not until Orlando looks into the mirror and sees the physiological changes in his body that he realises that *he* has become *she*. As we can see through the sanguine way in which Orlando views the changed body in the mirror, Woolf's androgynous subject is one whose mind is 'calm, stable, unimpeded by consciousness of sex' (Showalter, 1978: 289). Indeed, Woolf (2000: 88) reflects on the ways in which others might respond to these changes in Orlando by commenting 'let other pens treat of sex and sexuality; we quit such odious subjects as soon as we can'.

One of those 'other pens' is clearly that of Irigaray. Grosz (1990: 173, emphasis in text) notes that Irigaray's project:

like Alice's (A-Luce), is to pass *through* the looking glass into the 'wonderland' of women's own self-representations 'on the other side'. In place of the 'platitude'/flatness, of the platonic mirror, Irigaray substitutes the speculum, the curved, distorted medium of women's self-observation and self-representation.

In doing so:

> Irigaray reverses the mirror imagery employed by Plato and Lacan back on itself, as she works to produce a 'burning point' that would reflect back and destroy the metaphysical past.
>
> (Battersby, 1996: 263)

In *Speculum*, alongside the metaphor of mirroring, Irigaray uses:

> the language of bonding by blood. She opens up a division between 'sang rouge' (red blood, that is linked to matrilineal descent) and 'sang blanc' (white blood/anaemic blood which links with white sperm and patrilineality and is also homophonous with le semblant or semblance). 'Whiteness' is the language of purity, and a dead, static, *specularised* nature. Against this whiteness, 'redness' is used to suggest a form of identity that bleeds onto otherness. Irigaray is not providing an experiential report, nor an appeal to 'nature' as unmediated access to the body. Instead what is offered is a new (blurry) image of a female subject-position that (she claims) has remained un-represented in the history of the West.
>
> (Battersby, 1996: 263).

Thus, our reading of Irigaray (op. cit.) offers a glimpse of that 'form of identity that bleeds onto otherness' when Alice is alone and behind the screen of representation. Irigaray's politics are to 'revalue the pejorative label and celebrate woman's difference from man at all levels, psychic, physical and intellectual' (Belsey and Moore, 1997: 10). This is no mere essentialism, however, and it is to her mode of writing that we have to look for evidence of this.

Her writing, in the style of Derrida, and which alongside other French feminists is referred to as *écriture féminine*, seeks to 'displace old patriarchal truths, to rewrite their narratives and re-vision the role of language itself' (Belsey and Moore, 1997: 11). Through her writing Irigaray seeks to tell 'the men ... we are beyond the mirror of your languages in a new psychic space ... a realm – at once emotional and intellectual – in which woman is no longer defined in relation to man as his negative, other, or as lack' (Burke, 1994: 45). In addition, her deconstructive approach is 'chiefly concerned with questioning familiar modes of thought and interrogating the concepts of logic and the rules of discourse ... [and to] rethink woman without resorting to limiting or essentialist definitions' (ibid.).

The role of language in the politics of feminism is the major theme of this chapter. My purpose is to illustrate elements of post-structuralist politics with particular attention to the purpose and methodology of deconstruction and the development of critical literacies. These issues are therefore explored below in 'Beyond the mirror: deconstructive politics for contemporary feminisms'. Nonetheless, as a concluding chapter it also remains for me to draw together some of the threads of the text. The following section, 'Reflections in the mirror: deconstructing discourses for contemporary womanhood', provides such a summary.

Reflections in the mirror: deconstructing discourses for contemporary womanhood

Liberalism's characterization of the locus of power and domination – and thus the logical site of resistance – promises the impossible. That is, it claims that power resides in legal and governmental institutions; consequently, it views these institutions as the appropriate arena for resistance. In this view, engagement with formal governing or other policy-making institutions is the path to eventual liberation. This perception diverts attention away from the restrictive forces that emanate from sources other than those centralized, juridical institutions. Domination does not always take the form of outright prohibition; and resistance takes place in many different arenas.

(Young, 1997: 5)

The major argument of this text is that 'discourses and discursive practices provide subject positions, and that individuals take up a variety of subject positions within different discourses' (Moore, 1994: 55). To explore what this might mean in terms of women's everyday lives, I have framed the content and analysis of this text around five common phrases. In doing so, I have argued that the phrases selected should not be understood as applying only in the singular in terms that women, for example, *either* seek 'the best of both worlds' *or* they 'have it all'. Rather, I have sought to show that 'Individuals are multiply constituted subjects, and they can, and do, take up multiple subject positions within a range of discourses and social practices. Some of these subject positions will be contradictory and will conflict with each other' (ibid.). Thus, I have argued for a both/and analysis in which, for example, we consider womanhood as encompassing both 'making it' *and* 'caring'. Indeed, I have argued that we need to understand the phrases as a connected circle with each phrase running into the other and in which womanhood is constituted through all, and more, of the subject positions that can be ascribed to each phrase:

My choice of portraying the phrases as a circle is motivated by a desire on my part to illustrate something of the nature of these phrases. Thus, I am suggesting that the circularity represents both continuity and closure, repetition and occlusion. This is not to say that there is no escape from this circle. Nor, indeed, that the meanings ascribed to the phrases are unchanging. Rather, it is to say that one needs to be wary of being caught up within the confines of such circularity.

To illustrate my points further I want to return to, and expand upon, two questions I raised in the Introduction. With reference to the phrase 'women have made it' I asked 'How might success be defined through discourses that do not separate the economic from the social?' 'How might I "make it" without subscribing to either a competitive work ethic or selfless motherhood?' In exploring 'women have made it' as a discursive formation I noted that it accords with a liberal feminist agenda that has focused on the achievement of equal rights, freedom of choice and equal opportunities. Young (1997) refers to liberalism as canonised in studies of the women's movement. Certainly, it is commonly assumed that when one speaks of feminism one is referring to the aims and objectives of liberal feminism. These, of course, include getting women into positions of formal, institutionalised power in organisations and within the polity.

The success of a liberal feminist agenda in terms of, for example, an amelioration of social relations can certainly be read in terms of being a politics that is based on wanting 'what men have got, rather than questioning its value in any thorough sense' (Beasley, 1999: 52). Additionally, Browning (2000: 152–3) notes that 'The practical success of liberalism is highlighted in its close alignment with capitalism. Capitalism promotes consumerism and engenders calculating individualism on a global scale.' Is it any surprise therefore that predominant definitions of success continue to rest on economic and hierarchical values? Or that it is virtually impossible to 'make it' without subscribing to a competitive work ethic if these are ready-made aspects of the value system that a liberal feminist agenda has sought to colonise?

Indeed, the hegemonic nature of liberalism is indicated through the way that it is central to the meanings of the other phrases that frame this text. For example, I noted that the 'best of both worlds' is an amelioration of 1950s discourses of the 'good' mother who stayed at home to look after her children. The 'good' mother of 'best of both worlds' discourses is one who still ensures that her 'children come first'. However, the way that she does this is no longer through her continuous presence and attachment, as this is seen to create an overbearing mother who stifles her child's needs for independence and freedom. The 'good' mother, as evidenced in the 'best of both worlds', is one who continues in part-time employment in order to create space for her child. Of course, as Browning (2000: 161) comments 'Liberalism's key themes of individuality, reason, equality and freedom are well suited to the processes of continuous social and technological change generated by contemporary society'. Given the needs of the market for women as flexible labour, the 'good' mother of 'best of both worlds' therefore represents an accommodation towards the market.

It has been argued, however, that the 'good' mother represents a site of resistance to the competitive individualism of market-based economies. Certainly, the 'mother' enshrines aspects of caring, relationality and moral goodness. Drawing on such discourses and images, care ethicists have placed themselves within such a counter-discursive framework to propose an alternative conceptualisation of society. This society would eschew competitive individualism and would place care at its centre. The problems of an ethics of care in terms of its essentialist leanings are well rehearsed (see, for example, Diller, 1996). Such arguments can suggest that caring is an innate quality of womanhood and can continue to fix women into the caring roles they undertake in paid and unpaid work. Indeed, there is good evidence of the appropriation of these 'softer' discourses in management arenas, where they are posited not as offering a utopian vision of a caring society, but as offering the solution to maintaining competitiveness in global markets.

Discourses of 'doing it all' demonstrate the intransigence of assumptions that 'women are caring' and the practices and lived realities that arise from these. Despite women's greater participation in paid work, heterosexual women at least still continue to have the major responsibility for child, domestic and elder care. Through an analysis of 'doing it all' I have sought to illustrate how liberalist assumptions of equality as 'the same as' inform negotiations of household divisions of labour in heterosexual households. The fact that women are still 'doing it all' suggests something of the failure of these negotiations and, by corollary, the problems with assuming that equal must mean 'the same'. As I indicated, in such definitions the normative subject is a man. He becomes the benchmark against which we judge our actions or our aspirations. This maintains the hegemony of the masculine. In addition, calls for distributive justice that are based on sameness lead to a circularity of reasoning because same and different are so linked in the binary that we move from one to the other and then back again. For example, arguments that call for sameness of treatment use differences of outcome as their evidence. Differences of outcome call for sameness of treatment. And so we go round and round. Finally, arguments for 'sameness' tend to assume the androgynous subject. As Orlando exemplifies, this subject appears to be an amalgam of women's and men's 'best' qualities. Thus, women need to develop qualities of objectivity and detachment and men need to develop qualities of connection and caring. Indeed, this subject is a kind of utopian 'having it all' of humanist liberalism.

And so, turning to 'having it all', what we might say is that it is a phrase, *par excellence*, that confirms the deeply entrenched idea 'that we are autonomous human beings who can choose the kind of personal life we wish to live' (Plummer, 2000: 432). 'Having it all' not only speaks of freedom of choice, it also resonates with assumptions that one has a right to that choice. Indeed, a right to 'have it all'. Of course, rights, choices, freedom are central to liberalist ideologies. 'Having it all' also resonates with a kind of arrogant individualism in terms of 'I *shall* have it all'.

My analysis of each of these phrases has sought to explore how they work on our desires and aspirations and how they present certain 'truths' about who we are and the world we live in. These phrases, I argue, represent aspects of a hegemonic economic liberalism of market-based economies. 'Women have made it' is an aspirational discourse that confirms, rather than challenges, existing hierarchical relations. 'The best of both worlds' is a discourse of resolution to the difficulties of maintaining one's sense of identity as a career woman and as a mother. However, it is also a discourse that accords with the needs of capital for cheap, flexible labour. At first glance 'Women are caring' appears as a counter-discursive position to the predominance of market-based relations. Nonetheless, its incorporation into new managerial practices illustrates something of the ways in which dominant discourses maintain their hegemony. 'Having it all' is a utopian project, but rather than emphasise the freely choosing agentic subject of liberalism, I sought to illustrate the difficulties of transition at a personal and political level. In particular, I drew on the multiaxial nature of location to foreground its cross-cutting points of identification and resistance. These difficulties were confirmed in 'Doing it all', which, as a cautioning discourse, is spoken in tones of resigned acceptance or rightful injustice. It may be that Young (op. cit.) is correct when she says that liberalism has promised the impossible.

So how might we look beyond the mirror of representation? Gordon (1990) notes that the diversity of feminist debate in this regard is significant because, although the possibilities for alternatives are raised, there are no straightforward explanations or prescriptions that can be offered. Thus, Evans (1995) notes that the problems of equal/sameness issues have led liberal feminists to turn their attention to issues of difference. Alcoff (2000: 871) notes that 'Few feminist ethicists today hold naive concepts of the self or the capacity for agency'. Thus, care ethicists such as Sevenhuijsen (1998) have called for a deconstruction of liberal and justice-based ethical discourses. The implications of Foucauldian analyses of power have also led to a focus on local, specific concerns in which there is, albeit temporarily, a shared interest or identity (Young, 1997). Thus, within the field of post-colonialism, and drawing on Foucault, Brah (1996: 190: emphasis in text) provides a possible future through multi-locationality and dia-synchronic relationality:

> What I wish to stress is that the study of diasporic formations ... calls for a concept of diaspora in which different historical and contemporary elements are understood, not in tandem, but *in their dia-synchronic relationality*. Such analyses entail engagement with complex arrays of contiguities and contradictions; of changing multi-locationality across time and space.

Brah's concerns are to 'critique discourses of fixed origins while also seeking to reconstruct a space of identity from which a different kind of subject might speak and act' (Gedalof, 2000: 344). Thus, for Brah:

> ... identity is about hierarchies which are constantly in flux and need to be seen in context. ... She finds any politics constituted around the primacy of one axis of differentiation (gender, race or class) over all others limited in its ability to do justice to the everyday experiences of most individuals who – like herself – have mixed allegiances and move in and out of different identities.'
>
> (Davis and Lutz 2000: 369–70)

As I shall now more fully explore, in addition some post-structuralists have argued for an agenda that not only deconstructs the hierarchical binaries of language but also allows for the development of pedagogies for critical literacies.

Beyond the mirror: deconstructive politics for contemporary feminisms

Poststructuralist approaches to difference question the foundations of both global and trans-historical accounts of patriarchy and of essentialist forms of identity politics. In the former, women often appear as an obvious and unproblematic category. In the latter, identity comes from belonging to a specific group of women, rather than a category of women as such. Poststructuralism suggests that ideas of shared identity are not the obvious outcome of being of colour, lesbian or working-class but discursively produced in relation to hegemonic discourses which privilege whiteness, heterosexuality and the middle and upper classes. Moreover, they are open to change. New forms of identity are personally and politically important in resisting sexist, racist and hetereosexist definitions of individuals and for imagining a different future. However, the basis for a shared politics in poststructuralist approaches tends to be shared forms of social oppression rather than shared identities.

(Weedon, 1999: 106–7)

As I noted in Chapter 6, there has been considerable hostility to the implications of post-structural theorising. At the heart of this hostility is the problem of how a political movement can organise itself if the subject at its centre, i.e. woman, has disappeared. Early second-wave radical feminism was based on the idea that patriarchal oppression was primary and was experienced by all women. It was upon this basis that women could come together and work collectively for the 'cause' of women's liberation.

Identity politics highlights how this notion of a unifying identity arising from being a woman was put to the test. This was primarily through critiques from Black, working-class, lesbian and dis/ablist feminists, who variously indicated that the feminist voice that purported to speak for/to all was in fact only speaking for/to White middle-class women. Consequently, these other aspects of social division and shared experience became a focus for organising. Indeed, as Pratt (1993: 58) notes, post-structural theories do not represent the only threat of fragmentation as 'Serious divisions within feminism seem to have emerged as much through an identity politics that fails to adequately question the foundations, status and stability of experience'.

Moreover, while outwardly there may be the appearance of unity and solidarity, a post-structural perspective would argue that even within these groups 'female subjectivity and identity [are] internally fractured and often contradictory' (Weedon, 1999: 105). Identity politics have added a necessary caution and complexity to ideas that there are universal experiences that arise from being a woman, but they have not overcome the problems associated with finding a source of unity based on aspects of identity. These problems relate to the diversity of experience and subjectivities that rest within these more refined identity groupings. But they also relate to the meanings that we ascribe to the concept of 'difference'. Indeed, as I illustrate below, difference provides a useful exemplar of the problems of binaries and the multiplicity of meanings.

Butler (1990) highlights a further problematic issue in feminism's preoccupation with identity politics. Identity politics is, if nothing else, about signifying difference. Yet the apparent paradox that arises from attempting to be both inclusive – as feminists – while at the same time recognising difference can be seen in the ways that feminists have learnt to make a list. When writing this list feminists recognise how incomplete it is and so often end with an embarrassed 'etc.':

The theories of feminist identity that elaborate predicates of color, sexuality, ethnicity, class, and able-bodiedness invariably close with an embarrassed 'etc.' at the end of the list. Through this horizontal trajectory of adjectives, these positions strive to encompass a situated subject, but invariably fail to be complete. This failure, however, is instructive: what political impetus is to be derived from the exasperated 'etc' that so often occurs at the end of such lines? This is a sign of exhaustion as well as of the illimitable process of signification itself. It is the <u>supplement</u>, the excess that necessarily accompanies any effort to posit identity once and for all.

(Butler, 1990: 143–4, emphasis in text)

The post-structural view of the subject-as-process is one that has been seen as heralding the possibility of transformation and change. This appears a strange statement to make given that, as I have indicated, political feminism has relied on concepts of unified, albeit differentiated, identities for working toward change. Nevertheless, for Butler for example, rather than being exasperated with the impossibility of closing the list of embarrassed etceteras, the list's illimitability is its very potentiality. It signifies new spaces for new ways of being. Thus, 'The illimitable etcetera ... offers itself as a new departure for feminist political theorizing' (Butler, 1990: 144).

Extending the limits of the list is achieved through a process of deconstruction. Deconstruction sees social life as a series of texts that can be read in a variety of ways. Because of this multiplicity of readings there is a range of meanings that can be invoked. Moreover, through each reading we are producing another text to the extent that we can view the social world as the emanations of a whole array of intertextual weavings. Although there is this variety, as I have previously indicated, texts contain hierarchical concepts organised as binaries. Deconstruction does not seek to overturn the binary through a reversal of dominance. It does, however, seek to illustrate how language is used to frame meanings, as I shall now illustrate.

Deconstructing the binaries

Deconstruction does not say there is no subject, there is no truth, there is no history. It simply questions the privileging of identity so that someone is believed to have the truth. It is not the exposure of error. It is constantly and persistently looking into how truths are produced.

(Spivak, 2001)

Deconstruction rests on two strategies: overturning and metaphorisation (Garrick and Rhodes, 1998). Overturning seeks to change embedded hierarchies so that the marginal term becomes dominant and vice versa. For example, one might seek to change common perceptions through change at a discursive level. Slogans such as 'Black is Beautiful' or 'Gay Pride' would be examples of this. However, a key problem is that subverting the binary through reversal is an insufficient political act because, even if the positions are changed, this reversal retains domination. It would give rise to, for example, the feminine being more dominant than the masculine or homosexuality being more dominant than heterosexuality. A brief exploration of the binary difference–sameness illustrates this.

Gunew and Yeatman (1993) comment that difference is the central issue facing feminism as a social movement for change. As is clear, in political terms difference is often taken to be a negative element in this respect. In the binary of same–different, it is sameness that is imbued with positive meanings because of the linkage between sameness and unity of purpose or interests. In these terms, difference is taken to mean disunity and divisiveness.

Yet in other contexts the meanings of this binary are reversed. Do we all want to be the same? In ecosystems, for example, difference represents diversity and richness. By comparison, sameness implies uniformity and monotony. In an attempt to revalue these meanings of the binary, Dunne (1999) suggests that we might look to sameness as a way of moving away from compulsory heterosexuality. She notes how sameness implies dull, but reflects that this illustrates how the difference of heterosexuality exerts its claim as the only site of alluring excitement. In arguing for sameness, Dunne acknowledges other forms of difference yet remains optimistic that solidarity can be built between women in ways that would 'dissolve gender as a category of both content and consequence' (p. 80). Her vision also includes valuing women's traditional work, and she urges the necessity of finding ways that would facilitate and insist on change in men's lives.

Dryden (1999) also argues that it is unlikely that women will achieve equality if they remain in relationships with men. Her separatist agenda calls for women to resist marriage. Her agenda also goes in tandem with a parallel need for men to be willing to change. Dryden suggests that the questions that face feminism are those related to masculinity. For example, 'Is it possible to transform and produce non-oppressive masculinities? What could non-hierarchical gender difference look like? What form(s) could it take?' (p. 149).

Dunne's 'passion for sameness' can also be found in Felski's (1997) concerns that feminism has focused too much on woman's otherness. Felski argues for a recognition of the connections between sameness and difference. She suggests that feminism's tendency to configure woman as always the other means that the realm of the same is left untouched. Felski argues that we need to consider 'difference within sameness and sameness within difference' (p. 19). She argues that this will much more fully allow for the development of multiplicity that is at the heart of feminist politics.

Although we might seek to revalue sameness, in accord with Dunne's schema, and view sameness and difference as connected as Felski suggests, and also take up Dryden's call for men to change their ways through an exploration of alternative forms of masculinity, we are still keeping the power of the binaries intact. We are caught between the two poles and two different evaluations of sameness and difference. In consequence, we go back and forth between them. It appears to be a trap from which there is, seemingly, no escape.

As is clear from the foregoing discussion, whichever meaning of difference–sameness one takes, these meanings derive from their relationship to the opposite term in the binary. This is why the process of metaphorisation is important. Through metaphorisation the relation between the two binaried terms is held in play so that one can illustrate how each are dependent on the other for their meaning and how one continuously threatens the hegemonic power of the other.

Within feminist politics the significance of a deconstructive approach is that it challenges the idea of gender as a core category of womanhood. As I have indicated, for some this represents a challenge to feminism itself. Without a core 'feminism threatens to self-destruct as feminists deconstruct its central analytical category' (Pratt, 1993: 56). All we are left with, it is argued, is an individualist politics. Yet this very posing of the issue in terms of an either/or binary of collective versus individualist highlights the potentiality of a deconstructive approach. Binaries represent fixed and oppositional positions. As such they operate as boundaries of inclusion and exclusion. They lead us to making identity statements such as 'I am a feminist' or 'I am not a feminist' or 'I am gay' or 'I am straight'. The boundaries around these categories are also very fiercely policed. Through critically interrogating these boundaries, a deconstructive approach seeks to unpick them and the oppositional politics that it gives rise to.

Braidotti (1997) takes up one form of this. She comments that sexual difference cannot be perceived to be either unproblematic or autonomous. Rather, it is a name that we give to the ways in which various differences intersect and are activated against each other. It is the basis of subjectivities and accordingly is the site for political struggle. Using the metaphor of mimesis, Braidotti argues that the political task is one of repetition. This is accomplished deliberately, self-consciously and affirmatively. She demonstrates this in relation to the verb 'to be'. Braidotti argues that the verb 'to be' is the fundamental basis of phallocentric ontology. Within phallocentricism 'Being' is perceived as singular and male. By unravelling 'Being' and making it spin off its axis, feminists will shift it away from its dogmatic authority and thereby expose the multiple differences within. Braidotti expresses this as follows (p. 39):

> To illustrate this politics, I would like to take the (I hope) classical feminist axiom 'woman is a subject inscribed in power via class, age,

race, ethnicity, sexual orientation' and activate it as a set of inner differences that go on multiplying themselves. As in Gertrude Stein's operatic prose, the logocentric gravitational pulls of the sentences would implode under the strain of the repetition: 'Woman is a subject is inscribed is in is power is via is of is class is age is race is ethnicity is sexual is orientation is ...' and so on indefinitely.

Sargisson (1996) also points out how a deconstructive reading has produced the neologism of *différance*. This term, central to post-structuralist theorising, represents a new way of conceptualising issues of difference. Indeed, our difficulties in explaining and understanding *différance* can be understood to reflect the embeddedness of binaried language as an organising framework of meaning :

> The term *différance* is both part of and a result of a deconstructive reading. It creates new 'meaning' and is itself new in that it does not 'fit' into a hierarchical or dualistic conception of language: strictly speaking, it is unconceptualizable. Derrida's 'conceptualization' of *différance* is representative of a creative and transgressive utopian moment in his work.
>
> (Sargisson, 1996: 108)

The notion of the subject-as-process as indicating change and movement and the desire to resist the ways in which binaried terms fix us within them also means that a deconstructive approach pays significant attention to issues of closure and non-closure in the definition of concepts. Sargisson (1996) explores this issue within a broader discussion of utopianism. She notes how blueprints for utopias convey some kind of perfect resolution and represent a closing down of other options (see also Jaggar and Rothenberg, 1993). Sargisson argues for an open-ended conceptualisation of utopia that is perceived as a dynamic and unending process. There are two main reasons for her refusal of blueprints of closure. One of these rests on a distrust of universalism that has arisen from the debates outlined above with regard to the politics of difference. A second arises because 'The act of closing a debate or text is believed by those taking this approach (again, I include myself) to be a political act, the function of which is to impose a methodology that privileges sameness and oneness and favours self over other.' (pp. 64–5).

The politics of closure is, of course, also evident in the debates that surround the name of woman, as much of the discussion in this chapter testifies. How does the name 'woman' define and attempt to fix identity? The politics of difference have clearly shown that there is no literal referent that is embodied in the name 'woman'. In addition, the name 'woman' can be seen to inevitably lead us to some form of essentialism. Is 'woman', then, a term that we need to hold under erasure?

Certainly there are those who believe that because the term 'woman' is so critical to our understanding of social relations that it should be retained and reclaimed. For example, Tanesini (1996) argues that feminists should be concerned to develop new meanings of woman without abandoning the term altogether. Similarly, Hekman (1999) is concerned to define a new epistemological space for feminism. Her task is to contribute to the clarification of a new paradigm. She rejects the idea that the paradigm shift is one from modernism to post-modernism, in part because of the assertions of some post-modernists that post-modernism is beyond paradigms and because many contemporary post-modern theorists provide little guidance on key epistemological and methodological issues that are of concern for feminism. Nonetheless, Hekman does not seek to abandon the term 'woman'. Rather, one of the tasks that Hekman sets herself is to argue that concepts central to feminism, such as 'woman' and 'gender', should be understood in terms of Weberian ideal types. Her reasons for this are:

- This would retain their political character and maintain the visibility of values that are central to social science concepts.
- They would continue to testify to the partiality of all concepts by being non-universal in themselves.
- Such concepts contribute to our understanding of social reality.

As we have seen, Butler (1990) argues that the illimitable list of embarrassed etceteras has transgressive potential. It can add innumerable aspects of difference to our understanding of womanhood, some of which may not yet be known or yet named. Indeed, Spivak (1993) argues that 'woman' is a misnaming and that the political task is to naturalise the term in the way that Foucault has naturalised the term 'power'. Spivak's focus on the open-ended nature of meaning brings her to comment that the disenfranchised woman who does not recognise herself in the ways through which she is named 'reminds us that the name of "woman", however political, is, like any other name, a catchresis' (p. 137). She comments that 'If *we* lose the "name" of specifically woman for writing there is no cause for lament' (p. 136, emphasis in text).

Spivak conveys the deconstructive moves that surround the naming of woman in the following quotation. In addition, and although some readings are more privileged than others, Spivak draws on the idea that there is not 'a single, literal reading of a textual object, the one intended by the author' (Barone, 1995: 65) to keep in the foreground the notion that the future cannot be controlled or guaranteed:

> In other words, hidden agendas might pass themselves off as the goes-without-saying-ness of truth, to fools and knaves alike; but to show them up as writing *and mean it* is to buy into that very agenda,

unless we put scare-quotes around the word, and say: can't do better for the time being, must keep moving. To call by the name of man all human reality is move number one: humanism; to substitute the name of woman in that mode is move number two; to put scare-quotes around 'woman' is move number three, not a synthesis but a provisional half-solution that always creates problems because it is or is not mistaken for the second move; therefore always looking forward, while making do, toward a fourth move, that never happens but always might.

(Spivak, 1993: 131)

Change at a discursive level faces a key problem because such change can be superficial, leaving predominant meanings intact yet more hidden. For example, Griffiths (1995) discusses the significance of changing language for political purposes. She argues that the task of changing language needs to address both the surface level and the deeper structures of language. She notes how it has been possible to unpack the oppressive assumptions underlying many ordinary words. Pronouns such as 'we', 'he', 'she' and 'I' are now put under routine scrutiny.

However, as campaigners against 'politically correct' language signify, there can be intense resistance to such changes. At a deeper level, change is more difficult. Drawing on the work of Cameron (1992), Griffiths notes how the word 'person', as in 'chairperson' or 'spokesperson' has not become a catch-all phrase for both sexes. Rather, the term 'person' has become a euphemism for 'woman' signifying that when we use the term 'chairperson', for example, we *really* know this means 'chair*woman*'. Griffiths notes (pp. 169–70) that :

Coining a new word is more like driving a wedge into a crack in a wall than putting a torch on to a previously unilluminated part of the stonework. The wall may prove to be obdurate. Or the stone may shift to make room for the wedge – and indeed may break up all together, leaving room for new wedges. Thus ordinary, everyday language has now changed to accommodate some of the new words, changing their meaning in the processes. Other new words are in the processes of being excluded again.

Changes of meaning, therefore, need to go hand in hand with a broader development of critical literacies, as I shall illustrate.

Critical literacies

... literacy needs to be viewed within an ethical and emancipatory discourse providing a language of hope and transformation that is able to analyze, challenge and transform the ideological reference for understanding how people negotiate and translate their relationship with everyday life. It is also a form of social praxis that is directed at self and social transformation. In other words, it offers an alternative form of literacy to the dominant discourse, enabling a critical reading of how power, ideology and culture work to disempower some groups of people while privileging others.

(Brady, 1994: 142)

The pedagogic issues that arise from this focus on deconstruction have been labelled by some as the development of critical literacy. Brady (1994) notes how the concept of critical literacy draws on the liberatory pedagogies of the Brazilian educator and philosopher Freire. Freire's work has been criticised for its overemphasis on class struggle and its lack of attention to the gendered nature of oppression and domination. Nevertheless, the development of understandings of critical literacy have encompassed moves 'toward distinctively poststructuralist variants such as (textual) deconstruction, discourse analysis, and the like' (Lankshear *et al.*, 1997: 3).

In essence, the purposes of critical literacy are:

1 to generate a level of critical literacy that enables learners to recognise multiple discourses;
2 to facilitate a critical awareness of the ways in which the self is contradictorily positioned, as coloniser and colonised, as oppressed and oppressive, within these discourses;
3 to embrace, as one's own, the multiplicity of positions with which one wishes to identify.

Davies' (1997b) focus on critical literacy provides a classic example of the importance of equipping learners not simply with knowledge, but with the tools through which they can become their own knowledge producers. Her account also brings to the fore the two-stage nature of practices of deconstruction upon which critical literacy rests:

Davies offers an analysis of a lesson given by a teacher she names Mr Good. The pseudonym is apt because it suggests that this teacher is skilled and effective. In addition, it is clear from Davies' description that Mr Good draws on an emancipatory framework that is designed to disrupt traditional gendered identities. For example, Mr Good opens up the spaces in his lesson for boys to be literate and oral beings. He encourages boys to write and read poetry and to express their emotions. He also directly challenges assumptions that aggression and war solve problems.

One reading of Mr Good, therefore, is that he is opening up spaces for these children in which masculinity can be constructed in a range of ways beyond machismo. We might even say that he is reversing some common meanings of the binary of male–female according to which masculinity is hard and femininity is soft. Nevertheless, Davies illustrates how Mr Good's pedagogic approach is flawed. This is because Mr Good does not offer the students in his class the tools through which they can engage with and critique the discourses that are made available. Essentially, Mr Good does not hold in play the variety of meanings ascribed to masculinity. He does not explore the ways in which these meanings rely on each other. Nor does he explore the potential for the creation of new meanings. Thus, Mr Good is opening up for these children a range of alternative cultural identifications. However, he does not offer the children in his class 'the kind of reflexive knowledge that would allow them to see what is happening and to critique the various discourses that are made available to them' (p. 25).

Searle (1998: 10) sets out the necessary stages of the development of critical literacy through eight words beginning with the letter 'C'. These are: 'creation, consideration, consciousness, confidence, collaboration, consolidation, cultural action and crossover'. Thus, through the creation of new forms of words and language one's imagination is mobilised. This is consolidated through consideration or reflection of what has been produced and is seen to lead to a new consciousness of the previously unimagined. This, in turn, is seen to promote confidence in the creative self and in others when working in collaboration. Searle argues that cultural action may follow at a later time and that through working in a classroom where different languages are present 'and where cultural symbols and narratives are broad and different the crossover of culture becomes an emphatic objective of critical pedagogy and literacy development' (p. 10).

Of course, the notion that formal education of this kind should be the sole source of the development of critical literacies would ignore how education upholds, rather than subverts, existing social relations. It would also place rather too much emphasis on the ability of formal education to enact such widespread change. As Lankshear *et al.* (1997: 189) comment:

> There are no easy answers, quick fixes or magic bullets here. We certainly cannot expect 'Education' alone to do the job. History has been a long time in the making, and building new and more expansive human (and humanizing) histories is a long-term task.

Indeed, Searle (1998: 9) notes how recent policies in school education in the UK, together with the culture of post-industrial capitalism, have meant that:

> The development of a dialogue-based pedagogy and critical literacy is not an easy task in such a system where all is to be prescribed, outcomes are to be preordained, examined by ceaseless testing and overseen by OFSTED (Office for Standards in Education), the new schools inspectorate and curriculum police. The obstructions and

permanent surveillance are formidable and offer little space for democratic practice and creative sharing of knowledge and experience between student and teacher – the foundation of a truly progressive pedagogy. Then, beyond the curriculum confines of school, there is the 'predatory culture' of post-industrial capitalism in which an entire generation of young people are threatened to become immersed.

In this, therefore, we need to look beyond the formal education sector to other places where 'Language acts ... can play a crucial part in bringing about individual and collective change' (Young, 1997: 25). Young focuses on feminist publishing and feminist autobiographical writing as important sites for discursive activism and in consequence for enabling women to understand their situations and their perceptions of how these might change. She suggests that autobiographical and autotheoretical texts are significant in this regard for several reasons:

- They maintain the women's movement's longstanding focus on domination and resistance at the level of daily life – a contribution to progressive politics that distinguishes the women's movement from other social movements.
- They bring to this focus a complex understanding of a variety of forms of domination and resistance, and of arenas in which these forms of domination and resistance are enacted.
- They seek to understand women's different situations in ways that resist reducing the subordination of women and other marginalized groups to a monolithic cause or character.
- The texts reflect, as well as contribute to, developments in feminist analysis that arise out of feminist activism, and thus provide readers with ways of understanding and transforming their own lives.

We should also turn to Irigaray's *Speculum* for an example of 'language acts' that are designed to be transgressive. Whitford (1994: 380) describes Irigaray's politics as:

> ... a 'politics of the imaginary' or a 'politics of the unconscious' [whereby] 'the politics of the imaginary' contains the idea that imagination – the possibility of imagining that things might be different – could have a critical function in political thought [and] the phrase 'politics of the unconscious' foregrounds the idea that there is a sense in which you cannot know exactly what you are doing.

Thus, in addition to Irigaray's deconstructive style, she also refuses to write within the conventions of academic prose and grammatical construction:

Precise references in the form of notes or punctuation indicating quotation have often been omitted. Because in relation to the working of theory, the/a woman fulfills a twofold function – as the mute outside that sustains all systematicity; as a maternal and still silent ground that nourishes all foundations – she does not have to conform to the codes theory has set up for itself. In this way, she confounds, once again, the imaginary of the 'subject' – in its masculine connotations – and something that will or might be the imaginary of the female. Let all, then, male or female, dead or alive, recognize themselves as same according to their desire or their pleasure, even in the parody of capital letters. But if, in the resistance set up against the male imaginary, distortion gave rise to discomfort, then, perhaps?, something of the difference of the sexes would have taken place in language also.

(Irigaray, 1985: 365)

Of course, the development of critical literacies alone does not constitute total 'formulae for liberation. However, [it does] constitute resistance to manifestations of domination that go beyond legal and policy forms ... and underscore[s] the importance of looking beyond electoral politics and policy outcomes to analyze ideological forms of domination and resistance' (Young, 1997: 188). Significantly, a focus on the development of critical literacies focuses our attention on language as:

... an active form of cultural production for 'getting at' and understanding the things that shape our identity; it allows us to understand zones of cultural difference, and to create spaces where people can move beyond wooden topologies that lock them into rigid boundaries and identities ... language becomes a referent for understanding how institutional practices privilege certain forms of identity, how one reads the world, and also how one refigures one's own identity within a specific set of historical, social and economic configurations.

(Brady, 1994: 151)

Thus, the political purpose of critical literacy is that dominant discourses will be more open to challenge as they are no longer taken as representational of the natural order of things. This opens up further possibilities for the creation of multihued identificatory positions that carry the potential of creating new gender (and other) discourses. Walkerdine (1989: 206) offers one way of summarising how these points of creation might come into being:

By taking those stories apart and seeing how we are caught up in them, we can begin to tell our own. For example, by analysing how women's domestic labour is transformed into a prop for play and the nurturance of the rational unitary subject, we can examine the painful and oppressive work that goes into this; or we can show that rational discourse is produced not out of certainty but out of a terror of losing control. In other words, we can turn conventional stories on their heads and tell those which the current truths actively suppress.

Indeed, it may be, that in deconstructing the circle of:

we might well move beyond this particular mirror of representation. To what, of course, is post-structurally a question of becoming.

Summary

This chapter has explored the politics of post-structuralism through attention to the significance of deconstruction and the development of critical literacy. I have argued that through deconstruction we can recognise how discourses work to shape how we know and how we envisage what we might become. Our task is to learn to be critically literate in the ways that we read discourses because such literacy leads to the potentiality for change. This change is accomplished by inserting new discourses into the language that envisage new gendered, and other, possibilities.

REFERENCES

Adams, S (1996) 'Women returners and fractured identities', in Charles, N and Hughes-Freeland, F (eds) *Practising Feminism: Identity, Difference, Power*, London, Routledge, pp. 202–222.

Adkins, L (1995) *Gendered Work: Sexuality, Family and the Labour Market*, Buckingham, Open University Press.

Alberti, J (1997) 'A fantasy of belonging?', in Stanley, L (ed.) *Knowing Feminisms*, London, Sage, pp. 144–153.

Alcoff, I (2000) 'Philosophy matters: a review of recent work in feminist philosophy', *SIGNS: Journal of Women in Culture and Society*, 25 (3): 841–882.

Ang, I (1995) 'I'm a feminist but ... "Other" women and postnational feminism', in Caine, B and Pringle, R (eds) *Transitions: New Australian Feminisms*, Sydney, Allen & Unwin, pp. 57–73.

Anthias, F and Yuval-Davis, N with Cain, H (1992) *Racialized Boundaries: Race, Nation, Gender, Colour and Class and the Anti-Racist Struggle*, London, Routledge.

Apter, T (1993) *Professional Progress: Why Women Still Don't Have Wives*, Basingstoke, Macmillan.

Arber, S and Gilbert, N (1989) 'Men: the forgotten carers', *Sociology*, 23 (1): 111–118.

Arber, S and Gilbert, N (1992) *Women and Working Lives: Divisions and Change*, Basingstoke, Macmillan.

Arnot, M, David, M and Weiner, G (1999) *Closing the Gender Gap: Postwar Education and Social Change*, Cambridge, Polity Press.

Bacchi, C (2000) 'Policy as discourse: What does it mean? Where does it get us?', *Discourse: Studies in the Cultural Politics of Education*, 21 (1): 45–58.

Barkan, E and Shelton, M (eds) (1998) *Borders, Exiles and Diasporas*, Stanford, CA, Stanford University Press.

Barone, T (1995) 'Persuasive writings, vigilant readings, and reconstructed characters: the paradox of trust in educational storysharing', in Hatch, J and Wisniewski, R (eds) *Life History and Narrative*, London, Falmer Press, pp. 63–74.

Barrett, M (1987) 'The concept of "difference" ', *Feminist Review*, 26: 29–42.

Barrett, M (2000) 'Post-feminism', in Browning, G, Halcli, A and Webster, F (eds) *Understanding Contemporary Society: Theories of the Present*, London, Sage, pp. 46–56.

Bartky, S (1990) *Femininity and Domination: Studies in the Phenomenology of Oppression*, New York, Routledge.

Battersby, C (1996) 'Her blood and his mirror: Mary Coleridge, Luce Irigaray, and the female self', in Eldridge, R (ed.) *Beyond Representation: Philosophy and Poetic Imagination*, Cambridge, Cambridge University Press, pp. 249–272.

150

REFERENCES

Battersby, C (1998) *The Phenomenal Woman: Feminist Metaphysics and the Patterns of Identity*, Cambridge, Polity Press.

Beasley, C (1999) *What is Feminism? An Introduction to Feminist Theory*, London, Sage.

Beer, G (1997) 'Representing women: re-presenting the past', in Belsey, C and Moore, J (eds) *The Feminist Reader*, 2nd edn, Basingstoke, Macmillan, pp. 71–90.

Belsey, C (1997) 'Constructing the subject: deconstructing the text', in Warhol, R and Herndl D (eds) *Feminisms: An Anthology of Literary Theory and Criticism*, Basingstoke, Macmillan, pp. 657–673.

Belsey, C and Moore, J (eds) (1997) *The Feminist Reader: Essays in Gender and the Politics of Literary Criticism*, Basingstoke, Macmillan.

Benhabib, S (1992) *Situating the Self: Gender, Community and Postmodernism in Contemporary Ethics*, Cambridge, Polity Press.

Berry, P (1994) 'The burning glass: paradoxes in feminist revelation in *Speculum*', in Burke, C, Schor, N and Whitford, M (eds) *Engaging with Irigaray: Feminist Philosophy and Modern European Thought*, New York, Columbia University Press, pp. 229–248.

Bhopal K (1997) *Gender, 'Race' and Patriarchy*, Aldershot, Ashgate.

Blackmore, J (1997) 'Disciplining feminism: a look at gender-equity struggles in Australian higher education', in Roman, L and Eyre, L (eds) *Dangerous Territories: Struggles for Difference and Equality in Education*, New York, Routledge, pp. 75–98.

Blackmore, J (1999) *Troubling Women: Feminism, Leadership and Educational Change*, Buckingham, Open University Press.

Blackwell, L (2001) 'Occupational sex segregation and part-time work in modern Britain', *Gender, Work and Organization*, 8 (2): 146–163.

Blaxter, L and Hughes, C (2000) 'Social capital: a critique', in Thompson, J (ed.) *Stretching the Academy: The Politics and Practice of Widening Participation in Higher Education*, Leicester, NIACE.

Blaxter, L and Tight, M (1993) 'I'm only doing it to get in the black gown': dream and reality for adults in part-time higher education, *Journal of Further and Higher Education*, 17 (1): 13–21.

Blaxter, L and Tight, M (1994) 'Juggling with time: how adults manage their time for lifelong education', *Studies in the Education of Adults*, 26 (2): 162–179.

Blaxter, L and Tight, M (1995) 'Life transitions and educational participation by adults', *International Journal of Lifelong Education*, 14 (3): 231–246.

Bloot, R and Brown, J (1996) 'Reasons for the under-representation of females at head of department level in physical education in government schools in Western Australia', *Gender and Education*, 7 (3): 293–313.

Boehmer, E (1995) *Colonial and Postcolonial Literature*, Oxford, Oxford University Press.

Boris, E (1993) 'The power of motherhood: black and white activist women redefine the "political" ', in Koven, S and Michel S (eds) *Mothers of a New World: Maternalist Politics and the Origins of Welfare States*, New York, Routledge, pp. 213–245.

Bornat, J, Dimmock, B, Jones, D and Peace, S (1999) 'Generational ties in the "new" family: changing contexts for traditional obligations', in Silva, E and Smart, C (eds) *The New Family?* London, Sage, pp. 115–128.

Bowlby, J (1965) *Child Care and the Growth of Love*, 2nd edn. Penguin, Harmondsworth.

Brady, J (1994) 'Critical literacy, feminism, and a politics of representation', in McLaren, P and Lankshear, C (eds) *Politics of Liberation: Paths from Freire*, London, Routledge, pp. 142–153.

Brah, A (1996) *Cartographies of Diaspora: Contesting Identities*, London, Routledge.

151

REFERENCES

Braidotti, R (1994) *Nomadic Subjects: Embodiment and Sexual Difference in Contemporary Feminist Theory*, New York, Columbia University Press.

Braidotti, R (1997) 'Comment on Felski's 'The doxa of difference': working through sexual difference', *SIGNS: Journal of Women in Culture and Society*, 23 (1): 23–40.

Brine, J (1999) *Under Educating Women: Globalizing Inequality*, Buckingham, Open University Press.

Britton, C and Baxter, A (1999) 'Becoming a mature student: gendered narratives of the self', *Gender and Education*, 11 (2): 179–194.

Brooks, A (1997) *Postfeminism: Feminism, Cultural Theory and Cultural Forms*, London, Routledge.

Browning, G (2000) 'Contemporary liberalism', in Browning, G, Halcli, A and Webster F (eds) *Understanding Contemporary Society: Theories of the Present*, London, Sage, pp. 152–164.

Bulbeck, C (1997) *Living Feminism: The Impact of the Women's Movement on Three Generations of Australian Women*, Cambridge, Cambridge University Press.

Burke, C (1994) 'Irigaray through the looking glass', in Burke, C, Schor, N and Whitford, M (eds) *Engaging with Irigaray: Feminist Philosophy and Modern European Thought*, New York, Columbia University Press, pp. 37–56.

Butler, J (1990) *Gender Trouble: Feminism and the Subversion of Identity*, New York, Routledge.

Butler, J (1993) *Bodies That Matter: On the Discursive Limits of 'Sex'*, New York, Routledge.

Butler, J. (1995) 'Contingent foundations', in Benhabib, S, Butler, J, Cornell, D and Fraser, N (eds) *Feminist Contentions: A Philosophical Exchange*, New York, Routledge, pp. 35–57.

Butler, J and Scott, J (eds) (1992) *Feminists Theorize the Political*, New York, Routledge.

Cameron, D (1992) *Feminism and Linguistic Theory*, 2nd edn, London, Macmillan.

Carby, H (1982) 'White women listen! Black feminism and the boundaries of sisterhood', in Centre for Contemporary Cultural Studies (eds) *The Empire Strikes Back*, London, Hutchinson.

Chamberlain, M (1997) *Narratives of Exile and Return*, London, Macmillan.

Charles, N and Kerr, M (1999) 'Women's work', in Allan, G (ed.) *The Sociology of the Family: A Reader*, Oxford, Blackwell, pp. 191–210.

Clarke, J and Newman, J (1997) *The Managerial State*, London, Sage.

Clough, P (1994) *Feminist Thought: Desire, Power and Academic Discourse*, Oxford, Blackwell.

Colgan, F and Ledwith, S (1996) 'Women as organisational change agents', in Ledwith, S and Colgan, F (eds) *Women in Organisations: Challenging Gender Politics*, Basingstoke, Macmillan, pp. 1–43.

Collins, P (1991) *Black Feminist Thought: Knowledge, Consciousness and the Politics of Empowerment*, London, Routledge.

Connell, R (1987) *Gender and Power: Society, the Person and Sexual Politics*, Cambridge, Polity Press.

Coote, A and Campbell, B (1987) *Sweet Freedom*, Oxford, Basil Blackwell.

Corti, L, Laurie, H and Dex, S (1994) *Caring and Employment*, Research Series No. 39, Sheffield, Department of Employment.

Cotterill, P (1994) *Friendly Relations? Mothers and their Daughters-in-law*, London, Taylor & Francis.

REFERENCES

Coward, R (1993) *Our Treacherous Hearts: Why Women let Men Get their Way*, London, Faber.

Crouch, M and Manderson, L (1993) *New Motherhood: Cultural and Personal transitions in the 1980s*, Sydney, Gordon and Breach Science.

Davies, B (1997a) 'The subject of post-structuralism: a reply to Alison Jones', *Gender and Education*, 9 (3): 271–284.

Davies, B (1997b) 'Constructing and deconstructing masculinities through critical literacy', *Gender and Education*, 9 (1): 9–30.

Davies, B, Dormer, S, Gannon, S, Laws, C, Taguchi, H, McCann, H and Rocco, S (2001) 'Becoming schoolgirls: the ambivalent project of subjectification', *Gender and Education*, 13 (2): 167–182.

Davis, K and Lutz, H (2000) 'Open Forum: life in theory: three feminist thinkers on transition(s)', *The European Journal of Women's Studies*, 7 (3): 367–378.

Delphy, C and Leonard, D (1992) *Familiar Exploitation: A New Analysis of Marriage in Contemporary Western Societies*, Cambridge, Polity Press.

Diller, A (1996) 'The ethics of care and education: a new paradigm, its critics and its educational significance', in Diller, A, Houston, B, Morgan, K and Ayim, M (eds) *The Gender Question in Education*, Boulder, CO, Westview Press, pp. 89–104.

Dornbusch, S and Strober, M (eds) (1988) *Feminism, Children and the New Families*, New York, Guilford Press.

Drake, J (1997) 'Review essay: third wave feminism', *Feminist Studies*, 23 (1): 97–108.

Dryden, C (1999) *Being Married, Doing Gender: A Critical Analysis of Gender Relations in Marriage*, London, Routledge.

Dunne, G (1997) *Lesbian Lifestyles: Women's Work and the Politics of Sexuality*, Basingstoke, Macmillan.

Dunne, G (1999) 'A passion for sameness? sexuality and gender accountability', in Silva, E and Smart, C (eds) *The New Family?* London, Sage, pp. 66–82.

Eastmond, M (1993) 'Reconstructing life: Chilean Refugee women and the dilemmas of exile', in Buijs, G (ed.) *Migrant Women: Crossing Boundaries and Changing Identities*, Oxford, Berg, pp. 35–54.

Edholm, F (1992) 'Beyond the mirror: women's self portraits', in Bonner, F, Goodman, L, Allen, R, Janes, L and King, C (eds) *Imagining Women: Cultural Representations and Gender*, Cambridge, Polity Press/Open University, pp. 154–172.

Edwards, R (1993) *Mature Women Students: Separating or Connecting Family and Education*, London, Taylor & Francis.

Eisenstein, H (1991) *Gender Shock: Practising Feminism on Two Continents*, Sydney, NSW, Allen & Unwin.

Eistenstein, H (1984) *Contemporary Feminist Thought*, London, Unwin.

Eisenstein, Z (1993) *The Radical Future of Liberal Feminism*, Boston, Northeastern University Press.

Epstein, D and Johnson, R (1998) *Schooling Sexualities*, Buckingham, Open University Press.

Evans, J (1995) *Feminist Theory Today: An Introduction to Second-Wave Feminism*, London, Sage.

Evans, M (ed.) (1994) *The Woman Question*, 2nd edn, London, Sage.

Evetts, J (2000) 'Analysing change in women's careers: culture, structure and action dimensions', *Gender, Work and Organisation*, 7 (1): 57–67.

REFERENCES

Exworthy, M and Halford, S (1999) 'Professionals and managers in a changing public sector: conflict, compromise and collaboration', in Exworthy, M and Halford, S (eds) *Professionals and the New Managerialism in the Public Sector*, Buckingham, Open University Press, pp. 1–17.

Faludi, S (1992) *Backlash: The Undeclared War against Women*, London, Vintage.

Felski, R (1997) 'The doxa of difference', *SIGNS: Journal of Women in Culture and Society*, 23 (1): 1–21.

Ferrie, E and Smith, K *(1996) Parenting in the 1990s*, London, Family Policy Studies Centre.

Finlayson, A (1999) 'Language, in Ashe, F, Finalyson, A, Lloyd, M, MacKenzie, I, Martin, J and O'Neill, S (eds) *Contemporary Social and Political Theory: An Introduction*, Buckingham, Open University Press, pp. 47–87.

Firestone, S (1970) *The Dialectic of Sex*, New York, William Morrow.

Flax, J (1997) 'Forgotten forms of close combat: mothers and daughters revisited', in Gergen, M and Davis, S (eds) *Toward a New Psychology of Gender: A Reader*, New York, Routledge, pp. 311–324.

Foucault, M (1972) *The Archaeology of Knowledge*, London, Tavistock Publications.

Foucault, M (1977) *Discipline and Punish: The Birth of the Prison* (translated by Alan Sheridan), Harmondsworth, Penguin.

Foucault, M (1978) *The History of Sexuality: An Introduction* (Volume 1, translated by Robert Hurley), London, Penguin.

Foucault, M (2000) 'Las Meninas', in J Thomas (ed) *Reading Images: Readers in Cultural Criticism*, Basingstoke, Palgrave, pp. 184–197.

Francis, B (1998) *Power Plays: Primary School Children's Constructions of Gender, Power and Adult Work*, Stoke on Trent, Trentham Books.

Francis, B (1999) 'Modernist reductionism or post-structuralist relativism: can we move on? An evaluation of the arguments in relation to feminist educational research', *Gender and Education*, 11 (4): 381–394.

Fraser, N (1989) *Unruly Practices: Power, Discourse and Gender in Contemporary Social Theory*, Cambridge, Polity Press.

Freedman, J (2001) *Feminism*, Buckingham, Open University Press.

Friedan, B (1963) *The Feminine Mystique*, New York, Norton & Co.

Garrick, J and Rhodes, C (1998) 'Deconstructive organisational learning: the possibilities for a postmodern epistemology of practice', *Studies in the Education of Adults*, 30 (2): 172–183.

Gavron, H (1966) *The Captive Wife: Conflicts of Housebound Mothers*, Harmondsworth, Penguin.

Gedalof, I (2000) 'Identity in transit: nomads, cyborgs and women', *The European Journal of Women's Studies*, 7 (3): 337–354.

Gee, J (1996) *Social Linguistics and Literacies: Ideology in Discourses*, 2nd edn. London, Taylor & Francis.

Gee, J (1997) 'Forward: A discourse approach to language and literacy', in Lankshear, C with Gee, J, Knobel, M and Searle, C (eds) *Changing Literacies*, Buckingham, Open University Press, pp. xiii–xix.

George, R and Maguire, M (1998) 'Older women training to teach', *Gender and Education*, 10 (4): 417–430.

Giles, J (1990) 'Second chance, second self?', *Gender and Education*, 2 (3): 357–362.

Gilligan, C (1982) *In a Different Voice*, Cambridge, MA, Harvard University Press.

REFERENCES

Gilligan, C (1998) 'Remembering Larry', *Journal of Moral Education*, 27 (2): 125–140.

Goldscheider, F and Waite, L (1991) *New Families, No Families? The Transformation of the American Home*, Berkeley, University of California Press.

Gordon, T (1990) *Feminist Mothers*, Basingstoke, Macmillan.

Graham, H (1993) *Hardship and Health in Women's Lives*, Hemel Hempstead, Harvester Wheatsheaf.

Green, P and Webb, S (1997) 'Student voices: alternative routes, alternative identities', in J Williams (ed.) *Negotiating Access to Higher Education*, Buckingham, Open University Press, pp. 130–152.

Gregson, N and Lowe, M (1994) 'Waged domestic labour and the renegotiation of the domestic division of labour within dual career households', *Sociology*, 28 (1): 55–78.

Griffiths, M (1995) *Feminisms and the Self: The Web of Identity*, London, Routledge.

Grosz, E (1990) *Jacques Lacan: A Feminist Introduction*, London, Routledge.

Gunew, S and Yeatman, A (eds) (1993) *Feminism and the Politics of Difference*, NSW, Allen & Unwin.

Hart, M. (1992) *Working and Educating for Life: Feminist and International Prespectives on Adult Education*, London, Routledge.

Hartmann, G (1981) *Saving the Text: Literature, Derrida, Philosophy*, Baltimore, Johns Hopkins University Press.

Hatt, S (1999) 'Establishing a research career', in Hatt, S, Kent, J and Britton, C (eds) *Women, Research and Careers*, Basingstoke, Macmillan, pp. 89–108.

Haw, K (1998) *Educating Muslim Girls: Shifting Discourses*, Buckingham, Open University Press.

Hays, S (1996) *The Cultural Contradictions of Motherhood*, New Haven, CT, Yale University Press.

Hekman, S (1999) *The Future of Differences: Truth and Method in Feminist Theory*, Cambridge, Polity Press.

Henwood, F (1998) 'Engineering difference: discourses on gender, sexuality and work in a college of technology', *Gender and Education*, 10 (1): 35–50.

Higher Education Statistics Agency (HESA) (1996) *Higher Education Statistics for the United Kingdom 1994/95*, Cheltenham, HESA.

Hughes, C (1991) *Stepparents: Wicked or Wonderful?* Aldershot, Gower.

Hughes, C (1996) 'Mystifying through coalescence: the underlying politics of methodological choices', in Watson, K, Modgil, C and Modgil, S (eds) *Quality in Education: Educational Dilemmas, Debate and Diversity*, Volume 4, London, Cassell, pp. 413–420

Hughes, C and Tight, M (1995) 'The myth of the learning society', *British Journal of Educational Studies*, 43 (3): 290–304.

Hughes, C (2000) 'Is it possible to be a feminist manager in the "real world" of further education?', *Journal of Further and Higher Education*, 24 (2): 251–260.

Hughes, C, Taylor, P and Tight, M (1996) 'The ever-changing world of further education: a case for research', *Research in Post-Compulsory Education*, 1 (1): 7–18.

Ifekwunigwe, J (1997) 'Diaspora's daughters, Africa's orphans? On lineage, authenticity and "mixed race" identity', in Mirza, H (ed.) *Black British Feminism: A Reader*, London, Routledge, pp. 127–152.

Irigaray, L (1985) *Speculum of the Other Woman* (translated by Gillian Gill), Ithaca, NY, Cornell University Press.

REFERENCES

Irigaray, L (1993) 'The three genders', in Irigary, L (ed.) *Sexes and Genealogies* (translated by Gillian Gill), New York, Columbia University Press, pp. 169–181.

Irigaray, L (1997) 'The looking glass, from the other side', in C Belsey and J Moore (eds) *The Feminist Reader*, 2nd edn, Basingstoke, Macmillan, pp. 217–226.

Jackson, S (1998) 'In a class of their own: women's studies and working-class students', *European Journal of Women's Studies*, 5: 195–215.

Jaggar, A and Rothenberg, P (eds) (1993) *Feminist Frameworks: Alternative Theoretical Accounts of the Relations between Women and Men*, 3rd edn, New York, McGraw-Hill.

Jarrett-Macauley, D (ed.) (1996) *Reconstructing Womanhood, Reconstructing Feminism: Writings on Black Women*, London, Routledge.

Johnson, C (2000) *Derrida*, London, Phoenix.

Johnson, R (2000) 'Ascent of woman', *People Management*, 6 January 2000: 26–32.

Jones, A (1993) 'Becoming a "girl": post-structuralist suggestions for educational research, *Gender and Education*, 5 (2): 157–166.

Jones, D (1990) 'The genealogy of the urban schoolteacher', in Ball, S (ed.) *Foucault and Education: Disciplines and Knowledge*, London, Routledge, pp. 57–77.

Kaplan, E (1992) *Motherhood and Representation: The Mother in Popular Culture and Melodrama*, London, Routledge.

Kaplan, M (1992) *Mothers' Images of Motherhood*, London, Routledge.

Kearney, R (1988) *The Wake of Imagination: Ideas of Creativity in Western Culture*, London, Hutchinson.

Kelly, A (ed.) (1987) *Science for Girls?* Milton Keynes, Open University Press.

Kerfoot, D (1999) 'The organization of intimacy: managerialism, masculinity and the masculine subject', in Whitehead, S and Moodley, R (eds) *Transforming Managers: Gendering Change in the Public Sector*, London, UCL Press, pp. 184–199.

Kiernan, K (1992) 'Men and women at work and at home', in Jowell, R, Brook, L, Prior, G and Taylor, B (eds) *British Social Attitudes: The 9th Report*, Aldershot, Dartmouth.

Lane, N (2000) 'The low status of female part-time NHS nurses: a bed-pan ceiling?', *Gender, Work and Organisation*, 7 (4): 269–281.

Lankshear, C with Gee, J, Knobel, M and Searle, C (1997) *Changing Literacies*, Buckingham, Open University Press.

Laws, C and Davies, B (2000) Poststructuralist theory in practice: working with 'behaviourally disturbed' children, *Qualitative Studies in Education*, 13 (3): 205–221.

Lees, S and Scott, M (1990) 'Equal opportunities: rhetoric or action?', *Gender and Education*, 2 (3): 333–343.

Legge, K (1995) 'HRM: rhetoric, reality and hidden agendas', in Storey, J (ed.) *Human Resource Management: A Critical Text*, London, Routledge, pp. 33–62.

Leonard, P (1998) 'Gendering change? Management, masculinity and the dynamics of incorporation', *Gender and Education*, 10 (1): 71–84.

Letherby, G (2001) 'Researching non-motherhood in higher education: an attempt at a reflexive auto/duo/biographical approach', paper presented at the Politics of Gender and Education Third International Conference, Institute of Education, University of London, 4–6 April 2001.

Lewis, J (ed.) (1993) *Women and Social Policies in Europe: Work, Family and the State*, Aldershot, Edward Elgar.

Lewis, M (1993) *Without a Word: Teaching Beyond Women's Silence*, New York, Routledge.

REFERENCES

Lewis, S, Izraeli, D and Hootsmans, H (1992) *Dual-Earner Families: International Perspectives*, London, Sage.

Liff, S and Ward, K (2001) 'Distorted views through the glass ceiling: the construction of women's understandings of promotion and senior management positions', *Gender, Work and Organisation*, 8 (1): 19–36.

Lorde, A (1994) 'The master's tools will never dismantle the master's house', in Evans, M (ed.) *The Woman Question*, London, Sage, pp. 366–368.

Luke, C (1998) 'Cultural politics and women in Singapore higher education management', *Gender and Education*, 10 (3): 245–264.

Luke, C and Gore, J (eds) (1992) *Feminisms and Critical Pedagogy*, New York, Routledge.

McMahon, M (1995) *Engendering Motherhood: Identity and Self-Transformation in Women's Lives*, New York, Guilford Press.

McNay, L (1992) *Foucault and Feminism*, Cambridge, Polity Press.

Markson, E and Taylor, C (2000) 'The mirror has two faces', *Ageing and Society*, 20: 137–160.

Marshall, H (1991) 'The social construction of motherhood: an analysis of childcare and parenting manuals', in Phoenix, A, Woollett, A and Lloyds, E (eds) *Motherhood: Meanings, Practices and Ideologies*, London, Sage, pp. 66–85.

Marshall, J (1984) *Women Managers: Travellers in a Male World*, Chichester, John Wiley.

Maynard, M and Purvis, J (eds) (1994) *Researching Women's Lives from a Feminist Perspective*, London, Taylor & Francis.

Middleton, S (1998) *Disciplining Sexuality: Foucault, Life Histories and Education*, New York, Teachers College Press.

Mirza, H (ed.) (1997) *Black British Feminism: A Reader*, London, Routledge.

Mitchell, J (1974) *Psychoanalysis and Feminism*, Harmondsworth, Penguin.

Moody-Adams, M (1997) 'Feminism by any other name', in Nelson, H (ed.) *Feminism and Families*, New York, Routledge, pp. 76–89.

Moore, H (1994) *A Passion for Difference*, Cambridge, Polity Press.

Morris, L (1990) *The Workings of the Household*, Cambridge, Polity Press.

Moser, C (1996) *Confronting Crisis: A Comparative Study of Household Responses to Poverty and Vulnerability*, EDS Monographs Series 8, Washington, The World Bank.

Munro, P (1998) *Subject to Fiction: Women Teachers' Life History Narratives and the Cultural Politics of Resistance*, Buckingham, Open University Press.

National Statistics (2001(a)) *Labour Market Dataset*, http://www.statistics.gov.uk/ukin_figs/Data_labour.asp (accessed 15.01.2001).

National Statistics (2001(b)) *Labour Market Dataset: Cross-Sectional*, http://www.statistics.gov.uk/statbase/xsdataset.asp?vlnk=148 (accessed 15.01.2001).

National Statistics (2001(c)) *Social Trends, Spring 1999*, http://www.statistics.gov.uk/statbase/xsdataset.asp (accessed 15.01.2001).

Noddings, N (1984) *Caring: A Feminine Approach to Ethics and Moral Education*, Berkeley, CA, University of California.

Noddings, N (1994) 'An ethic of caring and its implications for instructional arrangements', in Stone, L (ed.) *The Education Feminism Reader*, New York, Routledge, pp. 171–183.

Norris, C (2000) 'Post-modernism: a guide for the perplexed', in Browning G, Halcli, A and Webster, F (eds) *Understanding Contemporary Society: Theories of the Present*, London, Sage, pp. 25–45.

Oakley, A (1974) *The Sociology of Housework*, London, Martin Robertson.

REFERENCES

Oakley, A (1981) *Subject Women*, London, Fontana.

Orr, D (2000) Success at Last? *Independent on Sunday (The Sunday Review)*, 2 January 2000: 4–16.

Orr, P (2000) 'Prudence and progress: national policy for equal opportunities (gender) in schools since 1975', in Myers, K (ed.) *Whatever Happened to Equal Opportunities in Schools? Gender Equality Initiatives in Education*, Buckingham, Open University Press, pp. 13–26.

Ozga, J and Walker, L (1995) 'Women in education management: theory and practice', in Limerick D and Lingard, B (eds) *Gender and Changing Educational Management*, Rydalmere, NSW, Hodder Education.

Paechter, C (2000) *Changing School Subjects: Power, Gender and Curriculum*, Buckingham, Open University Press.

Palmer, A (1996) 'Something to declare: women in HM Customs and Excise', in Colgan, F and Ledwith, S (eds) *Women in Organisations: Challenging Gender Politics*, Basingstoke, Macmillan, pp. 125–151.

Pascall, G (1997) *Social Policy: A New Feminist Analysis*, London, Routledge.

Pascall, G and Cox, R (1993) *Women Returning to Higher Education*, Buckingham, SRHE/ Open University Press.

Patel, P (1997) 'Third wave feminism and black women's activism', in Mirz'a H (ed.) *Black British Feminism: A Reader*, London, Routledge, pp. 255–268.

Pateman, C (1987) 'Feminist critiques of the public/private dichotomy', in Phillips, A (ed.) *Feminism and Equality*, Oxford, Basil Blackwell, pp. 103–126.

Pattanaik, B (1999) 'You nurtured me to be a carefree bird, O Mother', in Zmroczek, C and Mahony, P (eds) *Women and Social Class – International Feminist Perspectives*, London, UCL Press, pp. 185–198.

Phillips, A (ed.) (1987) *Feminism and Equality*, Oxford, Blackwell.

Phoenix, A (1991) *Young Mothers?* Cambridge, Polity Press.

Pilcher, J (1999) *Women in Contemporary Britain: An Introduction*, London, Routledge.

Piper, C (1993) *The Responsible Parent: A Study of Divorce Mediation*, London, Harvester Wheatsheaf.

Plummer, K (2000) 'Intimate choices', in Browning, G, Halcli, A and Webster, F (eds) *Understanding Contemporary Society: Theories of the Present*, London, Sage, pp. 432–444.

Pratt, G (1993) 'Reflections on poststructuralism and feminist empirics, theory and practice', *Antipode*, 25 (1): 51–63.

Press, J and Townsley, E (1998) 'Wives' and husbands' housework reporting: gender, class and social desirability', *Gender and Society*, 12 (2): 188–218.

Prichard, C and Deem, R (1999) 'Wo-managing further education: gender and the construction of the manager in the corporate colleges of England', *Gender and Education*, 11 (3): 323–342.

Procter, I and Padfield, M (1998) *Young Adult Women, Work and Family: Living a Contradiction*, London, Mansell.

Purdy, L (1997) 'Babystrike!', in Nelson, H (ed.) *Feminism and Families*, New York, Routledge, pp. 69–75.

Purvis, T and Hunt, A (1993) 'Discourse, ideology, discourse, ideology, discourse, ideology ...', *British Journal of Sociology*, 44 (3): 473–499.

Ramazanoglu, C (1993) 'Introduction', in Ramazanoglu, C (ed.) *Up Against Foucault: Exploration of Some Tensions between Foucault and Feminism*, London, Routledge, pp. 1–28.

REFERENCES

Reay, D (1998) 'Surviving in dangerous places: working-class women, women's studies and higher education', *Women's Studies International Forum*, 21 (1): 11–19.

Reed, L (1999) 'Troubling Boys and Disturbing discourses on masculinity and schooling: a feminist exploration of current debates and interventions concerning boys in school,' *Gender and Education*, 11 (1): 93–110.

Rich, A (1977) *Of Woman Born*, London, Virago.

Rothfield, P (1990) 'Feminism, subjectivity and sexual experience', in Gunew, S (ed.) *Feminist Knowledge: Critique and Construct*, London, Routledge, pp. 121–144.

Ruddick, S (1980) 'Maternal thinking', *Feminist Studies*, 6 (2): 342–367.

Sachs, J and Blackmore, J (1998) 'You never show you can't cope: women in school leadership roles managing their emotions', *Gender and Education*, 10 (3): 265–279.

Sargisson, L (1996) *Contemporary Feminist Utopianism*, London, Routledge.

Sarup, M (1996) *Identity, Culture and the Postmodern World*, Edinburgh, Edinburgh University Press.

Searle, C (1998) *None but our Words: Critical Literacy in Classroom and Community*, Buckingham, Open University Press.

Sevenhuijsen, S (1998) *Citizenship and the Ethics of Care: Feminist Considerations on Justice, Morality and Politics,* London, Routledge.

Sevenhuijsen, S (1999) *Caring in the Third Way*, Working Paper 12, Leeds, Centre for Research on Family, Kinship and Childhood, University of Leeds.

Sharpe, S (1994) *Just Like A Girl: How Girls Learn to be Women, From the Seventies to the Nineties* (New Edition). London, Penguin

Showalter, E (1978) *A Literature of their Own: British Women Novelists from Bronte to Lessing*, London, Virago.

Skeggs, B (1997) *Formations of Class and Gender*, London, Sage.

Skucha, J (1999) *Mature Female Graduates: Moving On?* University of Wolverhampton, Unpublished PhD thesis.

Smith, L (1999) *Decolonizing Methodologies: Research and Indigenous Peoples*, London, Zed Books.

Smith, M (1998) *Social Science in Question*, London, Sage/Open University.

Snitow, A (1992) 'Feminism and motherhood: an American reading', *Feminist Review*, 40, Spring: 32–51.

Soper, K (1994) 'Feminism, humanism and postmodernism', in M Evans (ed.) *The Woman Question*, 2nd edn, London, Sage, pp. 10–21.

Spelman, E (1988) *Inessential Woman: Problems of Exclusion in Feminist Thought*, London, Women's Press.

Spender, D (1980) *Man Made Language*, London, Routledge and Kegan Paul.

Spivak, G (1993) *Outside in the Teaching Machine*, London, Routledge.

Spivak, G (2001) *Political Discourse: Theories of Colonialism and Postcolonialism* (http://landow.stg.brown.edu/post/poldiscourse/spivak/spivak1.html, accessed 03/03/01).

Stanley, J (1997) 'To celeb-rate and not to be-moan', in *Class Matters: "Working-Class" Women's Perspectives on Social Class*, London, UCL Press, pp. 175–199.

Stanley, L (1990) 'A referral was made: behind the scenes during the creation of a Social Services Department "elderly" statistic', in Stanley, L (ed.) *Feminist Praxis*, London, Routledge.

Stanley, L and Wise, S (2000) 'But the empress has no clothes! Some awkward questions about the "missing revolution" in feminist theory, *Feminist Theory*, 1 (3): 261–288.

REFERENCES

Strachan, J (1999) 'Feminist educational leadership: locating the concepts in practice', *Gender and Education*, 11 (3): 309–322.

Summerfield, H (1993) 'Patterns of adaptation: Somali and Bangladeshi women in Britain', in Buijs, G (ed.) *Migrant Women: Crossing Boundaries and Changing Identities*, Oxford, Berg, pp. 83–98.

Tamboukou, M (2000) 'The paradox of being a woman teacher', *Gender and Education*, 12 (4): 463–478.

Tanesini A (1996) 'Whose language?', in Garry, A and Pearsall, M (eds) *Women, Knowledge and Reality: Explorations in Feminist Philosophy*, New York, Routledge, pp. 353–365.

Tanton, M and Hughes, C (1999) 'Editorial: gender and (management) education', *Gender and Education*, 11 (3): 245–250.

Tett, L (2000) ' "I'm Working Class and Proud of It" – gendered experiences of non-traditional participants in higher education', *Gender and Education*, 12 (2): 183–194.

Tizard, B and Hughes, M (1984) *Young Children Learning: Talking and Thinking at Home and at School*, London, Fontana.

Tong, R (1989) *Feminist Thought: A Comprehensive Introduction*, London, Sage.

Tronto, J (1993) *Moral Boundaries: A Political Argument for an Ethic of Care*, London, Routledge.

Tsolidis, G (2001) *Schooling, Diaspora and Gender*, Buckingham, Open University Press.

Umansky, L (1996) *Motherhood Reconceived: Feminism and the Legacies of the Sixties*, New York, New York University Press.

Visweswaran, K (1994) *Fictions of Feminist Ethnography*, Minneapolis, University of Minnesota Press.

Wajcman, J (1996) Women and Men Managers, in Crompton R, Gallie D and Purcell K (eds) *Changing Forms of Employment: Organisations, Skills and Gender*, London, Routledge, pp. 259–277.

Walby, S (1997) *Gender Transformations*, London, Routledge.

Walkerdine, V (1989) 'Femininity as performance', *Oxford Review of Education*, 15 (3): 267–279.

Walkerdine, V (1994) 'Femininity as performance', in Stone, L (ed.) *The Education Feminism Reader*, New York, Routledge, pp. 57–69.

Walkerdine, V and Lucey, H (1989) *Democracy in the Kitchen: Regulating Mothers and Socialising Daughters*, London, Virago.

Walkerdine, V and The Girls Mathematics Unit (1989) *Counting Girls Out*, London, Virago.

Walters, P and Dex, S (1992) 'Feminisation of the labour force in Britain and France', in Arber, S and Gilbert, N (eds) (1992) *Women and Working Lives: Divisions and Change*, Basingstoke, Macmillan, pp. 89–103.

Warhol, R and Herndl, D (1997) *Feminisms: an Anthology of Literary Theory and Criticism*, (revised edition), Basingstoke, Macmillan.

Weed, E (1994) 'The question of style', in Burke, C, Schor, N and Whitford, M (eds) *Engaging with Irigaray: Feminist Philosophy and Modern European Thought*, New York, Columbia University Press, pp. 79–110.

Weedon, C (1987) *Feminist Practice and Poststructuralist Theory*, Oxford, Basil Blackwell.

Weedon, C (1999) *Feminism, Theory and the Politics of Difference*, Oxford, Basil Blackwell.

REFERENCES

Whitford, M (1994) 'Irigaray, Utopia, and the death drive', in Burke, C, Schor, N and Whitford, M (eds) *Engaging with Irigaray: Feminist Philosophy and Modern European Thought*, New York, Columbia University Press, pp. 379–400.

Whitford, M (ed.) (1991) *The Irigaray Reader*, Oxford, Basil Blackwell.

Williams, J (1997) 'The discourse of access: the legitimation of selectivity', in J Williams (ed.) *Negotiating Access to Higher Education*, Buckingham, Open University Press, pp. 24–46.

Wilson, F (1999) 'Genderquake? Did you feel the earth move?', *Organization*, 6 (3): 529–541.

Wisker, G (2000) *Post-Colonial and African American Women's Writing: A Critical Introduction*, Basingstoke, Macmillan.

Wodak, R (ed.) (1997) *Gender and Discourse*, London, Sage.

Woodward, K (ed.) (1997) *Identity and Difference*, London, Sage/Open University.

Woolf, V (2000) *Orlando*, London, Vintage.

Woollett, A (1991) 'Having children: accounts of childless women and women with reproductive problems', in Phoenix, A, Woollett, A and Lloyd, E (eds) *Motherhood: Meanings, Practices and Ideologies*, London, Sage, pp. 47–65.

Wright, E (2000) *Lacan and Postfeminism*, Cambridge, Icon.

Wyatt, S with Langridge, C (1996) 'Getting to the top in the National Health Service', in Colgan, F and Ledwith, S (eds) *Women in Organisations: Challenging Gender Politics*, Basingstoke, Macmillan, pp. 212–244.

Young, L (1996) 'The rough side of the mountain: Black women and representation in film,' in Jarrett-Macauley, D (ed.) *Reconstructing Womanhood: Reconstructing Feminism*, London, Routledge, pp. 175–201.

Young, S (1997) *Changing the Wor(l)d: Discourse, Politics and the Feminist Movement*, London, Routledge.

INDEX

INDEX

INDEX